C A P S T O N E

G000123119

Stay Smart!

Smart things to know about... is a complete library of the world's smartest business ideas. **Smart** books put you on the inside track to the knowledge and skills that make the most successful people tick.

Each book brings you right up to speed on a crucial business issue. The subjects that business people tell us they most want to master are:

Smart Things to Know about **Brands & Branding**, JOHN MARIOTTI

Smart Things to Know about **Business Finance**, KEN LANGDON

Smart Things to Know about **Change**, DAVID FIRTH

Smart Things to Know about **Customers**, ROS JAY

Smart Things to Know about **Decision Making**, KEN LANGDON

Smart Things to Know about **E-Commerce**, MIKE CUNNINGHAM

Smart Things to Know about **Innovation & Creativity**, DENNIS SHERWOOD

Smart Things to Know about **Knowledge Management**,
TOM M. KOULOPOULOS & CARL FRAPPAOLO

Smart Things to Know about **Managing Projects**, DONNA DEEPROSE

Smart Things to Know about **Marketing**, JOHN MARIOTTI

Smart Things to Know about **Partnerships**, JOHN MARIOTTI

Smart Things to Know about **People Management**, DAVID FIRTH

Smart Things to Know about **Strategy**, RICHARD KOCH

Smart Things to Know about **Teams**, ANNEMARIE CARACCIOLO

Smart Things to Know about **Your Career**, JOHN MIDDLETON

You can stay **Smart** by e-mailing us at **info@wiley-capstone.co.uk**
Let us keep you up to date with new Smart books, Smart updates, a Smart newsletter
and Smart seminars and conferences. Get in touch to discuss your needs.

CAPSTONE

Smart

THINGS TO KNOW ABOUT

Innovation
& Creativity

DENNIS SHERWOOD

First published 2001 by
Capstone Publishing Limited (A Wiley Company)
8 Newtec Place
Magdalen Road
Oxford OX4 1RE
United Kingdom
http://www.capstoneideas.com

CIP catalogue records for this book are available from the British Library and the US Library of Congress

ISBN 1-84112-146-0

Typeset in 11/15pt Sabon by
Sparks Computer Solutions Ltd, Oxford, UK
http://www.sparks.co.uk
Printed and bound by
TJ International Ltd, Padstow, Cornwall

This book is printed on acid-free paper

Substantial discounts on bulk quantities of Capstone books are available to corporations, professional associations and other organizations. Please contact John Wiley & Sons for more details on 212 850 6000 or (fax) 212 850 6088 or (e-mail) info@wiley-capstone.co.uk

To Anny, Torben and Torsten, with thanks and love.

Contents

What is Smart?

The *Smart* series is a new way of learning. *Smart* books will improve your understanding and performance in some of the critical areas you face today like *customers, strategy, change, e-commerce, brands, influencing skills, knowledge management, finance, teamworking, partnerships.*

Smart books summarize accumulated wisdom as well as providing original cutting-edge ideas and tools that will take you out of theory and into action.

The widely respected business guru Chris Argyris points out that even the most intelligent individuals can become ineffective in organizations. Why? Because we are so busy working that we fail to learn about ourselves. We stop reflecting on the changes around us. We get sucked into the patterns of behavior that have produced success for us in the past, not realizing that it may no longer be appropriate for us in the fast-approaching future.

There are three ways the *Smart* series helps prevent this happening to you:

- by increasing your self-awareness

- by developing your understanding, attitude and behavior

- by giving you the tools to challenge the status quo that exists in your organization.

Smart people need smart organizations. You could spend a third of your career hopping around in search of the Holy Grail, or you could begin to create your own smart organization around you today.

Finally a reminder that books don't change the world, people do. And although the *Smart* series offers you the brightest wisdom from the best practitioners and thinkers, these books throw the responsibility on you to *apply* what you're learning in your work.

Because the truly smart person knows that reading a book is the start of the process and not the end ...

As Eric Hoffer says, "In times of change, learners inherit the world, while the learned remain beautifully equipped to deal with a world that no longer exists."

David Firth
Smartmaster

Preface

Every one dreams of having a magic, silver bullet – a blockbuster product that beats all the competitors, a fantastic process that delivers the ultimate in customer service, a brand image that never tarnishes. But we all know that sooner or later, every product passes its sell-by date; every process is an artifact of current technology; and even the most powerful brands can become valueless when things go wrong.

So, far, far better than having a single silver bullet is to own a *silver bullet machine* – a machine that can make silver bullets again and again and again and again.

And that's what this book is about. It is a design manual, a how-to guide, to help you build your own silver bullet machine in your own organization. A silver bullet machine based on one single, fundamental, concept.

Innovation.

I am passionate about innovation, and I hope that this book will make you passionate about it too. Generating ideas, being creative, and helping to make these ideas come to reality are immensely rewarding and enjoyable activities, and I trust that my enthusiasm will be contagious as you turn each page. Innovation – the ability to generate new ideas, to solve problems, to capture fleeting opportunities – is surely the most fundamental core competence, conferring on the organization that can truly make innovation happen the ultimate competitive advantage. That, surely, is the essence of a silver bullet machine.

This book, which is based on my experience building silver bullet machines in all sorts of organizations from media companies to government departments, manufacturers to service industries, comprises six chapters, plus an introductory prologue.

Very briefly:

Chapter 1 – *Target: Innovation,* sets the scene by describing innovation as a process embracing four sequential stages – idea generation, idea evaluation, development and implementation, leading to

Chapter 2 – *Applications,* which shows how the concepts of Chapter 1 can be applied to important business activities such as new product development, the design of improved processes, organization development, relationship management and corporate strategy.

Chapter 3 – *It's All About Patterns,* addresses, and answers, the central question, "What is creativity?" providing a framework for

Chapter 4 – *InnovAction!*, which describes a six-step process which you will soon be able to use to help you and your team generate stunning new ideas.

Chapter 5 – *How to be Wise*, discusses how new ideas can be evaluated in a fair and balanced manner, so that the best ideas are selected for further development, and

Chapter 6 – *The Unlearning Organization*, explores a broad range of cultural issues, all of which contribute to making your organization truly innovative.

In writing this book, I am indebted to many people with whom I have worked, or whose books and articles I have read. May I firstly thank my clients, and those with whom I have worked, in particular Arthur Day, Chelvin Hibbert, David Lyle, Deborah Howard, Evan Jones, Geoff Feasey, Greg Quakenbush, Janet Evans, Judith Argyle, Lin Kendrick, Marie Hogstedt, Mark Batten, Mark Selway, Paul Hernaman, Phil Bulley, and Tony Little.

Special thanks too to Judith Hackett, my colleague and partner in *Silver Bullet*, and extra special thanks to Anny, my wife, and Torben and Torsten, my two sons.

And thanks, in advance, to you too. I hope you will enjoy this book, and gain benefit from reading it. If you have any observations, comments or questions, do contact me via e-mail at dennis@silverbulletmachine.com!

Happy – and smart – innovating!

Dennis Sherwood
Brabourne, Kent
January 2001

Prologue

"Put it all on just one sheet of paper, will you?"

Once upon a time …

"Come in!"

"Good morning."

"Hello. Come in. Good morning. What can I do for you?"

"Well, I've got this great idea … I'm sure it's really important … and enormously valuable too … I was wondering … "

"Mmm. That's good. But I'm a bit busy right now: could you write me a paper on it?"

"Oh … well … if you think … "

"Yes, a paper will be really helpful.'

"Oh … well … er … yes … of course."

"And remember to put it all on just one sheet of paper, please."

"One sheet of paper? That's impossible!"

"Impossible? Of course not! If you really understand it, you must be able to capture it on one sheet of paper!"

"But it's quite complex … subtle … "

"You know I'm far too busy to read anything more than one sheet of paper. As I just said, if you really understand it, you can capture the essence on one sheet of paper!"

"Well … er … OK … "

* * *

"Come in!"

"Good morning."

"Ah. It's you again, is it?"

"Good morning – do you have a moment, please?"

"Yes, I do. How's your idea? Did you capture it on one sheet of paper?"

"No."

"Mmm. As I told you when I saw you last week, if you can't capture it on one sheet of paper, you don't understand it. And it's no use briefing me on it if you don't understand it yourself."

"I appreciate that. In fact, I do understand it."

"Then why can't you express it on one sheet of paper?"

"Because I don't need to."

"Don't need to? What do you mean?"

"I think I understand it so well that I don't need a whole sheet of paper – I can express it in just one line."

"One line? Are you sure it's not trivial?"

"I don't think so."

"Mmm. Well, OK then. Show me."

"Here it is: just one line!"

$$E = \frac{m_0 c^2}{\sqrt{(1 - v^2/c^2)}}$$

"Eh?? What's all this gibberish?? It's crazy!"

"Well, it's all about space and time, you see, and energy, and what happens when things move at speeds approaching the velocity of light … "

"Space? Time? Velocity of light? It's crazy! Nuts!"

"But you did tell me to put it all on just one sheet of paper … "

The "just one sheet of paper" fallacy

Whether or not this conversation actually took place between the young Albert Einstein and his boss at the birth of the theory of relativity – probably one of the half-dozen most creative concepts in human history – I don't know, but if it did, Einstein probably learnt three things. Whether or not his boss learnt anything at all, I don't know either, but I'm sure you'll get the drift.

Firstly, Einstein will have learnt that innovation is an intensely cultural activity. Few people with great ideas are inspired by the "I'm busy right now, write me a paper on it" response. Thankfully, Einstein had the tenacity not to give up in despair.

Secondly, Einstein will have learnt that what his boss said is deeply true. When you do understand something – intensely, intimately, profoundly – you can express its essence on just one sheet of paper, or indeed, sometimes, in just one line. That incomprehensible equation (a smarter version of the more familiar $E = mc^2$) really *does* capture much of the essence of the theory of relativity.

And thirdly – and rather more importantly – Einstein will have discovered the "just one sheet of paper" fallacy.

You've probably come it across it – busy, self-confident boss, no time for all the ancillary detail, attention span measured in milliseconds, a pile of twisted ex-paper clips on the corner of the desk – you know what I mean. These people always ask for just one sheet of paper. And that works really well when one condition holds true: *one sheet of paper is OK only if the boss is already very familiar with the subject matter, and so can immediately understand – deeply – the true significance of the carefully selected words on that one sheet.* But if the boss isn't particularly familiar with the material, or if great care has not been taken to brief her in a series of well-chosen sound bites over the last few weeks, then that one sheet of paper falls on deaf ears – or rather, into an inadvertently ignorant mind.

It's not that the boss isn't bright, or even smart – of course she is, or she wouldn't be the boss. Rather, it's because the world is full of complexity, and not even the brightest, smartest boss can have covered everything.

And if there is a body of knowledge that is both unfamiliar and non-trivial, not even the brightest, smartest person can immediately get the whole picture from just one sheet of paper. It takes more than one sheet to explain it, and it takes some effort on behalf of the receiver to think about it, internalize it, understand it, use it.

That's the "just one sheet of paper" fallacy. And it's not just a lame excuse for sloppy thinking and long-windedness. Rather, it's a recognition that a smart and succinct description of complex concepts, concepts that are new and unfamiliar to a particular audience, legitimately requires more than one well-crafted sheet.

And this applies to innovation, as much as it applies to relativity.

SMART PEOPLE
TO HAVE ON
YOUR SIDE:

ALBERT
EINSTEIN
(1879–1955)

Albert Einstein was born in Ulm, in Germany, and despite being very much middle-of-the-road at school and university, he is now recognized as one of the most creative human beings who has ever lived. In 1905, whilst working as a junior civil servant – Technical Expert (Grade III) – in the Patent Office in Berne, the Swiss capital, he wrote three truly seminal scientific papers. One was on the theory of Brownian motion, the incessant jiggling of molecules attributable to heat; in another, Einstein revolutionized physics by introducing what we now know as the special theory of relativity, one consequence of which is the possibility of transforming mass into pure energy, as expressed by the famous equation linking the energy (E) of a moving body to that body's mass (m_0, as measured when at rest), its speed (v), and the speed of light (c). But it was for the third paper that Einstein was awarded his Nobel Prize in 1921. This third paper included a theory that successfully explained the hitherto inexplicable observation that when light falls on certain metals, it causes an electric current to flow. This is the "photo-electric effect," used today in devices such as digital cameras.

Einstein's theory envisaged that the electric current is caused by a flow of electrons dislodged from their host atoms by the impact of a "particle" of light – just as a stationary billiard ball is caused to move by an impact from a moving ball. Current orthodoxy at the time was that light was a wave (like on the surface of water), but the idea that light might be a stream of particles was by no means new – Einstein's great predecessor Isaac Newton (1642–1727) had advocated that one, building on the ideas of the ancient Greeks. Furthermore, to determine the energy of the collision, Einstein drew on an idea first put forward by Max Planck (1858–1947) in a lecture given in 1900 on the radiation of heat – an idea we now call quantum theory. Einstein's Nobel-Prize-winning work combined two existing ideas – the old, but disregarded, particle theory of light, and the much more recent quantum theory, which so far had been applied to heat but not light – and so explained the photo-electric effect. This is just one instance of Koestler's Law (see page 95) that creativity is all about finding new patterns of existing components (see point 7 of "Twelve smart things you need to know about innovation" on page 8).

Innovation on just one sheet of paper

The bullet points on the accompanying two pages tell you everything you need to know about innovation on just one sheet of paper (both sides – I hope that's not cheating!). Take a look through them, and if you feel comfortable that you really understand them – deeply – then you don't need the rest of this book. On the other hand, if you find them interesting, challenging, maybe puzzling, perhaps intriguing, then this book really is for you, and I know you will enjoy reading it. For on the remaining 150 or so sheets of paper (using both sides again!), I've got enough space, and I trust you have enough time, to get to that level of understanding, and application, where all you'll need thereafter as an aide-memoire is just that one sheet of paper …

TWELVE SMART THINGS YOU NEED TO KNOW ABOUT INNOVATION

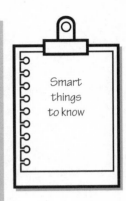

Smart things to know

1 Smart people recognize that **innovation and creativity aren't the same thing**, and they distinguish carefully between these two, often muddled, concepts. Creativity is about having ideas in the first place; innovation is a much broader concept involving not only having ideas, but also exercising commercial wisdom in identifying which are the smart ones, as well as having the capability of bringing the smart ones to full fruition.

2 Smart people appreciate that innovation **does not just apply to the invention of "the better mouse-trap"** – it applies to many other domains of activity, from processes to relationships, from strategy to the innermost working of our own minds.

3 Smart people know that **there is no such thing as a "creative" – or more importantly "non-creative" – person**. They know we are all born with inherent creativity, and they know we can all contribute to the process that lies at the very heart of innovation – the generation of stunning ideas.

4 Smart people know that **creativity is a skill that individuals can learn, practice and develop**, and smart people enjoy using the tools and techniques that can be applied to help.

5 Smart people also know that although individuals (and better, small groups) can be very effective in generating great ideas, to make something happen – to be innovative in addition to being creative – is very rarely something that individuals and small groups can do by themselves: **innovation requires the co-ordination of many organizational resources**. Smart organizations get this right.

6 But unsmart organizations don't: that's why unsmart organizations find innovation very, very difficult. **Not only is successful innovation a question of organizational culture, but it also involves all sorts of things from the ability of the organization to deploy a successful project team, to the subtleties of the promotion process.**

7 Many people feel that creativity is some sort of mystical process, requiring a special gift, which they, sadly, just don't have; many of those fortunate enough to possess this gift enjoy its benefits, but have no idea how it works – and often bask in the sunshine of being regarded by their peers as "wonderfully creative." Smart people have learnt that creativity can be vastly enhanced by following a deliberate and systematic process of **searching for new patterns of existing components**.

8 Smart people appreciate that **innovation in a business or organizational context is almost never on a green-field site, starting with a blank sheet of paper.** Only in the most rudimentary start-ups is the site genuinely green: for almost all of us, innovation takes place on a very muddy field indeed – and probably a field that we ourselves have "ploughed." For we have all developed new products, designed new processes, defined business strategies before.

9 Smart people consequently realize that the key skill for innovation in business and organizations is therefore **not** the capability to come up with stunning new ideas – rather, it is the **willingness to discard the old ones, to unlearn familiar habits**.

10 Smart people know that to transform their organization from a conventional one into a truly innovative one – to build **the unlearning organization** – does not happen overnight, and takes time, energy and leadership.

11 But smart people know that it can be done. And **they make the time, have the energy, and display the leadership, to make it happen**.

12 And as a result, smart people can reap the reward. For the true reward of building that unlearning organization, in which innovation really is "the way we do things around here," is the building of a **truly unassailable, ultimate, competitive advantage** – the ability to solve whatever problems might arise, and to grasp every available opportunity.

1
Target: Innovation

So, you want to be smart at innovation …

… in which case, the best place to start is to make sure we're all speaking the same language.

So, take a moment to reflect on your answer to our first *killer question*:

KILLER
QUESTIONS

> What, precisely, do you understand by the term *innovation?*

Most people reply "Doing something new," or perhaps "Inventing something novel," or maybe "Taking a new idea to market." These answers, and the many similar variants, are fine as far as they go, but they rate as "OK"; they do not rate as "smart." If you want to be smart at innovation, you want something richer, deeper, more insightful … so take a look at the next *Smart things to know*, for the "Innovation Target" sets the scene.

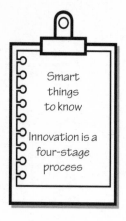

Smart
things
to know

Innovation is a
four-stage
process

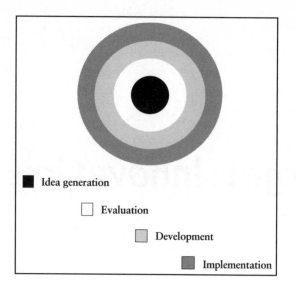

■ Idea generation

□ Evaluation

▨ Development

▨ Implementation

This diagram focuses attention on innovation as a process requiring four stages:

- *idea generation* – having ideas in the first place

- *evaluation* – selecting the ideas you wish to progress

- *development* – refining the idea from concept to working reality

- *implementation* – making the idea happen for real.

The purpose of this chapter is to explain, in detail, the thinking underlying the Innovation Target, and its significance.

"WE HAVE NO SHORTAGE OF IDEAS AROUND HERE – OUR PROBLEM IS TO MAKE SOMETHING HAPPEN!"

If this sounds like your organization, then you have no difficulty in generating ideas, but something is going wrong elsewhere.

Maybe the blockage is in **evaluation** – the white zone – for perhaps your organization is so risk averse that only the safest, and by the same token least innovative, ideas can win funding.

Or perhaps the problem is in **development**, the pale gray zone. To develop an innovative idea usually requires a project team, and some organizations with very strong line structures find it difficult to attract the best managers out of the line into project teams, then to manage the project, and ultimately to disband the team once the project is complete. If assignment to a "special project team" is perceived organizationally as the first "we don't want you around here" signal, then all the smart managers will find some very good reasons why they are far too busy doing their line job, and that although they would of course love to join the project team, well, they just can't right now. So the project gets staffed by the duffers, the people no one else wants, and – surprise, surprise – the project fails. This reinforces the organizational belief that special projects are for losers ... and innovation is dead for ever after.

Or the problem might be in **implementation**, the outermost, dark gray zone. If, for example, the innovation is the launch of a new product, what are the performance measures that determine whether the launch is a "success" or a "failure?" If the performance target for success is unrealistically high, then the product might be withdrawn from the market before it has had a chance to establish itself, and the project team will be tarnished with the indelible brush of failure. What does such a visible "failure" do to the organization's appetite for innovation? And for the morale of the team managing the next product launch – if indeed there is one? But where, precisely, is the "failure?" Was the original idea flawed? Was the product, as launched, a much-compromised version of the original concept? Was the pre-launch advertising campaign underfunded? Was the product launch managed badly? Was the product training of the sales force insufficient? Or was the performance target just unrealistic?

All these weaknesses in implementation (and many more too) can contribute to ultimate failure, and each weakness has a different cause, and a different solution. Smart organizations understand this complexity, and work hard to ensure each individual component process within implementation works, works well, and works in harmony with all the associated processes.

Idea generation

The center of the Innovation Target – the black zone – represents *idea generation*. In the absence of new ideas, there is nothing to evaluate, nothing to develop, nothing to implement, and so idea generation is truly the heart of the entire innovation process.

But in the business and organizational worlds, simply having ideas is not enough: not only must you have ideas, you must also make them come to successful fruition. Academics and dreamers, of course, can legitimately live solely in a world of pure ideas, but for smart business managers, having ideas is just the first stage in the process. That is one of the key messages of the Innovation Target.

Idea generation is synonymous with creativity, but as soon as the word "creativity" is mentioned, most people begin to make mental associations with concepts such as "creative people," "genius," "special gift" and the like, associations driven by the popularly-held belief that creativity – the personal ability to generate new ideas – is an especially rare talent, with which only the fortunate few are born.

One of the main objectives of this book is to debunk this myth, and to demonstrate – conclusively and convincingly – that the ability to generate new ideas is within us all. It is a skill that can be learnt and, as with all human skills, its application is enhanced with practice. Also, as with all human skills, some people will be better at it than others, some people will enjoy it more than others, and some people will wish to devote more time to it than others. These of course are all interlinked, for we all tend to spend more time on activities we enjoy, and as a result we become more proficient, so fuelling the virtuous circle to motivate us to devote yet more time.

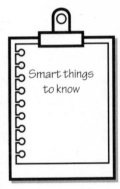

Smart things
to know

PRACTICE MAKES PERFECT

We all know that world-class athletes devote prodigious amounts of time to training, and so become perfect through practice.

What is less well-known is that people engaging in more "creative" activities are at least as dedicated, just three examples being:

- Most concert pianists have spent *at least* 10,000 hours practicing before they achieve the level of proficiency required to perform in public. To make that figure more real, that's the equivalent of practicing for 6 hours and 40 minutes on each of 300 days a year, for five years!

- 1847 was quite a year for sisters Charlotte (1816–1855) and Emily (1818–1848) Brontë, for it saw the publication of both their great novels *Jane Eyre* and *Wuthering Heights*. These works, however, were not just one-off flashes of literary genius – the Brontës had a family tradition of storytelling and poetry-writing, and Charlotte and Emily had been crafting tales and writing stories since their early childhood.

- In 1995, Andrew Wiles, a 42-year-old English professor of mathematics at Princeton University in the United States, presented a solution to Fermat's Last Theorem. This refers to the equation $x^n + y^n = z^n$, which is a generalized statement of Pythagoras's Theorem. If we think only of whole numbers (other than zero) for x, y, z and n, when $n = 2$, there are many possible sets of values for x, y, and z – such as 3, 4, 5 and 5, 12, 13 – which fit the equation. But what happens when n is greater than 2? Fermat's Last Theorem states that if n is any whole number greater than 2, then there are *no* sets of whole numbers x, y and z (excluding zero) that make the equation work. To most of us, that's not overly exciting; but to *prove* the equation cannot work for *any* whole numbers – however large, and in whatever combination – really *does* turn mathematicians on! Some time around 1637, the French mathematician Pierre Fermat (1601–1665) scribbled a note in a textbook alongside a statement of the problem: "I have assuredly found an admirable proof, but the margin is too narrow to contain it." For the next 350 years, this teaser stimulated the very best mathematicians in the world to seek to discover the solution – or rediscover it, if Fermat had indeed been right! – but to no avail. Until Wiles, that is. But this was no eureka-like strike of lightning – Wiles had been working on the problem, single-mindedly and exclusively, for about ten years.

If, for example, you enjoy playing golf, you will find all sorts of ways of finding the time, and your handicap will decrease accordingly, so increasing your enjoyment; conversely, if you don't enjoy long-distance running (as I don't!), you are unlikely to volunteer to run the London marathon, and you will never, as a result, become an Olympic athlete. But even if you don't aspire to those heights, and even if you don't particularly enjoying running, you still know how to do it, and can – if you wish (for example, to support a charity) – participate.

What is true for golf and long-distance running is also true for creativity and idea generation: it is a skill which can be learnt, and an activity in which we can all participate – but only if you know what to do, and personally wish to.

My assertion that idea generation is a skill that can be learnt might be something of a surprise, particularly to anyone who has been to school. School, after all, is where you learn things. But who reading this book was trained at school (or college or university for that matter) in idea generation or creativity? Many of us will have heard the term "creativity" used in connection with "creative arts"; very few of us, however, will have had explicit experience during our passage through the education system of being trained in idea generation and creativity in a more intellectual sense.

Most of us, however, have been trained explicitly how *not* to be creative, as we learn the difference between what is "right," and what is "wrong." Try, for example, the exercise in the box.

ARE YOU A GENIUS?

In Tony Buzan's *Book of Genius*, mind map guru Tony Buzan and International Chess Grandmaster Raymond Keene give their views on what genius is, and portray brief biographies of those whom they believe to be the top 100 geniuses of all time. They also feature a number of tests and exercises to help you determine your "GQ" – genius quotient – a richer version of the more familiar IQ, intelligence quotient. Here is one of the tests:

Which is the odd word out?
NOLI   TERIG   GROMNLE   NELFEI   ACT

SMART THINGS TO DO

What did you get?

The right answer, as given in the crib at the back of the book, is GROMNLE, this being an anagram of mongrel, the only de-anagrammed word referring to dogs, rather than cats (lion, tiger, feline, cat). Getting this answer contributes 150 points to your GQ; any other answer is wrong and contributes zero.

When I did this exercise, my ego dropped 150 points: I had chosen NELFEI on the basis that only FELINE is used primarily as an adjective, all the others being anagrams of words used exclusively or primarily as nouns. Oh well, I guess I never wanted to be a genius anyway...

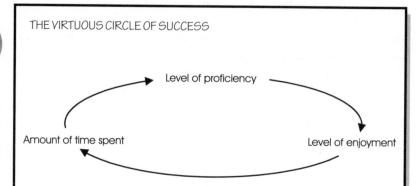

THE VIRTUOUS CIRCLE OF SUCCESS

This diagram captures the "virtuous circle of success": the more you enjoy something, the more time you spend on it, the greater your proficiency, and so you enjoy it even more ... This applies to many types of activity, from sports to the performing arts, from interpreting financial statements to idea generation. This virtuous circle perpetuates itself once it gets going in the right direction – but how do you get it going in the first place?

This, as we all know, is a problem encountered by every parent, who wishes to encourage a child to do something the parent believes is worthwhile. Take playing the piano, for example. Does the wise parent say, "You must practice everyday for half an hour," so kick-starting the circle by forcing the *amount of time spent*? Or is it better to say, "You will really enjoy this" (or its surrogate "This is good for you"), so forcing the *level of enjoyment*? Or is it wisest to say, "Well done! Fantastic! You played that piece really beautifully!" so heightening the perceived *level of proficiency* (regardless of the truth)? Or is it a mixture of all three? Or do you let it be altogether, hoping that the child will self-discover the virtuousness (if not virtuosity) of the circle, despite the allure of alternative attractions such as Sony PlayStations, TV and the Net? This example, of course, is not limited to playing the piano . . .

Diagrams of this type, by the way, are known as *causal loops*, and can be very powerful in understanding and analyzing complex problems, and in helping formulate policies (such as how best to encourage a child to learn the piano!). For more on this theme, and the related topic known as *systems thinking*, see my previous book *Unlock Your Mind*.

And what about:

- NOLI, because it is an anagram of lino, the floor covering, which is not associated in any way with animals, as all the other de-anagrammed words are.

- NOLI, because it's the only word as given that makes sense in Latin (it means "Don't"!).

- NOLI, because it is the only item with four English anagrams – lino, lion, loin and noil (a less familiar word, unless you happen to know the wool trade – it means a straggly waste bit of wool, often found on that part of a fleece near a sheep's nether end!).

- TERIG, because tiger is the only word that is a designated year in the Chinese calendar ("year of the tiger," but not "year of the mongrel").

- TERIG, because tiger is the only word that refers to a type of shark.

- TERIG, because it's the only item with five letters.

- GROMNLE, because it's the only item that contains four consecutive letters (L, M, N, and O).

- GROMNLE, because mongrel alone is a generic noun that can refer to all breeds of animal, whereas all the others refer exclusively to cats.

- NELFEI, because it's the only item with three vowels.

- NELFEI, because it's the only item with two letters the same.

- ACT, because cat has only one syllable, all the other de-anagrammed words having two.

- ACT, because it's the only word as given that makes sense in English!

I'm sure you can find some others!

These, I would argue, are all legitimate reasons for selecting the "odd word out." Some people, however, might argue that some reasons are "better" than others: for example, that the selection of TERIG on the basis of having five letters is "weak." This raises several points.

Firstly, what is the basis of selecting the "odd word out"? Is it driven by something very special about the selected item, without there needing to be anything in particular that links the others? Or is the selected item the odd word out, not because it is special in its own right, but because it is excluded from a club naturally formed by the other four? TERIG does indeed have five letters, but since all the others have different numbers of letters, there is no obvious club of this nature from which TERIG is excluded. Had the other four items been anagrams of three letters – ACT/CAT, GIP/PIG, WOC/COW, LEK/ELK – then the selection of TERIG as having five letters is arguably "stronger" by virtue of the fact that all the remaining items have only three.

The question "what is the odd word out?" is, I would argue, inherently ambiguous, for it embraces two very different approaches: "Can you identify any highly distinguishing features of a single item that makes it stand out from the crowd?" as opposed to, "Can you find a coherent thread linking any four of the items, thereby necessarily excluding the fifth?" Perhaps "odd word out" questions are a diagnostic not of GQ or IQ, but rather personality – would the "what stands out?" approach naturally be taken by rugged individualists who see themselves as standing out from the crowd? And, by the same token, would the "what's in common?" approach immediately appeal to the team player, or the conformist?

Secondly, the selection is highly dependent on specialist knowledge, which may or may not be arbitrary, and may or may not be an indication of any particular talent. I happen to have worked for some years in Bradford, the center of England's wool industry, and so I have come across the word "noil." So what? Another example of this occurred when I showed this chapter to my wife. She went for ACT on the basis that it is the only item that is an acronym for a UK tax – advanced corporation tax, no less. My wife is – you've already guessed – a tax accountant, so she would notice things like that!

And thirdly, whether or not a given reason is "good" or "bad" depends on context. If, for example, we were solving a crossword puzzle clue such as "an aggressive animal," and knew that we were searching for a five-letter word, then the fact that TERIG/TIGER has five letters becomes the most important feature in distinguishing it from the other aggressive animals in the list – certainly lion, and possibly cat and mongrel too.

If this test were administered at a school, it is likely that GROMNLE/ MONGREL would get marked "right," and all other answers wrong. Some kids will glow with pride; others will cower in their private corners, eyes down and perhaps moist, wearing their imaginary-but-oh-so-visible dunce's caps in shame. All will learn that saying "But ... Miss..." doesn't work; all will learn that all questions have only one "right" answer, and that all others are wrong; all will learn that the way to win in this system is to second-guess what someone else has predetermined the "right" answer to be.

And all will learn that being "creative," spotting something that no one has noticed before – especially the teacher – is decidedly not a clever thing to do. Einstein was not a star at school: but he was expelled from one – expelled for "being disruptive." Or was it for putting up his hand and saying "But ... miss ..." one time too many? Einstein, fortunately, was not crushed by the experience of being forced to accept the *status quo*, he merely bit his lip and bided his time.

Most of us, however, do not survive the experience so robustly, in that we not only lose the knack of being creative, but far more importantly we lose the self-confidence that, yes, we can spot things others haven't noticed, we can get out of the box of accepted wisdom. And as a consequence, we begin to believe that we are not creative, we fear to look outside of the box, and, worse still, we stop even noticing that the box is there.

Well, those are all fine words. It's all very well for me to claim that idea generation is a skill that we can all learn, but how do we actually do it? What is the basis of the method? What are the tools and techniques? How can I convince you that it really works? These are all good and valid questions, which, as we shall see in Chapters 3 and 4, have good and valid answers. For the moment, though, let's continue our discussion of the Innovation Target, and move on to the next zone, the white zone of evaluation …

Tony Buzan is the guru, par excellence, of mind maps: vivid, pictorial representations of associations, linkages and relationships. Mind maps can be very powerful in capturing much complex information in a very informative way, using very few words and very little space. As an example, the figure on p. 22 shows a mind map capturing the essence of this chapter.

The branching structure recognizes the fact that most concepts are not a linear succession of A follows B follows C, a form we are usually obliged to adopt when writing; the nesting of sub-branches immediately represents structures and hierarchies of relationships; the encouragement of visual images makes mind maps very compelling, and facilitates recall; also, the use of color (unfortunately not possible here) can highlight related features, and is a further mechanism for helping memorization.

My mind maps tend to be rather dull visually, and a bit wordy – for some wonderfully vivid examples of mind maps as art form, track down some of Tony's many books, including *The Mind Map Book: Radiant Thinking* and *Use Your Head*.

SMART PEOPLE
TO HAVE ON
YOUR SIDE:

TONY BUZAN

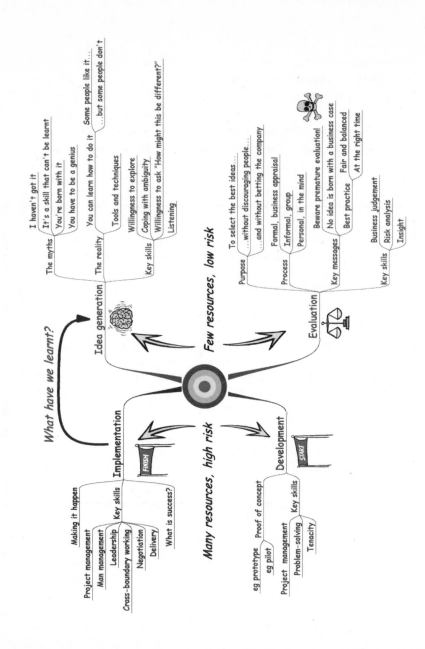

The myths
- I haven't got it
- It's a skill that can't be learnt
- You're born with it
- You have to be a genius

The reality
- You can learn how to do it
  - Some people like it...
  - ...but some people don't
- Tools and techniques
- Willingness to explore
- Coping with ambiguity
- Willingness to ask "How might this be different?"

Key skills
- Listening

Idea generation

What have we learnt?

Few resources, low risk

Evaluation

Purpose
- To select the best ideas...
- ...without discouraging people...
- ...and without betting the company

Process
- Formal, business appraisal
- Informal, group
- Personal, in the mind

Key messages
- Beware premature evaluation!
- No idea is born with a business case
- Best practice
  - Fair and balanced
  - At the right time

Key skills
- Business judgement
- Risk analysis
- Insight

Implementation

Key skills
- Making it happen
- Project management
- Man management
- Leadership
- Cross-boundary working
- Negotiation
- Delivery

What is success?

Many resources, high risk

Development

- eg prototype — Proof of concept
- eg pilot

Project management

Key skills
- Problem-solving
- Tenacity

Evaluation

Evaluation – the white zone of the Innovation Target – is the process by which ideas are selected for further development or, alternatively, rejected. Stated as simply as that, evaluation sounds as if it's a well-ordered and effective process that every business does in a professional way as a matter of course.

EVALUATION IN ACTION

As a result of a recent review of overhead expenditure, a study team has identified that your organization's recruitment process for middle managers (in the age bracket 30–35) is cumbersome (there are many interviews before a candidate can be given an offer), time-consuming (the process can extend over three months) and expensive (in terms of interviewer time, assessment centers, and candidates' expenses). This is causing a number of good candidates to withdraw before an offer is made, and there is also some disappointment with the quality of those candidates who do join, but don't seem to come up to expectations after a year in the organization.

You are a departmental manager attending a meeting to discuss this, and since you are not directly involved with recruitment, you have no particular axe to grind – your key objective is to help contribute to the discussion of ideas as to how to improve the recruitment process.

During the meeting, a junior manager, newly recruited herself, says: "What about this for an idea? Why don't we dispense with most of our process altogether, but offer three-month temporary contracts to candidates that have got particularly good CVs? If they work out, we can then make their contracts permanent; if not, they can go."

What is your immediate reaction to this idea?

Smart things to think about

Most people's immediate reaction is, "that's nuts." So, if that was your reaction too, you are not alone. And most people would have no angst about saying so in the meeting, either directly, or in terms of the umpteen reasons why that idea wouldn't work, such as:

- "As soon as word got out, we'd be flooded with crazy applicants."

- "We'd never be able to get rid of those that don't make the grade."

- "No good applicant would be willing to join on a three-month contract."

- "It's illegal."

- "We'd be taken to every employment tribunal under the sun."

I'm sure you can think of many more.

In all probability, after a few minutes, that idea will be dismissed as lunatic, and the meeting will move on to more "serious" suggestions. And, as a result, the junior manager will have learnt a very important organizational lesson: to be very careful about when to open her mouth, and even more careful about what she ever dares to suggest. But that's not the only result. The organization has lost out too, for by dissuading someone from making a suggestion, the organization is losing the opportunity for someone else to build on the original suggestion, and take it further, perhaps to a very good idea indeed. As we shall see in Chapters 3 and 4, an important part of the idea generation process is the way in which teams work together, with people springboarding off one another's contributions – a process that can work only if individuals are willing to make a contribution in the first place.

What is happening here, of course, is the process of evaluation – but few of us think of this natural, everyday business interaction in such formal terms. An idea has been tabled – that the organization might change its recruitment process in a very radical way – and as soon as the words are uttered, we immediately form a judgement as to whether the idea is "good" or "bad." What else is this but evaluation? And how do we make this judgement? Are we influenced by who made the suggestion? Are we influenced by whether or not we are potentially threatened by the suggestion? Or by whether we immediately like or dislike the idea? Or by whether or not we like the person who suggested the idea? Or whether or not we feel it is in our career interests to be seen to be supporting the idea, opposing it, or remaining detached?

My experience is that we are influenced by all of these things, and many more too. Our reaction to new ideas – especially radical ones – is a complex mixture of detached judgement and personal emotion, of business experience and organizational politics.

EVALUATION IN ACTION REVISITED

With reference to the box on p. 23, what would have been your own reaction, and the reaction of the meeting, had the same suggestion been put forward by:

- the company chairman?
- the company chief executive?
- the human resources director?
- the senior manager responsible for recruitment?
- the company lawyer?
- a recently recruited middle manager?
- a candidate?
- a secretary?

Smart things to think about

Mmm. Is evaluation in your organization ultimately a question of power? If it is, then this is very real, very human, very believable. But from a business point of view, the key question is "Is this smart?" Does it make good business sense for ideas to be evaluated in such a cavalier, off-hand, and political manner? And is it smart to build into the organizational culture all sorts of fears, all manner of subtle, unstated pressures that result in only the most banal ideas ever being tabled?

My answer to all these questions – of course – is "No – that isn't smart at all!"

But is there a way of conducting the process of idea evaluation in a more robust, more professional manner? A way that encourages people to continue to suggest ideas without feeling they are risking their careers, but one that still filters out the lulus, so we don't bet the company either? A way that clearly identifies the risks associated with the idea, enabling us to determine how those risks can be assessed and managed? Clearly, what we are seeking is a question of balance: a process that stimulates idea generation, but can still distinguish the pie-in-the-sky from the blockbuster; a process that avoids the worst of organizational politics, but rewards integrity and honesty; a process that passes the "due diligence" test that enables us to say with pride, even five years later, that the decision we took was the best possible, given the information we had at the time.

The good news is that such as process does indeed exist. I'll describe it in detail in Chapter 5, but let me highlight the key points here.

Firstly, we need to recognize that evaluation takes place in three different ways:

- *Formally, in the context, for example, of business cases and project approvals.* Each organization has its own way of doing these: typically, the process involves the review of written proposals by a panel that meets at defined intervals, say, every three months, with the outcome that approved projects are funded, rejected projects are shelved, and any on which decisions can't be taken are sent back to their originators for further work.

- *Informally, in small groups, in meetings and discussions.* This is the process of largely unconscious, inadvertent, and unwitting evaluation that takes place in all our group interactions – as the last two boxes illustrated. This is how more junior people learn what is right, wrong, accepted, unacceptable, dangerous, safe; this is how more senior people can exert subtle, and not-so-subtle influence; this is a major mechanism whereby organizational cultures become defined, are made explicit and are maintained.

- *Personally, in our own heads.* As a result of our experience with other people, we all learn what is safe to say, to whom, when. Our innermost censor plays a major role in determining what we choose to say, how we choose to say it, from whom we are most likely to receive the most favorable response, and just when the time is right to speak up or to stay silent. If this rings a bell with you, then perhaps it is this inner censor that is the most significant block to innovation in your organization; or, to express the same idea in a different way, what is it about your organizational culture that causes people to be so fearful of putting new ideas on the table?

HOW PERSONAL FEAR CAN STOP ORGANIZATIONAL INNOVATION

Here is another causal loop diagram, which captures a key aspect of the way in which the behavior of the individual both influences, and is influenced by, the organization. You will also see that the diagram incorporates two new symbols – *S* and *O*.

Since idea generation is driven ultimately by individuals, each individual's *personal willingness to suggest ideas* contributes to the *organizational capability to innovate*. The small *S* by the arrowhead stands for *same*, indicating that the two variables at each end of the arrow move in the *same* direction: as the *personal willingness to suggest ideas* increases, so does the *organizational capability to innovate*. This in turn drives *organizational success* (with an *S* again), which in turn boosts *organizational confidence*, so enhancing the *organizational willingness to take more risks*. The loop is completed by the feedback to *personal willingness to suggest ideas*.

Ideally, each turn of the loop reinforces, and grows, the organization's innovative capability as more and more individuals feel comfortable suggesting new ideas. But this *does not* necessarily happen: if the individual has *personal fear of failure or ridicule*, this diminishes the *personal willingness to suggest ideas*. This is shown by the small *O* by the arrow-head. *O* stands for *opposite*, indicating that the two variables at each end of this arrow move in *opposite* directions: as the *personal fear of failure or ridicule* **in**creases, the *personal willingness to suggest ideas* **de**creases.

An individual's *personal fear of failure or ridicule* therefore acts as a brake on the otherwise virtuous circle, and if many individuals have a similar fear, organizational innovation can grind to a halt.

In many organizations, the formal process of business cases and project approval is far too slow and ponderous and, in its worst manifestation, can act as the ultimate block to organizational innovation: by the time an idea reaches the project panel, it has been sanitized and made safe, with all the radical – and the most innovative – elements long since excised. Sluggish, long-winded and highly political processes, however, are not the only way of playing this game, and we shall see how to make this process far more effective in Chapters 5 and 6.

Much more important are the group and personal processes: smart managers of course, know that these interact intimately, for the private, personal process is heavily conditioned by what happens in public, in groups. They know that a culture in which the informal group process acts as a disincentive on individuals creates a climate of fear and embarrassment, and so discourages people from doing anything other than grunt their reluctant agreement with their boss's ideas. Smart managers know how to build a culture which strikes a wise balance between two apparently contradictory concepts: a culture which is supportive of the individual and of the individual's ideas, encouraging people to articulate ideas, however apparently half-baked, as well as one which is professional, rigorous and fair, in which all ideas, when well thought through, are subject to careful scrutiny, so enabling the selection of the very best ideas to be progressed. I discuss how to go about building such a culture in Chapters 5 and 6, and how this can be helped by the use of a number of tools and techniques. One key concept, however, is presented in the next box.

AVOID PREMATURE EVALUATION

Many people – especially dominant younger males – become overexcited when ideas are discussed. If it's their idea, they are incredibly enthusiastic, optimistic, persuasive; if it's someone else's idea, they are hypercritical, scathing, damning. This condition is known as "premature evaluation," and is very disappointing for all concerned.

Smart managers know that no ideas are born with a business case attached – they just aren't. And smart managers know that adversarial attacks such as, "That's crazy, we don't stand a hope of making money out of that!" "We tried that before you joined the company and it was a total failure!" and "How much revenue do you think that will make, then?" aren't smart at all, they're just put-downs. So smart managers don't evaluate prematurely, and they help build internal processes in their organizations, which allow time and space for ideas to be developed to a sufficient state of robustness that they can be evaluated fairly and professionally. That means that genuinely good ideas are backed, no matter who originated them; and when ideas are rejected, the originators are not damaged, but positively encouraged to come up with more and more new ideas.

Smart managers also know the importance of language and the power of phrases such as, "Tell me more about that," "What do we have to do to make that work?" and "What resources do you need to work that idea up into a full business case?"

By building a culture that avoids premature evaluation, but one that is still rigorously professional, the smart manager can gain the best of all possible worlds – an organization in which weak ideas are rejected without discouraging people from trying again, whilst the very best ideas are funded through to the next stage – development.

Development

Development – the light gray zone on the Innovation Target – is the process by which an idea is proven to be a practical reality. For some ideas, the development process might be very short, requiring only a feasibility study (many ideas for process improvement, for example); for others, however, the development process may take many years, and be very difficult. The archetypal example here is the development process for a new drug, for which the activities of pre-clinical investigation, clinical trials and the gaining of approval from the regulatory authorities can be enormously arduous, lengthy and expensive.

Indeed, as we cross the boundary between evaluation and development, something very important happens – the resources of people, time and money which are required to make the idea happen, to develop it, and subsequently implement it, are usually much, much more than resources required to generate the idea and evaluate it.

As we shall see in detail in Chapters 3 and 4, individuals can be very creative in generating great ideas, and small groups can be even more powerful; small project teams can successfully carry out even the most thorough evaluations. But when we come to development, and subsequent implementation, much greater resources usually need to be mobilized.

This has two consequences:

- Firstly, the deployment of resources usually requires organizational co-ordination and commitment: although an individual can have a great idea, only in the most trivial cases can the individual alone bring the idea to full fruition.

- Secondly, the risk to the organization, and perhaps also to the individuals working on the project, increases: there is much more at stake if the project should fail.

The first point is about organizational style, behavior and culture, and the ease with which the organization can form, manage and subsequently disband project teams. It is also about the skills of the organization in managing projects, and its experience and expertise in managing project uncertainties. The second point is about risk – and indeed the themes of risk and risk management underpin much about innovation.

Innovation is fundamentally about risk. Innovation, by definition, is doing something you have not done before. And, as a consequence, this must entail risk. The unwillingness of some organizations, or some people, to take all but the safest risks is one of the reasons why those organizations, and those people, shy away from innovation. In today's business climate, however, there is a strong argument that the perceived low-risk option of maintaining the *status quo*, or of following others, is in fact more risky than stepping into the unknown by innovating!

Smart organizations, and smart managers, however, are not daunted by the existence of risk: rather, they are much more concerned about the mechanisms and processes by which the risks inevitably associated with innovation can be:

- *identified*, so we know what and where they are;

- *understood*, so we know how they are likely to arise, and the impact each is likely to have should any in fact crystallize;

- *monitored*, so we can have as early warning as possible of the likely occurrence of the risk; and

- *managed*, so we know how to reduce the likelihood of the risk, and what we need to do should the risk in fact come to pass.

And – more significantly – they do not wait until one of the risks hits to identify, understand, monitor and manage it: they have done this in advance. When?

During evaluation.

One of the most important functions – if not *the* single most important function – of the evaluation process, is to understand the risks of the innovation project, and to define how those risks are to be managed. How this can be done we shall see in Chapter 5; what we need to note here is that the organization should not even contemplate embarking on development unless it has the appetite, conviction and resources to see the project right through both the development and implementation stages – a commitment made in the full glare of anticipating all the risks.

INNOVATION IS ALL ABOUT RISK

An entrepreneur had a great idea, but needed a lot of funding – so much, in fact, that he realized he had to have government support. So he went about finding a backer.

He was disappointed when the authorities in Portugal, where he had for some time been resident, turned him down, but being globally-minded, he decided to try further afield. Alas, a setback in England was followed by one in France too, but his luck was in when he approached Spain – at last, he had found someone willing to take the risk on his idea.

This story took place about 500 years ago, for the entrepreneur in question is known in his adoptive land as Christóbal Colón, and to the English speaking world as Christopher Columbus.

His idea was a western sea route to the spice islands we now know as the East Indies, and, if his measure of success was achieving this, he failed. But in 1492 he did land in what we now know as America instead, and the subsequent benefits to himself of taking the risk were enormous – he became ennobled, and personally very wealthy. Spain and, later, the Hapsburg dynasty, didn't do so badly either.

Had Portugal, England or France been willing to take the risk, the history of the entire world for the last 500 years would surely have turned out very differently.

The evaluation zone therefore acts as a filter; the exercise of business wisdom in selecting those ideas which bring sufficient business benefit, even in the light of the well-researched risks, from those that do not.

Implementation

The outermost zone of the Innovation Target – representing implementation – concerns all those activities that take a proven idea into full fruition. For ideas concerning process improvement, this usually – these days – involves the building of a new IT system; for a new product, this can involve new factory facilities, an enhanced supply chain, training of sales and support staff, as well as all the marketing activities heralding the launch. There is clearly a lot that needs to be done.

Certainly, all the remarks already made concerning organizational co-ordination, the demand on organizational resources, and managing risk, apply even more to implementation than they do to development, and from the point of view of "making innovation happen," development and implementation dovetail smoothly into one another.

There are, however, two particular aspects of implementation which are unique to this stage, and merit attention: criteria of success, and learning.

Criteria of success

Every new idea carries high hopes, especially in the mind of the idea's originator. But when an idea receives the full organizational backing required for development and implementation, these hopes are often magnified and augmented until they become not only expectations, but the performance measures by which the idea, the development and implementation project, and – much more importantly – the individual members of the project team, are judged as successes – or failures.

What are the criteria by which the implementation is to be regarded as a success, or indeed a failure? What are the performance measures? Where do they come from? What is their validity? Given that innovation is all about moving into uncharted territory, how do you know when you've got there (as the Columbus example makes crystal clear)?

During the year 2000, there was an outstanding example of a botched implementation, and the problems caused by ill-considered criteria of success – the UK's Millennium Dome project.

THE MILLENNIUM DOME PARADOX

The Millennium Dome, an exhibition held within a stunningly innovative dome-like structure built close to the Greenwich Meridian in London, was intended as Britain's flagship project to mark the Millennium Year. The idea originated under the Conservative Government in the mid 1990s, and was vigorously adopted by the Labour Government following their general election victory in May 1997.

Between its opening on January 1, 2000 and its closure on December 31, 2000, the Dome attracted some 6.5 million visitors, making it significantly the most popular attraction in the UK, and second in Europe as a whole: only Disneyland in Paris pulled a greater crowd.

Was the Dome a success or a failure?

Smart things to think about

By attracting so many visitors the Dome, surely, must have been a success.

But, in the eyes of the British media, many politicians, and probably much of the public too, the Dome was more than a colossal failure – it was a true laughing stock. As well as requiring seemingly endless cash handouts from the British government (through the vehicle of the Millennium Commission, a body that distributed funds from the UK's National Lottery), the early days of the Dome were beset by technical difficulties – the celebrity opening night, for example, was a disaster as many "big names" queued for hours for their tickets. It was also a graveyard for senior managers. First to go, in February, was Jennie Page, the civil servant who was the project manager during the initial stages, and subsequently became the chief executive of the New Millennium Experience Company, the organization created to manage and operate the Dome and all its facilities. In May, the chairman, Bob Ayling, former chief executive of British Airways, was replaced by David Quarmby, who for eight years had been joint managing director of the leading British supermarket chain, Sainsbury, as well as subsequently serving as chairman of the English Tourist Board for three years. Quarmby himself relinquished the chairmanship in September to David James, a "company doctor" specializing in corporate turnarounds and recovery.

These senior figures are by no means inexperienced in business: so how could an attraction which ranked number two in Europe be such a disaster?

The answer can be traced back to the original business plan completed in May 1997, in which the number of visitors was projected as 12 million. This figure was not only a key measure of performance, but it was also the prime driver of the business plan itself: it was on the basis of this number that the accountants forecast the revenue (in terms of both ticket sales and merchandising), and from this, the managers determined how much they could spend. In the event, the actual numbers of visitors was way below the forecast, as was the revenue. But by that time, most of the money had been spent ... Hence a huge operating loss, hence the continuing demand on the UK's lottery funds for more cash, hence the embarrassment.

Where did the original forecast of 12 million visitors come from? This figure has been the subject of a number of investigations, including one by the UK's National Audit Office, whose chairman, Sir John Bourne, said on November 9, 2000:

"Building and opening the Millennium Dome on the very short timescale required was a tremendous achievement. But the New Millennium Experience Company has experienced severe financial difficulties this year and has required considerable additional lottery funding.

"The main cause of these difficulties is the failure to achieve the visitor numbers and income required. The targets were highly ambitious and inherently risky leading to a significant degree of financial exposure on the project. In addition, the task of managing the project has been complicated by the complex organizational arrangements put in place from the outset, and by the failure to establish sufficiently robust financial management."

In short, the original forecast was way too optimistic, and everything else follows from that.

Evidence that the forecast was optimistic can be seen by comparing the target of 12 million visitors with two benchmarks: benchmarks that would have been available at the time the business plan was compiled in 1997. During 1996, the most-visited attraction in the UK was the theme park, Alton Towers, with 2.79 million visitors; and in Europe was Disneyland, Paris, with 11.7 million. The 1997 business plan therefore assumed that the Dome, from a standing start, would capture *four times* the number of visitors who had attended the UK's top attraction, and rather more than Disneyland – a tourist magnet, drawing on a catchment area across the whole of continental Europe, bearing the globally-recognized Disney brand name, and supported by years of marketing hype. As it turned out, during 2000, the actual visitor numbers at each of these attractions was: the Dome, 6.5

million (of whom only 5.4 million paid to enter – the remaining million or so were largely schoolchildren who were invited to go free); Alton Towers, 2.6 million; Disneyland, Paris, 12.0 million.

I do not relate this story in defense of the Dome, its concept, its managers, the way the project was directed, or its standing as an artistic monument. Nor do I have any objections in principle to ambitious targets. But if you are going to set an ambitious target, the least you can do (or rather should do) is to understand the risks, and determine in advance what actions you need to take if in fact the worst should happen. Like what should be done if there are fewer visitors than had been hoped; like what should be done if there is bad press? Whether or not this was all discussed with regard to the Dome, who knows? In practice, it is abundantly clear that the risks were not adequately assessed, with the result that the only actions that were taken were to ask the government for more cash, and to fire the senior managers. Oh dear.

The original business plan was wildly over-optimistic, had not been subject to a balanced risk analysis, and was probably accepted in a rush of political euphoria. The hopelessly over-egged sales forecast overstated the sales revenue, and from this all the other problems stemmed. Overall, a set of performance measures was created which had almost no chance whatsoever of being achieved. So the whole thing is perceived as a dismal failure, and heads rolled.

But where was the failure? And did the right heads roll? Was the real failure way back at the business plan? If the sales forecast had been realistic, but the level of costs too high to be commercially viable, then either a different cost base had to be determined, or the project should have been cancelled then. This, of course, is a question of evaluation – and, as we saw in our earlier discussion, and will explore in more detail in Chapter 5, evaluation is all about understanding, taking a view on, and managing risk.

The Millennium Dome is just one, highly visible, and very public example of an idea that "failed," to my mind not because the idea itself was flawed, but because the performance measures of success and failure were profoundly wrong.

What are the performance measures you apply to implementation? And how do the performance measures applied to implementation relate to the commitments implied way back when the idea was evaluated?

Learning

This discussion of performance measures leads naturally to the topic of learning. However thorough the development process, it isn't until the idea is fully implemented that you can assess the extent to which the idea truly works in practice. You should not be surprised if the outcome is different from what you expected; smart managers seek to learn new things from each new experience, rather than forcing their previous learning onto a new world. What would have happened, for example, if Columbus, when he eventually came to terms with the realization that he had not in fact discovered a westward route to the East Indies, had said "Well, that was a colossal failure – I'll fire the whole crew, recruit a new one, and then see what happens if we sail the other way!"? A bizarre example, perhaps; but you might like to take a look at the last few innovative projects carried out by your organization, using the questions in the next box as a guide, and see if there are any parallels.

KILLER QUESTIONS

HOW GOOD IS YOUR ORGANIZATION AT INNOVATION?

Here are some questions that will help throw some initial light on how good your organization is at innovation.

- What new ideas have successfully been implemented by your organization in the last three years?
- Who originated those ideas?
- What was the nature of the process by which those ideas were evaluated?
- What were the plans and budgets originally agreed for the development and implementation of each idea?
- How did the actual outcome of the development and implementation compare to the original plans and budgets?
- What were the originally targeted performance measures for success?
- For those projects regarded as a success, what happened to the members of the project team?
- And for those projects that were regarded as failures?
- What was learned from the successes?
- And what from the failures?
- How has that learning been captured, internalized, communicated and used?

You may not know the answers to these questions as you read this, but you will know immediately if they strike a chord. If they do, then it might be worth asking a real killer question:

KILLER QUESTIONS

Why don't we set up a diagnostic project to identify, in detail, just what we are, and are not good at, as regards making innovation happen?

It is most unlikely that things are "wrong" across the board: far more likely that you are good at some things, poor at others. If you can identify the things you are relatively weak at, and fix those, then you are well on the way to making your organization effective at managing the entire innovation process – a topic I discuss in more depth in Chapter 6.

"Unlike cutting costs, or making an acquisition, innovation does not happen just because the chief executive wills it. Indeed, it is confoundedly difficult to come up with new ideas year in, year out – especially brilliant ones. Underneath the gurus' diagrams, lists and charts, most of the available answers seem to focus on two strengths that are difficult to create by diktat: a culture that looks for new ideas, and leaders who know which ones to back."

The Economist, December 4, 1999, page 90

Managing the Innovation Target

What are the key skills required to deliver success in each of the four stages represented by the Innovation Target?

And what is the likelihood that each of these skills is present to the appropriate degree in a single person?

The quick answers to these two questions are "Different ones" and "Pretty unlikely"; let's spend a moment or two on the longer answers too.

Working from the outermost zone of the Innovation Target inwards, the key skills required for successful *implementation* are all concerned with *project management* – skills such as the ability to co-ordinate a broad range of diverse resources; planning; the ability to deliver on time, within budget; strong leadership to keep things going when they get tough. There is a heavy emphasis on managing people: "downwards," in view of the often large project teams; "sideways," since many innovation projects cross organizational boundaries; and "upwards," in terms of negotiating for resources, and reporting progress.

Many of these project management skills are also important during *development*, but perhaps with less emphasis on the management of people (usually, the project teams required for development are smaller than those required for implementation), and rather more on *ingenuity in problem solving*. Development, remember, is the phase in which an idea that has already been formulated, is made real and tested for fitness-for-purpose, perhaps – in the case of new products – by means of prototypes or models. The key question being addressed during development is therefore "How can we get this to work?" and this usually requires the team to identify and successfully solve any number of problems. Certainly, this demands some creativity, but the nature of the creativity is well focused on finding answers to specific questions: "How can we machine this part to the required tolerance?" "How can we minimize the costs of packaging?" and "What is the best way of testing the market?"

Evaluation is very, very different. The role of the evaluation stage is to filter the good ideas from the not-so-good; to decide how the organization can best allocate the inevitably limited resources which can be committed to development and implementation; and to assess whether or not the organization is willing to accept the risk of making real what is at this stage just a new idea. The way in which the evaluation process works sends signals throughout the organization as to what is "good" or "bad," "acceptable" or "too risky," and so is probably the most important determinant of how innovative the organization wishes to be.

What are the key skills here? I'm tempted to say *business wisdom*, for that's what it is – but that's rather too ethereal. So let me make that more concrete by reference to *judgement, risk assessment, insight*, all applied to matters such as the *selection and quality* of the proposed development and implementation team; the *realism, and robustness as regards uncertainty*, of the proposed development and implementation plans; the *value to the organization* of the idea once successfully implemented.

These are all hard-nosed business skills, often gained through experience – and such a different set from those that deliver success in the innermost zone of *idea generation*, the true heart of innovation. As we will see more clearly in the Chapters 3 and 4, the key skills here are *a willingness to cope with ambiguity, the ability to imagine circumstances very different from today's, a delight in challenging "the rules," a passion for asking "How might this be different?"* These all imply that those who enjoy idea genera-tion – and so are likely to be good at it – are comfortable in unstructured contexts, prefer open-ended situations to those with predetermined out-comes, and always seek to question the *status quo.*

So, as we can see, the skills required for success in the different stages of the innovation process are indeed very, very different – from the pragma-tism of the project manager driving implementation, to the free thinking underlying the question, "What would happen if we did this differently?" as required for successful idea generation; from the doggedness of the engi-neer trying the umpteenth different approach to solving a particular prob-lem during development, to the broadly-based business wisdom applied to the risk assessment required for effective evaluation.

This has two important implications.

Firstly, it is extremely unlikely that any single person possesses all the skills required for success across all the stages of the Innovation Target. Not only that – some of the skills are in direct conflict: the last thing the implemen-tation project manager wants to hear is the idea generator's voice saying "Hey, I've just had a great idea – why don't we change …"; likewise, during an open-ended, exploratory, idea-generation session, project-manager-style remarks such as "We've only got ten minutes left, and we still need sixteen new ideas" are pretty unhelpful.

Managing the Innovation Target is therefore a team effort, with leadership being passed from one person to another as the stages progress. That's one reason why many innovative start-ups fail – the scientist with the great idea just doesn't have the management skills (and maybe interest too) for successful development and implementation, nor does the start-up company have a broad enough team for the baton of leadership to be passed from one person to another. But that raises a personal point too – sometimes the originator of an idea is so much in love with it (and maybe himself too) that he is positively unwilling to allow leadership to pass to someone else – and so a project rolls on to doom with the inevitability of a Greek tragedy.

The second implication concerns structures and hierarchies. Most organizations promote people on their success in getting things done; their ability to deliver things on time, within budget; their political skills in not rocking any boats. Their personal styles often correspond to the ESTJ or ISTJ Myers Briggs types, or the "shaper" or "completer-finisher" classifications in the Belbin scheme (see the next two boxes). These are the skills and personal styles that play best in the outermost zone of implementation, and worst in the innermost zone of idea generation. As a consequence, most "bosses" tend to respect and reward implementation skills, so perpetuating the hierarchy.

Unfortunately, though, some bosses – usually those who do not understand the Innovation Target, and especially the innermost zone of idea generation – get very intolerant of the behavioral styles best suited to idea generation, and stop them from happening. They may, for example, refuse to authorize budgets for idea generation sessions, or workshops for sharing knowledge – "What do you mean, you're just going to talk and exchange ideas? If I'm going to authorize an off-site, I want to see the detailed agenda beforehand, and the twenty action points that you are committing to as a result!" They will probably describe people who dare to challenge the (boss's) rules as "dangerous" or "terrorists," and they will almost certainly be premature evaluators.

Katherine Cook Briggs and Isabel Briggs Myers were a mother-daughter team who worked together from the late 1920s to develop some of Carl Jung's theories of psychology into a framework for classifying individual behavioral styles. This resulted in the definition of the *Myers Briggs Type Indicator*, abbreviated to MBTI.

Their classification system is based on four scales:

- *Extroversion (E)–Introversion (I)*. This indicates the degree to which an individual seeks stimulation from the external environment, or is quite content from within.
- *Sensation (S)–Intuition (N)*. This indicates the degree to which an individual relies predominantly on evidence from the senses, or is more inclined to follow intuition, even if this might at times conflict with "harder" evidence.
- *Feeling (F)–Thinking (T)*. This indicates the degree to which an individual takes decisions predominantly by reference to how others might feel, or on the basis of logic and reason.
- *Perceiving (P)–Judging (J)*. This indicates the degree to which an individual feels comfortable with ambiguity and letting it be (P style) or prefers clarity and certainty (J style).

As a result of the appropriate tests, an individual can determine his or her own preferred style, expressed as one of sixteen possible combinations such as ESFP. It often happens that individuals, when under pressure, adopt a different style, and this can be determined too.

Different roles and professions tend to correlate with different Myers Briggs types – many business leaders, for example, are ESTJ, while their lawyers and accountants are ISTJ; doctors are often ISFP, teachers and psychologists, INFP. Those who like innovation, and especially idea generation, are likely to be ENTP (with a preference for the dreamier) or ENTJ (with a preference for the more pragmatic).

SMART PEOPLE TO HAVE ON YOUR SIDE:

KATHERINE COOK BRIGGS (1875–1968) AND ISABEL BRIGGS MYERS (1897–1980)

SMART PEOPLE
TO HAVE ON
YOUR SIDE:

DR MEREDITH
BELBIN

An alternative classification of personal behavioral styles, with an emphasis on how individuals behave in groups and teams, was developed by Meredith Belbin during the 1970s. His original research was based on observing successful and unsuccessful teams competing in a series of business games being run by Henley Management College in the UK. Belbin distinguishes between nine different styles, thumbnail sketches of which are:

- *The co-ordinator*: the person who is a good chair, co-ordinating activities, managing the discussion without dominating it.
- *The shaper*: the self-confident, highly action-oriented person who enjoys taking a dominant role in discussions, and driving through obstacles.
- *The plant*, who often prefers thought to action, and is often looked to by the group for "bright ideas."
- *The monitor-evaluator*, who analyzes, criticizes, judges, challenges.
- *The resource-investigator*: the people-person, who enjoys active interactions with others, such as selling, influencing, developing contacts, and building teams.
- *The implementer*: the person who enjoys developing the ideas of others, and translating them into actionable plans.
- *The teamworker*: the person who can hold teams together, for example, by encouraging, mentoring, listening and resolving conflict.
- *The specialist*: the person who is happy to provide specialist input.
- *The completer-finisher*: the person who ensures things get done, who reminds you that, yes, there is a deadline to meet, and who questions whether that last tweak is really necessary.

Balanced, emotionally mature people know how to adapt their personal styles to context, and feel perfectly comfortable shaping in one meeting, making the coffee in another. But we all have our preferred styles, and indeed the style we revert to when under pressure. Plants, clearly, love innovation, especially idea generation; for shapers and finishers, though, it's often a very different story!

For further information, try the Web page www.belbin.com/home.html.

In my experience, bosses of this type do not usually do this deliberately, out of malice, as a willful and intentional way of killing innovation in their organizations – rather, it happens inadvertently, and as a result partly of their own personal style, and partly of their ignorance. No, I'm not saying that bosses are dumb or "ignorant"; what I am saying is that very few people have an intuitive understanding of, or have been trained in, innovation in general, and idea generation in particular. Alas, they know not what they do.

How do you handle this one? Maybe some of the ideas in the following boxes will help.

HOW TO EDUCATE AN IGNORANT BOSS

Smart managers don't need to be told, of course, that it is not a clever thing to suggest that your boss is "ignorant," or that she needs "educating." But handling an ignorant (in the nicest possible sense, of course) boss who really does need educating requires the most subtle upwards management.

Here are some ideas:

- Get involved on the organizing committee of the next annual conference (or whatever), and suggest that innovation might be a topic for, say, an after-dinner speech. Then invite me as the speaker!
- Look through the criteria used for staff appraisal, and see if any refer to creativity and innovation. If they do, ask the HR department to do an analysis of recent appraisals to identify whether the scores for these attributes are lowish, rather than highish. If they are low (compared to other scores), work with the HR function to define a program designed to enhance these scores, and involve your boss.
- If creativity and innovation do not appear on your criteria for staff appraisal, get your boss's permission to incorporate them within the criteria you wish to apply to your own staff (don't try to change the whole organization's criteria – that's too big a hurdle to jump). If your boss expresses interest, involve her in what the criteria should be, and how your team can be equipped with the appropriate skills. This will lead the discussion into training and "master classes" (training for those who believe they are too senior to warrant training!).
- Find out if your organization uses "the Balanced Scorecard" – a method of measuring organizational performance using a set of indicators much broader than those that relate just to finance. As the next box shows, measures of innovation feature under the generic heading "Internal business processes." If your organization uses the Balanced Scorecard, your boss is likely to have innovation as a personal performance measure, and so will be motivated to want to be better at it. And if your organization isn't yet using the Balanced Scorecard, maybe it should start thinking about it!

Robert Kaplan, a professor at Harvard Business School, and David Norton, the president of consulting firm Renaissance Solutions Inc., are co-authors of business best-seller *The Balanced Scorecard*, as well as three related articles in *Harvard Business Review*.

The thinking behind the scorecard is the recognition that performance measures based solely on (often short-term) financial results can erode the longer-term health of a company by encouraging only those behaviors that have short-term financial impact. Kaplan and Norton argue that, since people tend to behave in accordance with the metrics by which they are measured, then the portfolio of performance measures used within a smart firm should extend beyond the purely financial.

The Balanced Scorecard suggests a framework for this, under four main headings:

- *Financial*, including revenues, profits, profitability, asset utilization and so on.
- *Customer*, including market share, customer acquisition, customer retention, customer satisfaction and customer profitability.
- *Internal business processes*, including operations, after-sales service and – importantly from this book's point of view – the innovation process itself.
- *Learning and growth*, including employee capabilities, motivation, empowerment, alignment and information systems.

Since the publication *The Balanced Scorecard* in 1996, many organizations have seen the wisdom of measuring their managers on a much more broadly-based set of metrics, so that long-term objectives are not blithely sacrificed to meet this month's target.

SMART PEOPLE
TO HAVE ON
YOUR SIDE:

ROBERT
KAPLAN AND
DAVID NORTON

INNOVATION AS A COMPETENCY

Many organizations wish to become more innovative, and seek to do this by training – specifically training in idea generation. As the Implementation Target demonstrates, however, organizational innovation is much more than idea generation, and to train people in idea generation tools and techniques may in fact turn out to be counter-productive: people who have been trained, and then generate great ideas, might become frustrated at the organization's subsequent inability to manage the innovation process as a whole, from evaluation, through development to implementation.

A helpful way of looking at this is in terms of a competency grid:

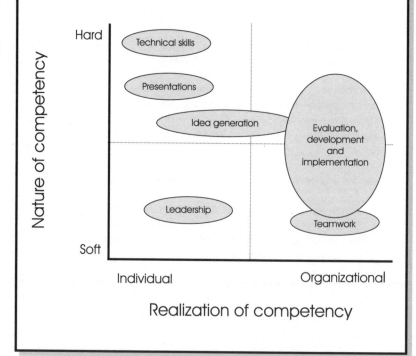

The vertical axis distinguishes between those skills that are "hard" (strongly supported by tools, techniques and methods which can be "taught" and "learnt") and those that are "soft" (determined largely by personal and inter-personal behaviors, requiring inter-personal sensitivity, and based primarily on experience); the horizontal axis distinguishes between skills that can be fully exercised by an individual, and those that require organizational co-ordination and co-operation. As an example, people can be trained in the technical skill of interpreting financial statements, and can then exercise that skill by themselves; as we shall see in this book, much the same applies to idea generation – but the positioning more towards the center captures the concept that the exercise of this skill is far more powerful in small groups.

Innovation, however, in all the richness of the Innovation Target, requires a mixture of hard and soft skills, and is absolutely dependent on organizational co-ordination and co-operation.

Smart organizations know this, and do not initiate a huge training program in idea generation before the organization is ready to cope.

THE POWER OF EDUCATION

Here is another grid – this one captures the issue of the boss who just doesn't understand what innovation in general, and idea generation in particular, are all about.

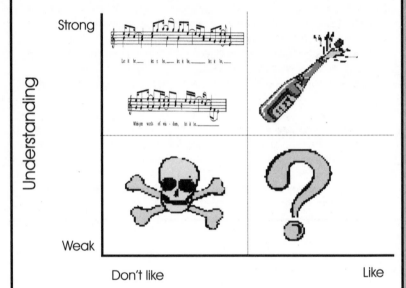

The vertical axis represents an individual's understanding of idea generation on a spectrum from "weak" to "strong."

The horizontal axis represents that individual's empathy with the process of idea generation on the basis that some people like it, and some don't.

Those who like it, but don't understand it (the bottom right quadrant) are those whom most of the rest of us call "naturally creative": they are naturally good at coming up with great ideas, but they can't describe the process that they are using, and, as a result, they don't know how to transfer their skill to others. The question mark represents the realization that such people could be so much more effective: "Wouldn't I and my team be so much better at this if only I knew, consciously, what I am doing!?"

This awareness moves you into the top right quadrant, where you like it, and know exactly what you are doing, so you can transfer the skill to others and exercise the skill, as a group, again and again and again and again. Whoopee!

People who occupy the upper left quadrant – those who understand idea generation, but don't personally like it – understand idea generation well enough to give them the wisdom of allowing it to happen for others. They don't like it personally, so they choose not to participate, but they do not stop it from happening – indeed they encourage it, since they understand its importance. Hence the music from The Beatles's song Let it Be.

People in the bottom left quadrant don't understand it, and if they are in positions of authority, and don't like what they see when others try to exercise the skills of idea generation ("No, that's the way we've always done it! And let me remind you that I was responsible for the design of that process!"), then that is death.

One of the objectives of this book is that everyone who reads it should very easily move up the vertical axis to a position of strong understanding. Whether or not you will like the process is up to you, and I have no axe to grind either way. If you do like it, great; if you don't, well, such is life – but I have every confidence that your understanding will allow you to let it be for others.

Mark Selway is a veritable dynamo within the automobile industry, having been managing director of the Rear Vision Systems Division of Britax International, and also of Schefenacker Vision Systems, a German-based global company with a very significant share of the world market for the manufacture of car components such as lights and rear view mirrors.

Mark is one of the most task-oriented managers you could ever meet: he sets and meets his targets, he drives his team fairly and hard. And he hates, just hates, the process of idea generation: all that faffing around, all that open-endedness, all that talk – strike a light, cobber (Mark is Australian), when is anything ever going to get done!?!

But Mark understands it – deeply. So, even though he can't stand the process itself, he knows why it is important, and he now never says "I want five new ideas on my desk this afternoon!" – he has learnt that "by next Friday" works much better.

But he wasn't always like that. He moved himself from the bottom left to the top left of the empathy grid, and uses his energy and drive to be the true champion of innovation throughout his company, encouraging those who like it to do it.

2
Applications

Innovation is not just a better mousetrap

Many people map the term "innovation" onto the discovery and successful launch of the "better mousetrap." Certainly, the invention, development and successful launch of new products and services is very important, but it is by no means the sole domain where innovation creates value in a business.

As the enhanced version of the Innovation Target shown in the next box indicates, innovation can play a vital role in a variety of domains, including:

- new *product* development;

- the design of new *processes*;

- new *organization* structures;

- new forms of *relationship*;

- new, breakthrough, *business strategies*; and

- new ways of thinking for *you*!

The purpose of this chapter is to discuss these applications more fully.

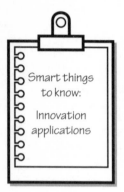

Smart things
to know:

Innovation
applications

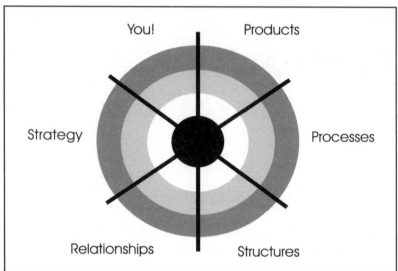

Smart
things to
think about

PRODUCT POSITIONING

"I've got it! I've got it!"

Heads turned; eyes opened wide. Yes, we were all at an idea generation session, but none of us were expecting quite such a *Eureka!* moment. What made the event even more dramatic was the fact that as the words were uttered, in a deep, resonant voice, the speaker leapt out of his chair (no, this latter-day Archimedes was not in a bath!), flung his arms in the air, and started bouncing about the room. And when Dr K bounces around a room, he sure bounces, and everyone takes notice.

"We've got it wrong! We've had it wrong for years!" he continued, gesticulating wildly.

"What have we had wrong for years?"

"The sales approach. The marketing approach. The positioning. Everything. Wrong. For years!"

Wry looks on faces. Eyes catching one another. Thought bubbles coming from everyone (everyone, that is, expect Dr K) saying "But we've been doing this for years. And we've been successful for years. What is this guy on about?".

"What *do* you have in mind?" I ask.

"Who are our buyers?"

"Well, we sell about 60 percent of our volume on prescription . . . and the rest is sold over-the-counter at farm stores."

"And who buys at the farm stores?"

"People from farms. People that want to treat their animals themselves, and who don't need a prescription from the vet."

"And these people, these farmers. What do they do all day? What do they look like?"

"Mmm . . . they're farmers; they run their farms. What do they look like? Well . . . I suppose they're pretty big guys, with check shirts, cowboy boots and a big hat. They look a bit like you, Dr K!" (Chuckles round room.)

"And these big guys. What do they drive?"

Chorus from around the room: "Four-wheel-drive pick-up trucks, Dr K!"

"And these big guys. What do they smoke?"

Chorus: "Marlboros, Dr K!"

"So why the hell are we selling our product in these stupid little containers, with all this scientific small print, and our long, fancy brand name? We should call this stuff **TERMINATOR**, with a strap-line like **KICKS BUGS BUTTS**. The pack should be big, and heavy, so only a real man can carry it. It shouldn't have any small print. The pack should be a vigorous, male colour – say bright red, or maybe yellow and black. And there should be a big image, like a raging bull. If we're selling our product to people who buy Marlboros, why don't we brand it like Marlboros?"

New product development

Sooner or later, every product or service reaches its sell-by date: perhaps a competitor has introduced a similar product with better features; perhaps the impact of a new technology has made an existing product obsolete.

The continuous invention, development, and successful introduction of new products and services is undoubtedly an imperative of every business, and the process that has to be followed comprises the now-familiar four stages of idea generation, evaluation, development and implementation.

An issue that often arises in new product or service development is expressed by the two questions, "When is a new product or service genuinely new? Does it have to be truly radical, or are incremental improvements OK?" These two questions capture the polarization between those who have very high thresholds of what they consider "new," so that only a truly revolutionary new product or service is good enough, and those who are content with apparently more modest achievements.

Those who espouse the "incrementalist" view have to withstand the accusation of being small-minded, unambitious, over-cautious. The "radicalists," on the other hand, certainly have high aspirations, but risk missing out on any number of potentially commercially valuable opportunities by rejecting ideas that "are not bold enough." They might also end up betting their companies – and losing – by introducing products or services so bold and revolutionary that they are way ahead of their markets. This is the archetypal technology-led syndrome, as shown, for example, by the English inventor and entrepreneur Sir Clive Sinclair. No one would deny the innovative and radical nature of his inventions; commercially, however, Sinclair's fortunes have cycled through periods of spectacular boom, only to be followed by even more spectacular bust.

Sir Clive Sinclair was, for a time, Britain's hero entrepreneur. Born in 1940, he did not attend university but left school to join the editorial staff of *Practical Wireless* magazine. A few years later, in 1961, he founded his first company, designing and manufacturing radios and audio equipment.

In 1972, he launched Britain's first pocket calculator, the Sinclair Executive, which, in its day, was a major breakthrough. A later model, the Sovereign, had a design so chic it could be found in all the smartest handbags, and on the smartest executive desks. Unfortunately, Sinclair's success with calculators and audio equipment was ruined by the failure of the digital "Black Watch," leading to a massive bale out by the government of the day. Undaunted, in 1980, he brought out Britain's first true personal computer – the Sinclair ZX80. Here he was ahead of his time. The commercial market for PCs was still very immature, and largely dominated by technical enthusiasts for whom the Sinclair ZX80, and the later models ZX81 and ZX Spectrum, were far inferior to other (admittedly much more expensive) products such as the Commodore Pet and Apple II. What Sinclair did do, however, was to create the UK market for home computers, selling to schools and to parents who wanted their children to have the latest gizmo. 1983 was a good year for Sinclair: the Spectrum achieved a rate of sale peaking at 12,000 units

SMART PEOPLE
TO HAVE ON
YOUR SIDE:

SIR CLIVE
SINCLAIR

a week, he had become a very successful and visible businessman, and UK Prime Minister, Margaret Thatcher, awarded him a knighthood.

Sinclair's second downfall came on two fronts. In the domestic PC market a new model, the QL, was launched in 1984 before it was technically ready and suffered from some very public teething problems. Then, in 1985, came the Sinclair C5 – undoubtedly a revolutionary product: a battery-powered one-passenger vehicle, designed for local transport, such as shopping trips. A few C5s were purchased by avant-garde eco-warriors, and one or two (I suspect) by design museums. But a handful of sales was not enough.

Sinclair sold his computer interests in 1986, but he continues inventing – his most recent concepts being the Zeta III, an electrical power pack to assist cyclists, and the X1, the world's smallest FM radio, which is about the size of a coin, and fits into the ear.

Were some of Sinclair's ideas ahead of their time? Or was he trying to be too clever by half?

Which school of thought is right?

To me the radical–incrementalist debate is a non-argument, based on the twin false premises that only radical ideas can be commercial blockbusters, and that incremental improvements can bring only incremental revenues.

Surely, the key objective in introducing new products and new services is to generate profitable new revenues, and the criterion of success can only be measured in these terms. I know of no law that states that commercial success is attributable only to radical new ideas; but I do know plenty of examples of seemingly relatively simple, or even banal ideas, that have proven to be enormous commercial successes.

WHO WANTS TO BE A MILLIONAIRE?

Here is a description of some of the key features of a TV game show:

- The contestant is given the answer to each question, in the form of a choice of four options.
- The contestant can elect not to answer the question, and leave the show with all the accumulated winnings, without penalty.
- If the contestant is unsure of which of the four presented answers is correct, he or she may seek help.

The show in question is *Who Wants To Be A Millionaire?* – undoubtedly *the* current commercial blockbuster, worldwide, of TV game shows.

Stated in such bald terms, what could possibly be duller as a game show? The contestant is given the answers in advance, with a one in four chance of getting it right? And can even ask for help? And can quit without penalty? What a yawn!

For sure, there are some other features, such as a top prize in the UK of £1,000,000, a charming host, and the drama of the *mano a mano* conflict between smart quizmaster and lone contestant. But there have been plenty of game shows with big money prizes (I remember *The £64,000 Question* from my childhood!); charming hosts are two-a-penny; and the dramatically lit, sweating contestant is familiar from *Mastermind*. Even the concept of multiple-choice questions is not new – many children's competitions have used that idea before.

Who Wants To Be A Millionaire? is undeniably a huge commercial success. But is the underlying idea radical, incremental, or even innovative?

Its commercial success is undeniable. But I would argue it is very much in the incremental camp.

Smart things to think about

Smart managers, therefore, don't fall into the trap of being precious about what is "radical" and what is "incremental": their criterion of success is a commercial one, not an intellectual one. And smart managers also know, as a result of their deep understanding of the Innovation Target, that, in the first instance, in the innermost zone of idea generation, all ideas are by definition "good." It is only later, when the ideas have had some time to mature, during the evaluation process, that a judgement is made on which ideas to back. As we shall see in Chapter 5, the smart evaluation process is designed to examine the idea from all angles, and to avoid acceptance or rejection solely on the judge's personal view of "radicalism" as opposed to "incrementalism."

Process innovation

Processes refer not to what you do, but to how you do it. And as a result of the quality revolution, businesses began to wake up to the fact that value can be created by process improvement as well as by new product development. Sometimes this value is created by cost reduction without compromising quality or product features, with the enhanced value being captured either by the company or passed on, at least in part, to the consumer. Alternatively, the value can be created in terms of enhanced customer service benefits – faster order-processing times, increased customization, more prompt responses to enquiries, or whatever.

This culminated in the business fad of the 1990s, business process re-engineering. Following the publication in *Harvard Business Review* of "Re-engineering Work: Don't Automate – Obliterate" by Michael Hammer and James Champy, organizations around the world suddenly became aware of their processes, and began re-engineering like crazy.

One of the key features of most business processes – such as "order processing," "new product development," "purchasing," and indeed "innovation" itself – is that they cross internal organizational boundaries. If you track the sequence of events for such a process – what happens, who does it, when – and do this completely from end-to-end, you will usually find that the process hops from one part of the organization to another, from one manager's domain to the next, from one directorate to a second. Also, for the most part, it is a fundamental business truth that the activities under the control of a single manager are more likely to be reasonably efficient and effective – after all, that's what the manager is paid to do.

It is very rare, however, for an entire business process to be under the control of a single manager below board level – the process is often just too extensive, and necessarily crosses conventional organizational boundaries. Boundaries, however, can often act as organizational no man's land, for there is no single individual whose legitimate role is to ensure that what straddles any given boundary is fully efficient and effective; furthermore, there is a strong disincentive on the managers on either side of the boundary to look over the fence for fear of being accused by the neighbour as meddling. So where processes cross organizational boundaries, you will often find queues, piles, muddle.

Process re-engineering throws a highly-focused spotlight onto these boundary zones, identifying the technical issues of how to make any given process smarter in principle, and bringing into sharp relief all the associated political issues such as turf disputes, lack of trust, and the absence of teamwork. As a result of diagnosing the problems, the re-engineering team then redesigns the process, making it slicker, smarter, quicker; often, the relevant managerial roles and responsibilities are changed too, with the intention of making the formal organization structure more consistent with the processes, so that there are fewer cross-functional boundaries, as well as a much clearer managerial ownership of processes as a whole, and of their major component parts.

So far, so good: this is all valuable stuff. But as the 1990s progressed, a number of things happened that damaged the reputation of re-engineering.

Firstly, there was the hype. Early on, there were a number of well-publicized case studies of this company reducing the costs of its purchasing process by 40 percent, or that company reducing its time to market for new products by 70 percent, or whatever. Everyone was talking about "step-changes," "quantum leaps" and "breakthroughs." Naturally enough, if there is an opportunity of knocking half of my overhead costs out at a stroke, I'll have one, please. And so the consultants entered the market, claiming to deliver breakthrough-quantum-leap-step-change. Armies of consultants then started rampaging through organizations, preparing process maps, recommending expensive IT solutions, dismissing all objections on the grounds that the objectors "are just far too resistant to change."

Secondly, there was, in the early 1990s in the UK, an economic downturn. This put pressure on profits, and so many organizations needed to cut costs. Cost-cutting sounds like bad news; process re-engineering is far more acceptable. The result of this was that the term "process re-engineering" was used as a politically correct title for plain, old-fashioned axe waving, with the inevitable consequence that the objectives, methods, and results of true process re-engineering became compromised.

The overall consequence of all this was disappointment. After the re-engineering exercise was completed, and the consultants' bills paid, yes, the process was better – but was it that much better? Was it a quantum leap? A step-change? A breakthrough? In some instances, yes it was; but in many it wasn't – it was more realistically a highly expensive and organizationally invasive way of changing older processes into newer ones, just as we did in the early 60s when computers first came in; in the 70s, with terminals; and in the 80s with PCs.

Unfortunately, this has discredited the power and value of process innovation. Here I use the term "innovation," rather than "re-engineering," for, if you have had experience of a less-than-fully-successful re-engineering project in the past, you might like to compare that experience to the Innovation Target, and ask yourself the question in the next box:

In your last major re-engineering project, how much time was spent in the innermost zone of idea generation, so that the project was based on a compelling, truly significant, new idea?

KILLER
QUESTIONS

It may be that your answer is "not a lot," for many of the disappointing re-engineering projects simply re-engineered (or rather tweaked) the *status quo*. In the absence of a compelling new idea, it is of course inevitable that the re-engineered process will be a lookalike of the old process, but with more modern technology. What else could it be? And if the old process was reasonably efficient, the new process will be more efficient, but probably not hugely so; if the old process was a mess, the new process is much more likely to be a step-change quantum-leap breakthrough. But more as a result of the muddle of the old, than the innovation of the new.

Process innovation can be extremely valuable. But only if it is based on truly new process concepts; only if real effort is put into the innermost zone of the Innovation Target, only if real effort is put into the generation of a truly compelling new process idea.

Organizational innovation

Organizational innovation is harder than process innovation because it is closer to people in general, and maybe you in particular. Doing something structurally new in the organization implies changing people's roles and responsibilities, their rights and obligations. And so people will feel anxious, fearful; maybe joyous; perhaps empowered at last.

Organizational innovation is also another good example of an extension of the issue which we first met in our discussion of new product development – is innovation doing something absolutely new, that literally no one else has done before?

My answer to this is "no": I'm in the camp that is happy with the concept that innovation is what is new to you. This may be new to everyone else too – but it doesn't have to be. In the case of product or service innovation, absolute novelty in certain key features may be the means of differentiating yourself from the competition; in the case of organizational innovation, however, the likelihood is that the idea has been tried elsewhere.

A highly centralized organization, for example, might choose to become decentralized; a heavily silo-based structure might be replaced by a more process-related one. Many organizations will have done this before, and many more will in the future. But for the organization considering this idea for real, and for many of the individuals within it, such a change might be perceived not only as innovative, but revolutionary.

I would argue strongly, however, that well-managed organizational innovation needs to go through all the four stages of the Innovation Target. Ideas need to be generated, and then evaluated; the development stage is usually short, but might involve a pilot study; implementation is bound to be a major exercise, especially as regards managing people, and sorting out all the ancillary processes such as performance measures, and reward and remuneration structures, so that they are fully fit-for-purpose in the new structure.

My experience with organizational innovation is that it is usually short on idea generation, and even shorter on evaluation. Given the proximity to people's personal interests, premature evaluation, particularly from those in positions of relative power, is omnipresent. Maybe that's why consultants are a primary vehicle for making organizational innovation happen.

AN ALTERNATIVE, RELATIONSHIP-BASED, ORGANIZATION STRUCTURE?

Here is a thought on organizational innovation in a professional firm.

Most professional firms are always struggling to define their organization structure: should it be geographical, with self-contained units serving defined territories (London, Midlands, the North)? Should it be organized by function or by technical expertise (marketing, IT, HR)? Or by market sector (financial services, pharmaceuticals, retail)? Or functional within market (marketing within the London region)? Or market within function, with a geographical overlay (IT, subdivided into financial services, pharmaceuticals and retail, with teams in multiple locations)? And once this is sorted out conceptually, who should be assigned to each unit? And who really has the power – the leader of the technical discipline, the market or the geographical region?

There is no right or wrong answer to this, and much time can be spent sorting it out.

But there might be a way of tackling the issue differently.

The ideal of any business unit is that it works cohesively, especially at the senior levels. Conversely, if there is no cohesion at the top, the dysfunction is all too plain.

Given a community of senior people, why not organize the business units on the basis not of technical skill, market sector, or where they are located, but on the basis of who likes, or enjoys working, with whom? In any community, people naturally cluster in affinity groups, and there may be some loners too. Is it necessary to force the loners into a structure? And if there are natural affinity groups, isn't it likely that they will work naturally well together, sharing information and clients without being forced to? Once the affinity groups have been established, then you can determine how the client base can be best handled, and the technical skills kept well honed. In this case, people are the drivers of the structure, not its victims.

What do you think of that idea? Did you notice any premature evaluation?

Relationship innovation

Relationship innovation is all about designing new interactions between people, independent of the organization structure. In general, these relationships are of two types: across the boundaries between organizations, and within the organization itself.

External relationship innovation applies to all parties outside your organizational boundary: suppliers, customers, competitors, shareholders, the public, the government, the regulator, the analysts, the media, and all the rest.

This land is full of "rules," some of which may be valid. But many may be arbitrary, and almost all continue for years unchallenged: "we do not share information with our competitors," "our relationship with the regulator is to keep him as far as possible at arm's length," "the whatever-it-is-journal always give us bad press." So relationship innovation is about exploring what would happen if we did share information with our competitors, if we invited the regulator in, if that journal started to give us good press. And in this exploration, maybe a new idea will emerge ...

EXTERNAL RELATIONSHIP INNOVATION IN MANUFACTURING

"There's a real shortage of skilled labour now that we've put robots on our production line."

"Yes, that's right. The robots have certainly made us more productive, but one side effect of their implementation has been to change the balance between skilled and unskilled staff: we have far fewer unskilled staff than before, and those staff we've retained are even more specialised and highly skilled than before."

"Which causes real problems whenever someone is off sick or on holiday. In the old days, we could arrange cover simply by switching in someone else, but these days, the roles are so specialised that this is increasingly hard to do."

"What we need is flexible access to a larger pool of highly skilled labour. That would really help."

"Where might these people be? In the local college perhaps ... or even at the schools."

"They've got the right sort of labour, of course, at the factory down the road. With exactly the right skills too."

"Yes, but they're the competition, aren't they?"

"Yes they are. But I wonder if there is some way we might collaborate: after all, they are probably facing exactly the same problems too. If we could discover some way of sharing our skilled labour forces ..."

"Don't be crazy! They're the competition!"

Crazy? Or a powerful opportunity for some external relationship innovation?

Internal relationship innovation is about what happens for real within organizations. Every professional firm – lawyers, accountants, consultants, for example – will say that "effective knowledge management is a good thing." But everyone within a professional firm also knows that the possession of knowledge can confer enormous power – if I can preserve my special knowledge of a particular subject, then anyone who needs to know something about it will have to come to me; if my personal network of client contacts is strong and exclusive, then I can protect my billings. So why on earth should I share my knowledge, or my client contacts, with anyone else? Especially someone I don't like?

Such a firm needs to think through how to initiate some relationship innovation pretty hard. The themes that underpin relationship innovation, by the way, are usually pretty obvious – teamwork, communication, shared objectives, shared rewards, shared values, trust, respect. But as I'm sure your own experience testifies, that doesn't make them any easier to put into action.

Smart things to think about

INTERNAL RELATIONSHIP INNOVATION IN A PROFESSIONAL FIRM

In 1993, I attended one of the regular meetings of the UK consulting partners in the firm then known as Coopers & Lybrand. There were about 100 partners in the room, all highly educated, articulate, self-confident, successful. The theme of the day was "teamwork," and the agenda was the usual stuff: "state of the nation" presentations, break-out groups, feedback.

Towards the end of the day, Malcolm Coster, the boss of the consulting firm, gave his "rah-rah" address – something he did very well, for he was a good speaker, always holding the audience's attention; charismatic, even. The territory he was covering was familiar – how we should all work together more, share leads, use each others' staff. As Malcolm was talking, my eyes drifted around the room, and I watched the faces of many of my fellow partners. And as I did this, one thought kept coming into my mind. "Who's that fellow, over there?" "What's the name of that lady sitting next to Tony? I don't think I've ever seen her before." "Who are all those people from Edinburgh, and why are they sitting in a huddle?"

At the end of the presentation, Malcolm asked for questions. There was the usual silence, which went on for rather longer than usual – he clearly hadn't planted any. So I put my hand up.

"Dennis?"

"May I ask a question, please? Not of you, Malcolm, but of everyone here? Thanks. I reckon there are about 100 of us in the room today. Is there any person here who knows the names of all the other 99?"

I paused, and looked around the room. No one put up a hand. No one.

"If we don't even know each others' names, how on earth can we operate as a high-performing team?"

Smart things to think about

RELATIONSHIP INNOVATION IN A GOVERNMENT DEPARTMENT

Not long ago, I was asked to run an idea generation workshop with the senior team of a UK government department. Idea generation workshops usually work better when there is a specific issue to address, and the one chosen for this workshop was "How can we release time from the day job for all the other things we really want – and need – to do?" This issue, for sure, is not limited to government departments!

During the discussion, everyone quickly agreed that one of the most time-consuming activities is "ministerial briefings." At any time, the telephone can ring, and they will be asked to prepare a "ministerial briefing" on whatever subject the Minister has requested. As soon as the phone call arrives, they launch into a well-oiled process of defining the structure of the brief, drafting the text, review, redrafting, more review, more redrafting, final review, print. And then the ten-page document, crafted in finest Jane Austen English, finds its way to the Minister.

I set the challenge that the team would not be let out of the room until they had discovered ways of reducing the time and effort of this process by a factor of ten – so 20 man-days of effort over ten elapsed days becomes a maximum of two man-days in just one – without compromising quality. How we went about this we'll discuss later in Chapter 4 – let me skip to the answers.

The first answer was "don't do it" – recycle the one on the same subject we did two weeks ago. That only works, of course, when there is a suitable briefing already on the shelf. What if there isn't? But during the discussion, an important light bulb went on. The realization was that an instruction for a brief *never* comes directly from the Minister – it always comes from the Minister's private office. So, maybe there is a possibility that the Minister might not actually *want* a ten-page brief – perhaps a one-paragraph sound bite would be acceptable. Or a two-pager. In fact, we don't know – every time we get an instruction for a brief, we just do the same, standard thing. So, instead of producing briefs on autopilot, maybe we could ask the private office what the Minister might actually want. But the private office is staffed by very busy people, who – because they're working directly for a Minister – assume that their requests will take priority over everything else. How on earth can we go back to them and ask, "Are you sure the Minister wants a ten-page briefing?" Won't they feel it to be some kind of challenge? Maybe … but maybe not. But if we don't even initiate the conversation, we'll never find out …

That's exactly what relationship innovation is all about.

Strategy innovation

I've recently been reading a companion volume in this series, *Smart Things to Know about Strategy* by Richard Koch. And a good read it is too, full of pragmatic wisdom, and sound common-sense advice. But what I really noticed was the fact that creativity and innovation underpin the whole book. Without wishing to do any injustice to an excellent book, my summary of the argument is that strategy is all about securing competitive advantage, and that competitive advantage comes from doing things differently from the competition.

Smart quotes

"To be really different you have to *do* things differently, you must make courageous decisions that defy conventional wisdom. Sources of competitive advantage do not grow on trees. They have to be created, and there can only be one creator."

Richard Koch, *Smart Things to Know about Strategy*, p. 6

The importance of strategic innovation is the fundamental theme of Gary Hamel's latest book, *Leading the Revolution*, but rather than referring just to "strategy," Hamel talks of something deeper: "business concept innovation," by which he means a total re-think of all aspects of a business model simultaneously – products, services, competitive position, organization, the lot.

Smart quotes

Innovation, in its richest sense, is therefore the holy grail of many business strategies – how can we be distinctive, to stand out from the crowd, to be fundamentally different from the competition? And we all need to be creative in the exploration and determination of the strategy itself, for if we are not we will get stuck in the same strategic rut we have been in for years.

Strategy and innovation are therefore intimate bedfellows, and more insights as to how to use the tools and techniques of idea generation to formulate truly innovative strategies will be presented on pages 284–292.

SMART PEOPLE
TO HAVE ON
YOUR SIDE:

GARY HAMEL

Gary Hamel is the fast-talking *enfant terrible* of the management guru community. Author of two best-selling books, *Competing for the Future* (with CK Prahalad) and *Leading the Revolution*, as well as some prize-winning articles in *Harvard Business Review*, Hamel is also the architect of concepts such as "core competencies" and "strategic intent." His academic credentials include professorships at the University of Michigan and London Business School, and he is the chairman and founder of the consulting firm, Strategos, headquartered in Menlo Park, the heart of Silicon Valley.

INNOVATION AS A STRATEGIC GOAL

Innovation maps on to strategy in three different ways. The first is as applied to your strategy itself – an innovative strategy is one which is significantly different from your competitors – IKEA's approach to the furniture market being a very good example.

The second is as applied, not so much to the end result of the strategy, but to the process whereby the strategy is formulated – for example, you might find that the process described on pages 284–292 is an innovative approach to strategy development as far as your organization is concerned.

And the third is to make innovation itself your strategic goal – that the heart of your (innovative) strategy, which you (of course) formulated in a fully innovative way, is to make innovation the very heart of your strategy.

Why on earth would you do that?

Because you have a belief, a deeply held belief, a belief reinforced by reading this book.

A belief that innovation – the capability to solve problems in a fresh way wherever, whenever and however they might arise – is the ultimate competitive advantage. You know that new products are of course important, but all products have a shelf-life, and more important than an individual product is the capability to create new ones. You know that processes are important too, but you also know that processes are artifacts of technology, and need to be replaced as technology offers different opportunities. And you also know that even brands can become tarnished over time – what, after all, happened to British Airways and Marks & Spencer?

Yes, as a smart manager, you know that innovation – innovation as a fundamental capability, as a core competence – is the only truly ultimate competitive advantage. And that's why innovation itself is your fundamental strategic goal.

e-novation

There is a very wild-looking French author named Georges Perec, who does innovative things in literature. He has written, for example, an entire book – yes, an entire book – which does not contain the letter "e." The title of the book, in its original French, is *La Disparition*; even more remarkable is Gilbert Adair's English translation, entitled *A Void*, which doesn't contain any "e"s either – no "the," no "he," no "she," no verbs in the past tense ending -ed, no "e"s at all. Amazing.

Georges Perec is an innovator in literature. From his picture, you may not particularly choose to have him on your side, but he is fun to know about.

In 1960 (when else?), a group of French writers and mathematicians got together to create a group known as Oulipo. Their mission was to discover new ways of writing, in accordance with certain self-imposed constraints. As an example of what this means, suppose you happen to be Shakespeare, and you want to write a sonnet. This is not a free-format, open-ended exercise – a Shakespearean sonnet is a Shakespearean sonnet because it conforms

SMART PEOPLE
TO HAVE ON
YOUR SIDE:

*GEORGES
PEREC
(1936–1982)*

to a very strict structure, obeying a host of rules, three of which are: there must be 14 lines, no more, no fewer; the first line must rhyme with the third; and the second line must rhyme (differently) with the fourth. Writing a sonnet is a highly constrained activity, and the wonderful skill of the great sonnet writers is how powerfully, imaginatively and innovatively they write, even within such tight constraints.

The Oulipo movement took this idea, and widened its scope. Take the letter "e," for example. What about imposing a constraint such as not using it, in any words at all, throughout a particular work? How long a manuscript can you construct within this limitation? Is it just a paragraph or two? Or could it, with brilliant flair and startling imagination, turn out as a short story, stylistically similar to a famous author such as, say, Maupassant or Maugham? Or might you craft a truly significant, substantial and important work of fiction, non-fiction, or possibly biography, of a quality worthy of a Tolstoy, a Proust or a Dumas? Georges Perec did indeed do it for a whole book – I could just about manage five short sentences!

One of Perec's other works is entitled *Life A User's Manual* (I wish I could think up titles like that!), and, if you really are a committed e-freak, try *Les Revenentes*, known in English as *The Exeter Text*. Throughout its entire length, you will find no "a"s, no "i"s, no "o"s, no "u"s – the whole text, in both the original French and its English translation, has as its only vowel the magic letter "e"!

The reason I mention this odd fact here is that, up to now, you might have been thinking, "How come, in a book written in the year 2000 on innovation, why isn't it full of e-commerce, e-business, e-B2B, e-B2C, e-this, e-that, e-everything? Isn't "e" the essence (or even e-ssence) of business these days? Is this guy some kind of management Georges Perec, with an aversion to the letter 'e'?"

Well, it is true that e-mania has had little visibility so far in this book, but this is not because I have an aversion to the letter "e"; rather it is because I do not see e-novation as the be-all and end-all of innovation. Indeed, as this chapter in particular makes clear, my view is that innovation applies to many domains, from new products to new strategies, from new organizations to new forms of relationship. There is much space for truly stunning innovation in all sorts of places beyond the e-world. And there are many examples of companies who have been innovative and successful in "conventional" ways – Virgin Atlantic Airways continually enhances its customer service package, from introducing limousines to ease the burden of travel to and from the airport, through in-flight massages, to the availability of ice creams during the movies; retailers such as Wal-Mart and Toys "R" Us steadily increase their share of the pedestrian (in the literal sense of the word!) retail market. Conversely, there are any number of unknown e-business failures, as well as some very public ones.

What makes e-novation special, I believe, is its potential scope – for the ease of passing messages around the Internet creates the opportunity of causing highly disruptive change, simultaneously, in many different aspects of business activity.

The ability to pass messages from one computer to another has, of course, been around for at least three decades. But to make this happen, you have to solve two major problems. Firstly, the machines at each end have to be compatible: it's no use being able to send a message that the recipient can't understand. One solution to this is to have the same type of computer, and the associated software, at each end, which is easily done if both ends are within the same organization, but less easy if the messages cross organizational boundaries. In this case, the only solution was to agree, amongst all the different organizations party to the message, a set of standards for how messages will be structured. The definition and agreement of such cross-industry standards is time-consuming, but by no means impossible, just one important example being the standards agreed in the UK to allow banks to transfer funds electronically through the CHAPS system, which has been in operation since 1984.

The second problem concerns the knowledge the sender of a message required about the receiver. In the past, if I wanted to send a message to a specific recipient, I needed to know the recipient's telephone number. That's fine if I know the name of the person I want to send a message to, and if I can find their telephone number; not so good if I don't know the person's name, and even less so if I know the name, but can't discover the right number. The only assistance I might have had is Directory Enquiries if I knew the name but not the number, or the Yellow Pages if I had some idea of the nature of the organization I wanted to contact. But these are limited in their nature, and also their geography – at home I have only my local directories.

If e-business is defined as the ability for organizations to transfer computer messages over long distances, then it has been around for a long time. But what has happened in the last five years has changed the scene dramatically.

Firstly, the problem of compatibility has been largely cracked. The use of infrastructure standards such as html, the widespread adoption of the programming language Java, and the dominance of Microsoft, have together enabled messages written on the laptop computer I am using now to be read by almost any other computer in the world – without the necessity of that computer being from the same manufacturer, and without the need for me to agree, bilaterally, a set of standards with anyone else.

Secondly, the availability of Web browsers and search engines has solved the problem of the requirement for prior knowledge of telephone numbers. On my laptop, I have one telephone number that connects me to the Internet. Once connected, I then have access to all the other computers in the world that are also connected, and I can find them, and communicate with them, using Web browsers and search engines. These act as very sophisticated forms of Directory Enquiries and Yellow Pages, but with the significant benefits that I no longer need to know a specific name, nor am I restricted to a short description such as "car tyre retailers," nor am I limited geographically: my Web browsers and search engines allow me to use a huge range of keywords and descriptive phrases to search computers all over the world. In seconds, I can discover the computer I want to connect to, no matter where it is, then make the connection directly, and so send and receive the messages I want.

And in addition, the number of people to whom I might wish to send messages to, or receive messages from, is vast. In the 1970s, when the major businesses were developing their own internal networks, the only places where you found computers were in other businesses. No one had computers at home, or on their laps. Today, the number of computers in private ownership, used primarily from the home, is huge. And the need for a stand-alone computer is diminishing fast, as televisions and mobile phones increasingly become available as providing direct Internet access.

The inter-connectivity of an enormous, and growing, number of computers, combined with the increasing ease of finding what you need, stimulated by the reducing cost of the equipment and the communications, together form the basis of the e-revolution.

At one level, e-business is an opportunity for process innovation: instead of doing my purchasing by face-to-face contact, negotiation, ordering and invoice payment, I can streamline the process using electronic messaging. This applies as much to businesses (the B2B world is driven by purchasing process innovation) as it does to the personal shopper (as delivered by suppliers such as Amazon.com).

At another level, e-business offers much scope for product or service innovation. If you are looking for the lowest price airline ticket, for example, there are now many Web sites that draw together the prices of all the airlines that fly between the appropriate two cities, and offer you a direct price comparison on a single screen. In the past, the only way you would have been able to do this was either to contact each airline one-by-one – a tedious thing to do – or by reference to an agent whom you trust. Now this service is available instantaneously, at any time of day or night.

But it doesn't stop there: e-business is driving organizational innovation too, in at least two ways. Within established organizations, functions that hitherto had shuffled all the paper are now no longer needed; and within the new dot.com companies, there are all sorts of organizational innovations being explored – flatter, non-hierarchical structures, more flexible working régimes, different forms of remuneration.

But perhaps the biggest impact concerns relationship innovation. Relationship innovation concerns changes in internal relationships independent of the formal, official organization structure, and in external relationships. The fact that I can easily discover which airline offers the cheapest tickets profoundly changes my relationship with my "favorite" airline. In the past, I might have contacted that airline, as first choice, simply because I was in a hurry, and hadn't the time (or, more likely, just couldn't be bothered) to shop around. But if shopping around is made much easier for me to do, then I'll do it. So much for customer loyalty. Or rather, the greater the incentive for my favorite airline to do even better in keeping me happy, so I'll continue to buy their tickets even if they're not the cheapest. The Internet has provided – and will continue to provide – consumers with an increasing amount of relevant information, and so gives consumers, both as a group and individually, hugely more power.

Another key relationship that is in the process of changing is that between an organization and its key stakeholders, such as shareholders or a wider public. Only a few years ago, listed companies produced a glossy annual report, just once a year, and perhaps a few flimsy interim reports during the year. Many annual reports are now published on the Internet, so creating pressure for more information, more often. How long will it be before companies begin to publish their management accounts, or even their budgets?

The umbrella concept of e-business therefore straddles product innovation, process innovation, organizational innovation and relationship innovation – and as a consequence, strategic innovation too, for the existence of the Internet must influence the strategy of all organizations. The e-world encompasses the whole of the Innovation Target, and that's why it is especially significant right now.

INNOVATION AND YOU!

The purpose of this chapter has been to demonstrate convincingly that innovation is not just about inventing a "better mousetrap," but applies to process improvement, organizational development, internal and external relationships, and strategy too. But if you look back to the enhanced Innovation Target on page 56, you will see that there is a sixth segment, labeled "You!" What does this mean?

It's there to remind you that the richest form of innovation, and maybe the hardest to accomplish, is when you accept the possibility that maybe, yes, there is a different – and perhaps better – idea out there than the one you thought of. Or, to put it the other way round, the biggest blocker to innovation, by far, is the unwillingness of someone in authority to do just that.

Smart things to think about

3
It's All About Patterns

LET'S BE CREATIVE!!

Gather together a small group – say, five or six. Go to a blank flipchart and try this: as a group, see how many ideas you can generate for a new game.

Give yourself just twenty minutes.

SMART THINGS
TO DO

How did that go? Fun?

Now try this:

LET'S BE CREATIVE – AGAIN!!

Gather together a small group – say, five or six. Provide everyone with a pad of paper and a pencil.

SMART THINGS
TO DO

Then ask them to spend just five minutes writing down, as a series of bullet points, everything they know about the game of chess. Encourage them to write down simple things, as if they were sending an e-mail to a Martian so that when the Martian lands, he would be able to distinguish chess from draughts, Scrabble, line dancing, and any other activity. If anyone says "But I don't know anything about chess!" reassure them that they know enough to make a valuable contribution – even if the total extent of their knowledge is that it is a game in which two players move funnily shaped pieces on a board.

Then go to a flip chart, and compile an aggregate list of the group's bullet points – different people are likely to have different lists, albeit with some common points.

Then choose any item on the list and say, "How might this be different? What would happen if [whatever] were not the way it is now, but [something else]? How would we play a game like that?"

To make this more concrete, take the feature of chess that it is played by two people. How might this be different? Well ... there might be only one person, or maybe four, perhaps sixteen or even thirty two ... How would we organize a game of chess if there were, say, four players?

Then see what happens. And when you naturally run out of steam on one item on the list, try another ... and then another.

Keep an eye on the time, and be sure to allow only twenty minutes from when you first asked, "How might this be different?"

How did that one go? And how did it compare to the first exercise? Which exercise generated the greater number of ideas? And of good ideas? Which exercise did you find easier? More effective? In which of the two exercises did you participate more? And your colleagues? In which exercise did you listen more? And in which were you listened *to* more? Which exercise was the more judgemental? And which more empowering? Which exercise showed better teamwork?

I often do the first exercise as a "shocker" when I run training courses: "Right, we're here to be creative, so be creative. Go to a flipchart and write down as many new games as you can in twenty minutes. Go!!" You get the idea.

The first exercise is enjoyed by extrovert, dominant characters, and can quickly revert to the silly – games such as "executive toys" in which company directors are progressively deprived of their company car, their credit card, their expense account, until you see which director squeals first.

The second exercise usually starts off in puzzled silence: "But I don't know anything about chess!" "Why am I doing this?" "Is there some trick?" No, there is no trick. The starting point is simply about cataloging what you know about chess – it's as easy as that. And then, when you share what you have written down about chess with your colleagues, amazingly, you discover that other people have thought of things you didn't! "Good Lord, why didn't I think of the fact that only one piece can occupy a square at any one time! Yes, of course I know that! But why didn't I think of it?"

And then the question "How might this be different?" That's where the fun starts.

"Don't be silly, chess is played by two people, not four."

"Yes, but that's true for chess as it's played now. But let's just imagine what would happen if it were played by four people. How might the game be organized?"

"Well ... you could have two teams of two ..."

"Perhaps one person could control the back row, and the other the pawns."

"Or what about one person controlling the pieces on the left hand side of the board, and the other person, those on the right?"

"The players could play alternately…"

"… or perhaps you could roll a dice to determine which player on each side goes next."

"But doesn't all that assume that the same players are on each side all the time? What about having one 'core' player on each side, and the other two players have to play on whichever side they are assigned to for any given move?"

"Wow, that is different!"

Did you see how many different games have been invented there?

Most people find the second exercise much more successful and satisfying, and, as we shall shortly see, literally hundreds of new games can be invented in this way – the record by groups I have worked with is about 150 in twenty minutes!

Why does this second method work?

Well, that's what this chapter and the next are all about – how to make the process of idea generation deliberate, systematic and safe.

Just a quick health warning. These two chapters are demanding. My assumption is that smart people like you, although in a hurry, are not satisfied by long lists of arbitrary bullet points, or unstructured instructions of the type: "If you do this, it works, trust me, I'm a doctor." So my intention is to provide you with a thorough intellectual explanation of what the creative process actually is, how it works, and how you can make it work. This will therefore provide you with a framework of understanding – understanding that you can apply to a very broad range of situations, and that you can tailor to your own needs. But to get there, you will need to get engaged. My task is to make it engaging, and this I trust I have done. Also, I've structured these chapters, which are quite a full meal, into what I feel confident you will find tasty bite-sized chunks! Bon appetit!

The heartland of innovation

Welcome to the heartland of innovation – idea generation. In this chapter and the next, you will discover how to release the latent creative power that has lain dormant in your mind ever since it was squashed flat by your school's pressure on you to get the "right answer."

Our starting point is an examination of just what creativity is, and what better place to look than at what some highly creative people actually do?

Take Beethoven, for example, a true creative genius if ever there was one. But what did he actually do? Composed great symphonies, yes: great musical works of art, yes too. But what, precisely, was the nature of his art? Well, he used music as a profound medium of expression, but not just any old music – he used music in what we recognize as the Western classical tradition. His music is not – by any means – an arbitrary jangle of random noises: on the contrary, Beethoven's music was written in the context of a well-established musical "language."

All his music, for example, was written within the framework of major and minor scales, those doh-re-me runs of notes that children practice when they learn to play the piano. These scales originated with the so-called "modes" which date back to antiquity, were further developed by the monastic communities in their Gregorian Chants, and reached the peak of their most evolved form with the work of JS Bach, who died in 1750, twenty years before Beethoven was born.

More fundamentally, the notes which comprise all of Beethoven's works are drawn from the same set of notes used by Bach, Mozart and Stravinsky; by Jelly Roll Morton, Glenn Miller and Dave Brubeck; by Burt Bacharach, Andrew Lloyd Webber, and the Beatles. In fact, given a piano – which acts as a repository of all those notes – it is quite possible to play a tune that you would instantly recognize as Beethoven, the Beatles, or whoever.

All music in the Western tradition has the remarkable characteristic of sharing the *same* notes, and so one thing that Beethoven, the Beatles (and any other composer for that matter) did *not* do was to invent any new notes.

So if Beethoven didn't invent any new notes, what *did* he do?

Given that Beethoven didn't invent any new notes, a moment's reflection will convince you that what Beethoven actually did was to invent very many, wonderful, emotionally powerful *patterns* of notes. The essence of Beethoven's creative genius was in taking some basic elements that already existed – the notes that you can find on a piano or any other musical instrument – and combining them simultaneously in time, and sequentially over time, into a host of astonishing patterns: patterns of rhythm, patterns of melody, patterns of harmony, patterns of dynamic intensity; patterns that we give names to such as Beethoven's Fifth Symphony, the "Moonlight" Sonata, and Ode to Joy.

John Lennon and Paul McCartney, about 150 years later, did essentially the same thing – they took the same basic elements, the notes, and combined them into another set of new patterns, with names such as "She Loves You" and "Penny Lane." The notes are the same as Beethoven's – it's the patterns that are different.

In music, then, the creative act is well focused: it is the discovery of a new pattern of elements – the notes – that already exist. What is truly amazing about this is that the number of different elements from which all Western music is formed is incredibly small: a standard piano has only 88 different notes, and of these, only 48 are in frequent use – the very high and very low notes (the ones out of the range of the human voice) are hardly used at all. And more fundamentally still, these 48 are in fact four related groups of twelve, these being the tones and semitones in a single octave, as represented by the repeated groups of the seven white, and five black, notes on a piano keyboard. Just twelve fundamental elements therefore combine and recombine in a myriad of different patterns, creating the diversity of Beethoven and the Beatles, Bach and Bacharach, Handel and Holly.

Smart things to think about

HOW YOUR ORGANIZATION COULD WIN THE EUROVISION SONG CONTEST

If, as I assert, creativity in music is the discovery of a new pattern of existing notes, then here is a way in which your organization might create a winning song for a future Eurovision Song Contest. (If you happen to live outside Europe and have never heard of this annual ritual, let me explain that, ever since 1956, a competition, televised right across the continent, has been held to find the "best" purpose-written popular song in Europe.)

This is how you do it. Get everyone in your organization to ask their families, friends and acquaintances to go to a piano, and, randomly, plink twelve notes, and write that twelve-note pattern down. Do this again a further nine times, so that each person creates a total of ten twelve-note tunes. To make it easier, (and since this does refer to the European Song Contest!), you can encourage people to keep only to the white notes, and to include sequences of the same note, or adjacent notes.

Let's assume that each individual in your organization can persuade a total of 20 people to do this, and let's assume again that your organization is relatively large, say, 1000 people. That means that you will gather together 200,000 tunes.

Don't you think that somewhere in there will be one of a caliber suitable of winning the contest?

Well, you never know, it might win! Now I'm not saying that this is an efficient process of musical composition, or one that will produce great art. But what I am saying is that it is a well-structured and deliberate process in which everyone, even the musically ungifted, can participate; a process that will generate, systematically and deliberately, many new patterns of notes. For sure, the great majority of these patterns will sound truly awful, but some of them might be quite tuneful. What makes great composers great, of course, is that they don't have to go through this random process of trial-and-error: their genius is in forming marvelous patterns at will. Certainly, I am not suggesting that those of us who have no flair whatsoever for musical composition might develop a talent by randomly plinking on a piano. But maybe the insight that musical composition is in essence a process of pattern formation, patterns built from pre-existing component parts, will help us along our journey of discovery into the nature of creativity.

Art, literature and life too

Is the example of music – that creativity in music is about building new patterns of existing elements – a unique case? Let's see ...

And talking of seeing, and of patterns, one of the most obvious examples of pattern creation is visual art, as expressed in paintings. I recognize that it is somewhat demeaning to describe Michelangelo's ceiling at the Sistine Chapel, Monet's water lilies, and Mondrian's *New York Boogie Woogie* as different "patterns of color on a flat surface," but that's what they are. The basic elements from which these different patterns are formed are the colored pigments we call paints, and the number of basic colors is very few – fundamentally the primary colors of red, yellow and blue, along with black and white. Mixing these in different proportions creates the wealth of the artist's palette, and applying these in different spatial patterns on a surface can result in anything from a meaningless mess to a masterpiece. Michelangelo did not invent any new colors, but he did create the most magnificent patterns.

Likewise literature. Novels, essays, plays, poetry – in any given language, these are all composed of different patterns of another basic, pre-existing element, the word. Most of our verbal communication takes place using quite a small number of different words – a vocabulary of 2000 words gives a good working knowledge of any language, and 5000 words or more is well-educated. Our libraries are full of the patterns created by just these elements. Subject to one important point: from time to time, some authors do invent new words – much of the pleasure we derive from Lewis Carroll, for example, is his invention of new words:

Twas brillig, and the slithy toves
Did gyre and gimble in the wabe;

Language evolves, and new words, to represent new concepts, are coined continuously: ginormous, hot-desk, road rage. This in itself reveals a deeper truth – not only are many new words very obviously new patterns based on existing words (gigantic + enormous = ginormous), but, more fundamentally, all English-language words, including all the new ones, are themselves different patterns of just 26 different elements, elements we call letters. The marketing manager who seeks a new brand name, or the poet who seeks a new metaphor, do not invent any new letters – rather, they discover a new pattern of letters that already exist.

And so to life. Life is the most remarkable manifestation of innovation – every human being is a unique individual, and the diversity of living species is breathtaking. What is the basis of this diversity?

The answer lies in the chemical structure of our DNA – the giant chemical molecules in the chromosomes of every living being, from a tree to a tarantula, that carry hereditary information from generation to generation. Each individual DNA molecule is composed of a sequence of four chemicals, collectively known as "nucleotide bases," and individually as adenine (A), thymine (T), cytosine (C) and guanine (G). These sequences can be represented as a chain of letters such as …ATTCGTATTCC…, and the purpose of the "Human Genome Project" is to map these sequences for each of the 24 different chromosomes in the human body. This is no trivial task: human DNA molecules are truly colossal, being formed of sequences several *billions* of nucleotides long.

This length, however, can generate incredible diversity. Each position along the DNA chain can, in principle, be occupied by any one of the four different nucleotides, and so a two-nucleotide sequence can represent $4 \times 4 = 16$ different patterns; a three-nucleotide sequence, $4 \times 4 \times 4 = 64$ patterns, and so on. A sequence of a billion nucleotides can therefore represent a truly astronomic number of patterns: four multiplied by itself *one billion* times. Biologically, a huge number of these are "meaningless," but a sufficiently large number of meaningful patterns still remain to account for the difference between you and me, and between me and a tree. Just different patterns of the same components.

Koestler's Law

I trust I make my point. The essence of creativity is the discovery of a new pattern of elements that already exist. It is not a strike of lightning, a bolt from the blue, an act of God. Rather, it is a deliberate and systematic search for a new pattern, a new combination, formed from pre-existing component parts. The words used by Arthur Koestler, in his book *The Act of Creation*, are more elegant than mine:

KOESTLER'S LAW

The creative act is not an act of creation in the sense of the Old Testament.

It does not create something out of nothing; it uncovers, selects, re-shuffles, combines, synthesizes already existing facts, ideas, faculties, skills.

The more familiar the parts, the more striking the new whole.

Arthur Koestler, *The Act of Creation*

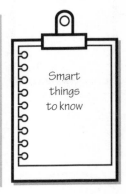

Smart things to know

The Act of Creation is neither a management textbook, nor a popular guide along the lines of "Twenty Ways to Improve Your Brain Power" as you might find on the "self-help" shelves of you local bookshop. It is in fact a philosophy book, which investigates in depth the nature of artistic creativity, with particular reference to literature, drama, intellectual endeavor and humor.

Born in Budapest, Arthur Koestler was educated at the University of Vienna, and subsequently became a journalist. In 1937, when acting as a correspondent for a British newspaper during the Spanish Civil War, he was arrested by Franco's troops, and sentenced to death, to be released only after intervention by the British Government. This experience was the basis for his novel, *Darkness at Noon*, first published in 1940, certainly one of the most spine-chilling books I have ever read.

During World War II, Koestler served in the French Foreign Legion as well as in the British Army, returning to journalism in 1945. *The Act of Creation*, published in 1964, is the second in a trilogy on the mind of man, the two others being *The Sleepwalkers* (1959) and the *Ghost in the Machine* (1967). Koestler is the author of more than thirty works, and was nominated for the Nobel Prize on three occasions.

Koestler's insight, however, is to me profoundly true. As the examples of music, art, literature and life all demonstrate, creativity is all about finding new patterns of existing components.

But all this talk of music, art, literature and life is all very well, and is quite a fun mind-game. What does it mean, though, to a smart manager who wants to enhance innovation in a business context?

Smart
things to
think about

TWO BUSINESS IMPLICATIONS OF KOESTLER'S LAW

Koestler's Law is important to business for two main reasons.

Firstly, it is a *statement of empowerment*. It does this by debunking the myth that creativity is an act of God, or something that requires special powers. Once this myth has gone, the door is open for us *all* to contribute.

Secondly, it describes a *process by which creativity can be made to happen*. A process that is all about uncovering, selecting, combining existing parts

> into a new pattern. That sounds very much like a jigsaw puzzle: the pieces are all there, and all we have to do is to uncover them (perhaps by turning them right-side-up), selecting the ones we want (maybe, in the first instance, those with a straight edge), and then combining them together to form a particular pattern (the outer frame of the picture).

As a statement of empowerment, Koestler's Law is immensely valuable. Just imagine how vibrant your business could be if all that latent creative talent, bottled up in the minds of yourself and your colleagues, could be unleashed. Koestler's Law shouts: "There is no such thing as an 'uncreative' person, nor is creativity the private reserve of so-called 'creatives.' We can all participate."

But as a statement of a process, Koestler's Law is something of a tease. Yes, any smart manager can see the jigsaw puzzle analogy, but few smart managers – save perhaps those who happen to be in the jigsaw business – sit at their desks playing with jigsaws. How can a smart manager actually apply Koestler's Law in a real business context? What are the "patterns"? What are the component "parts"? And if – as Koestler's Law indisputably states – the component parts already exist, where are they now?

Smart things to think about

KOESTLER'S LAW IN HINDSIGHT

Think of any innovation you like, and see if you can retro-fit it to Koestler's Law by identifying the pre-existing "parts" which have been combined into the new "pattern." Here are just a very few examples:

An old one is the printing press, first developed in China, but "reinvented" in Europe by Johann Gutenberg around 1440. This combined two technologies, which had been around for a very long time indeed: the die punch, used for minting coins, and the wine press.

More recently, the Sony Walkman is a good example of pattern formation. To create the Walkman, Sony discarded one part of the then-existing tape recorders (the recording mechanism), rearranged a second (the loudspeakers were moved into the earphones), borrowed a third (the cassette was originally developed by Philips in the Netherlands), and miniaturized the rest.

More recently still, Amazon.com breathed new life into a very old business indeed – mail order for selling branded goods. But, instead of using the mail for distributing catalogs, taking orders and distributing goods, they were one of the very first commercial users of the Internet for the first two parts of this process – the ones that depend on messages rather than physical goods – the publication of the catalog, and the entry of orders. Amazon.com, of course, did not invent the Internet – that was already there. They just spotted the opportunity offered by a "part" which, at that time, was not within the general learning, knowledge and experience of most business managers.

All these examples verify, with hindsight, the validity of Koestler's Law. Hindsight, though, is no surrogate for what we seek in business – and that is foresight. How can we use Koestler's Law not just to rationalize someone else's ideas after the event, but proactively, to create stunning new ideas for ourselves?

Learning

So, in business, where are the patterns? And what are the component parts? Do they exist at all? Where is my "business piano" that I can plink on to generate as many ideas as I like? Or is Koestler's Law of no practical business value? As we shall see, Koestler's Law is of enormous (if not ginormous!) practical value, and begins to become so as soon as we realize that, yes, the component parts relevant to business do indeed exist. And their location is ... *in an existing pattern*! That may sound strange, or even trivial, but a moment's reflection will show that this must be true. If, as we are now agreed, creativity is about finding a new pattern of existing components, then those components must exist now. But where should we look to find them?

The answer to this question emerges as soon as we recognize that, in principle, the individual components from which new patterns can be made can exist in two very different forms: they might exist in a "free," easily accessible, state, like the notes on a piano, or they might exist *bundled together* in an existing pattern, like the notes bundled together in, say, Beethoven's Fifth Symphony. In fact, for the components to be readily accessible in a "free" state is rather unusual: far more often, the components are bundled together in existing patterns. And because of the bundling, the individual components themselves are less easily observed, and might at first sight appear to be hidden. The existing patterns, though, are very visible, and the patterns themselves have familiar names: in music, for example, the patterns are called "symphonies," "operas" or "pop songs"; in literature, "novels," "plays" or "poetry"; in chemistry, "molecules"; and in business, "learning," "knowledge" and "experience."

Smart things to think about

THE NATURE OF LEARNING

We spend our entire life learning, accumulating more knowledge, adding to our experience.

But what is the nature of learning?

Learning enables us to apply an experience of the past into a situation in the future – it builds a "memory" of the future, so whenever we meet a particular set of circumstances, we don't have to work out what to do: we know what to do.

A trivial example of this is getting dressed. This is a process so automatic we no longer even think about it. But imagine what would happen if, each morning, you had to work out how to put on a shirt, how to tie a tie, where to put your shoes. Getting dressed would take literally all day! As indeed it does, as every parent who has ever "helped" a toddler to do it knows! But once we've learnt how to do it, we can do it again and again and again, often without conscious thought.

Some learning is about facts – the names of capital cities, chemical formulae, which accounts are usually debits, and which credits. But a lot of learning is about behaviors, about acquiring skills, about solving problems. All learning, however, shares a common characteristic feature: we learn that a particular trigger ("What is the capital of France?" "How do I drive this car?") stimulates a particular response ("Paris," "I've learnt how to do this: first I fasten the seat belt, then I check that the gears are in neutral, next I put the key in the ignition …").

But how does learning actually work? To answer this, we need to have a look at the structures within our brains – structures that we are now beginning to understand, thanks to recent breakthrough research in neurophysiology.

Smart
things to
think about

"NEURONS THAT FIRE TOGETHER WIRE TOGETHER"

Our brains consist of billions of individual cells called neurons. A single neuron, by itself, doesn't do much – all it does is carry an electric current from one place to another. But when neurons are connected together, truly amazing things happen. And the billions of neurons in our brains make billions upon billions of interconnections, forming an astronomical number of electrical circuits.

Current research shows that "learning" is in fact the creation of specific electrical circuits in our brains, circuits that, once formed, can be triggered into action given the appropriate stimulus. "Memory" is much the same:

human memory isn't a physical "thing," or a sequence of ones and zeros as it is on a CD-ROM or in a computer's memory; rather, memories can be invoked by triggering a neural circuit.

The creation of these neural circuits is an active, continuous process, which occurs when interconnected neurons pass an electric current from one to another: indeed the act of "firing" together increases the likelihood that they will fire together on another occasion, thereby creating circuits that can be invoked again and again and again. But if we don't invoke the circuits, over time, they can break apart – hence we forget.

In many respects, learning is a result of our brains becoming "hard-wired": a concept that inspired Nobel Prize winner Gerald Edelman, one of the major figures in current brain research, to coin the memorable phrase "neurons that fire together wire together"!

"Learning," then, is a process by which the neurons in our brains become wired together to the extent that we can invoke that learning whenever we wish; in this way, the "state of having learnt something" represents the existence of the appropriate, pre-formed, neural circuit.

LANDSCAPE AS A METAPHOR FOR LEARNING

All this talk of neurons and neural circuits is a bit abstruse. Much more concrete is the "landscape" metaphor for learning.

Imagine a flat plain; and imagine a raindrop falling onto it. If the landscape is absolutely flat, the raindrop just stays where it lands. But if the landscape is gently undulating, then the raindrop rolls down a slope. This is not a passive process, but rather an active one – as the raindrop rolls, it carves a very faint depression in the surface, the most rudimentary of valleys. But once this initial depression has been formed, other raindrops falling in the neighborhood are attracted into the valley, and, with each raindrop, the valley becomes

Smart things to think about

more deeply carved, attracting more raindrops, making the valley deeper still … until, over long periods of time, the landscape becomes richly carved with a network of mountains, ridges, valleys and plains, like the Alps, the Rockies or the Himalayas.

The creation of this landscape is a powerful metaphor for learning. Imagine now a newborn infant. What happens as she experiences the world, and learns how to suck mother's milk, how to attract attention, how to recognize faces, how to make sounds? As we saw in the last box, a neuro-physiologist would describe this in terms of the infant's neurons become increasingly more strongly connected in particular circuits. But from a metaphorical point of view, if we compare the mind of the newborn infant to a gently undulating plane, then the process of learning is just like the raindrops carving their valleys. And so, over a period of time, as the infant grows into a toddler, a child, a teenager, a young adult, she carves an increasingly rich landscape in her brain, with each "valley" associated with a label such as "sucking mum's milk," "recognizing dad's face," "getting dressed," "crossing the road," "playing a particular piece on the piano," "driving a car," or whatever.

By the time we become adults, our brains have a uniquely carved, personal landscape – the landscape of our learning, knowledge and experience.

Many people find the landscape metaphor more accessible than the concept of neural circuits, but they amount to the same thing: the neural circuits are the valleys, and the action of the raindrop in carving the valleys is a metaphor for the neuro-physiological mechanisms of connecting neurons together during the process of learning. Likewise, carrying out a learned action by invoking one of the resulting circuits corresponds to a raindrop flowing down a particular valley; and the intricately interconnected web of billions of circuits in an adult brain corresponds to a richly carved landscape.

Donald Hebb was for many years a professor of psychology at McGill University in Montreal, Canada, and originated the idea that the connections within neural circuits become reinforced during learning. This was one of the central themes of his important book, *The Organization of Behavior*, first published in 1949. At that time, there was no direct experimental evidence that this was indeed the case, but over recent years, research methods have enabled scientists to examine individual neurons, and their related circuits, as well as to study the behavior of artificial systems such as computers and robots. One of the leading figures in this field is Gerald Edelman, who, with British professor Rodney Porter, shared the Nobel Prize for Physiology or Medicine in 1972 for their work on the chemical structure of antibodies. Edelman is now the Director of the Neurosciences Institute in La Jolla, California.

SMART PEOPLE TO HAVE ON YOUR SIDE:

DONALD HEBB (1904–1985) AND GERALD EDELMAN

So, if we want to get dressed in the morning, we zoom down the "getting dressed" valley; if we want to cross the road, we zoom down the "crossing road" valley; as we drive to work, we are deeply, probably quite unconsciously, in the "driving to work" valley; and as we read our e-mails and prepare for the first meeting of the day, we begin to slide into the "how to manage staff" valley, the "how to negotiate with clients" valley, the "business strategy" valley, or the "why does he always write such stupid e-mails?" valley …

"Oh no I don't!" I hear you think. "I'm not some pre-programmed automaton, some brainless robot! Oh yes, I accept that I can go into auto-pilot when I'm getting dressed, or when I'm driving – those are totally trivial tasks after all. But no way am I on auto-pilot when I'm managing staff, negotiating with clients, or developing a strategy!"

Smart
things to
think about

THE LEARNING TRAP

Learning is immensely valuable, for it means that we don't have to waste time and effort diagnosing a situation and working out what to do whenever the situation might arise. Without having learnt how to cross a road, for example, we'd either stay on the kerb all day, or be killed by the traffic.

This is fine when we wish to repeat behaviors we have already learnt; but it isn't so fine when we want to do things differently – in particular, when we wish to innovate.

The pull of the valley is very powerful, and we are often sucked into the valley of the familiar, only to become trapped by the known.

If we wish to innovate, we have to find a way to get those raindrops out of the valleys, to unwire those neurons. But how?

Well, as the box says, that's something to think about. Are you sure? Really sure? When did you last say "no"? And was that anything to do with someone or something trying to push you out of a valley, a valley you have carved with your own bare hands, a valley in which you have, hitherto, been successful?

Smart
things to
think about

WE ARE ALL PRISONERS OF OUR SUCCESS

The more often you do something – particularly if you are successful at it – the harder it is to find new ways of doing it. We become trapped by familiarity, programmed by habit.

To find new ways of doing things – to innovate – we have to break out of the familiar; we must "unlearn" our habits.

The problem is how.

Unlearning

There is one, and only one, way to escape from the learning trap, to get our raindrops out of our valleys, to disentangle our hard-wired brains. And that is to be willing to "unlearn," to be willing to have our learning, knowledge and experience challenged. That is no easy thing to do, for it is a result of our learning, knowledge and experience that we have been successful, that we are smart. But really smart managers know that being willing to unlearn is one of the smartest things they could ever do.

Smart things to think about

INNOVATION IN BUSINESS NEVER TAKES PLACE ON A GREEN-FIELD SITE

Flip back for a moment to look again at the second Target Diagram (page 56), the one which shows the domains where we need to be innovative: domains such as new product development, process redesign, organizational development, relationship management, strategy.

These all have one important thing in common. They are all familiar territory – we've been there before, and been there successfully. We've developed products, redesigned processes, evolved the structure, built relationships, defined strategy. We know how to do all these things.

That, of course, is the problem. If we want to be innovative, to do any of these differently, we must unlearn how we have done them before.

And a big problem it is too. It's rather like an experienced golfer who decides he wants to improve his swing: his problem is not to learn how to swing properly – it's how to unlearn his current swing. For before he can learn the correct new action, he has to unlearn, unwind, unravel his old, well-entrenched, bad habits.

But the comparison of the smart manager to the ageing golfer breaks down in one very important respect. The golfer has a problem which he knows he wants to fix. The smart manager, in contrast, often doesn't have a problem at all – in fact, the smart manager is usually doing things well and successfully. Which makes doing them innovatively even harder, for to do things innovatively, you must do them differently, which means you must unlearn how you're doing them now. *Even if they're successful.*

AN EXERCISE IN UNLEARNING

Take a sheet of paper, or (better) stiff card, and cut out four shapes:

- shape A – a square, about 3 × 3 cm
- shape B – a small rectangle, 3 × 6 cm
- shape C – a large rectangle, 3 × 9 cm
- shape D – an L-shape, formed from a large square (6 × 6 cm), from which a smaller square (3 × 3 cm) has been removed from one corner.

Then say to a colleague, "I have a number of shapes, and what I would like you to do is to combine the shapes to form the simplest possible overall shape: here's the first one."

As you say "Here's the first one," place shape C, the long rectangle, on the table in front of your colleague. Then give your colleague shape B (the small rectangle), and after the shapes have been arranged together (don't interfere with this – let your colleague do whatever he or she wishes), hand over shape A, the square. Finally, give your colleague shape D, the L-shape.

Now ask for a second colleague, and say the same thing, but this time, give shape D, the L-shape, first. Then shape A (the square), then B (the small rectangle), then shape C (the large rectangle).

Did these two exercises result in the same final shape?

This exercise, which is based on an example given in Edward de Bono's book *The Mechanism of Mind*, demonstrates simply but vividly the power of learning, and the difficulty of unlearning.

SMART PEOPLE
TO HAVE ON
YOUR SIDE:

EDWARD
DE BONO

Typically, the first person, given shapes C (long rectangle), B (short rectangle) and A (square), arrives in one of two positions:

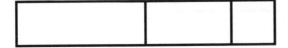

or

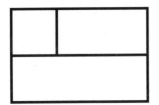

The L-shaped piece causes a problem, since it is neither a natural extension of the "wall," consistent with the upper shape, nor a "brick" easily fitted into the second pattern. Typically, there is some hesitation, as the person tries a few alternative positions, usually settling for either:

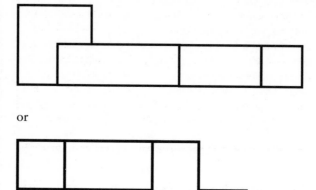

or

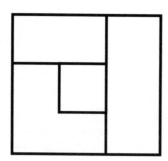

There are some other possibilities, but these are the most frequent occurrences.

The second person invariably ends up with a square:

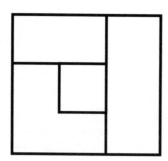

The pieces given to both people were the same, as was the instruction – to form the simplest possible overall shape. How come we ended up in two different places?

The *only* difference between what happened in each case was the sequence in which the pieces were offered. In the first instance, the sequence was long rectangle, short rectangle, square, leading either to a "wall" or a "brick." When the final L-shape comes along, it doesn't easily fit, and so it's tacked onto the end.

In the second, the L-shape came first, and then the square, which is almost invariably placed in the "hole" of the L to complete a larger square, allowing the small rectangle to fit alongside, and then finally the large rectangle – everything slotting neatly into place in sequence.

In the first case, the sequence in which the pieces are presented leads the participant to think in terms of either "walls," or "bricks": they are in fact being gently nudged into a "wall valley" or a "brick valley." And when they are given the L-shaped piece, they vainly try to fit it in as best they can.

Having built a "wall" or a "brick" with the first three pieces, and then being presented with the L-shaped piece, there is but one and only one way in which the L-shape can be made to fit most neatly. But this way *requires* that the existing pattern of either the "wall" or the "brick" is *taken apart, and broken into its component pieces*. Only then can the four parts be recombined into a new pattern – the square.

Very rarely, this actually happens: on being given the L-shaped piece, about one person in a hundred breaks the existing pattern apart, plays around a little, and then discovers the square. But on 99 times out of 100, this just doesn't happen.

Why not?

Well, there are several reasons.

Firstly, many people feel it is not in the "rules" to break the pattern apart. What rules? The instructions simply say, "what I would like you to do is to combine the shapes to form the simplest possible overall shape." They make no reference whatsoever to whether or not the pieces can be rearranged. But the fact that a pattern has been formed by the first three pieces often leads people to create their own box, a box from which they find it very difficult to escape.

Secondly, there is love. The "wall" or the "brick" is *mine* – I created it, I made it happen. How dare anyone challenge it? How dare anyone break it apart?

Thirdly, there is fear. People might spot that they are not prevented from breaking the existing pattern, but unless they have very powerful perceptive skills, they can't immediately see that an alternative is a nice, regular square. So, in breaking the existing pattern apart, they don't know that there is a better pattern out there to find. Better to play safe and leave things be.

And fourthly there is pressure: we don't have time to monkey around with all the bits, especially if the boss comes in and asks what the hell we're doing. Better to play safe and leave things be.

But unless the existing pattern is pulled apart, given the new L-shaped piece, it is simply *impossible* to discover the new pattern.

I'm sure every smart manager gets the message. Unless we are willing to have our existing patterns of learning, knowledge and experience pulled apart – unless we are willing to unlearn – we will never discover the new realms of innovation. Especially when the L-shaped piece is something from the outside world, such as the Internet.

Smart things to think about

IT'S QUIZ TIME!

You are in the final stages of compiling the final presentation for a major, complex study. The presentation takes place the day after tomorrow, and you know the audience, which is very senior, will be hostile, challenging and aggressive. You want to do the very best you can, and that is why you are putting the presentation together personally, rather than delegating it to others in your team. Right now, you're feeling good: you have a well-structured format, and a compelling argument. Everything is clear in your mind.

And then, the most junior person on the team comes to see you with some information which suggests a different solution.

Do you:

- explode, and tell the junior in no uncertain terms that he has found the wrong information, and should go away and find the right information?
- thank the junior, disregard the information, and go back to your presentation?
- throw the information into the presentation as an after-thought, and hope that no one notices the resulting inconsistency?
- stop, convene the team, and rework the solution in the light of the information, even at the risk of having to defer the presentation?

What answer would be given by:

- Attila the Hun?
- your boss?
- Inspector Morse?
- a smart manager, who really understands the message of the puzzle?

The reference to Inspector Morse – the fictional detective created by novelist Colin Dexter, and wonderfully portrayed on television by John Thaw – is not mere padding. About three-quarters of the way through a Morse novel, or at about the equivalent point in the television program, there is usually a scene featuring a dialog between Morse, and his long-suffering assistant Sergeant Lewis, during which Morse announces he has solved the mystery – his superior brain power has done what no one else could ever do, and he, Morse, declares the murderer to be Dr Edwards. Lewis then rubs his chin, and says something like "I understand all that, sir, but wasn't Dr Edwards having dinner with Mrs Miller at the critical time?" Morse disdainfully gives Lewis the 27 reasons why he is wrong; undaunted, Lewis presses on, and suggests that maybe the villain is Professor Sherry. "Professor Sherry, Lewis," Morse retorts, "Professor Sherry? How on earth could you think that?"

But there is still a quarter of the book to go, and, as the story evolves, Dr Edwards's alibi holds fast …

This is another example of a person in a position of authority who is unwilling to allow his patterns to be unraveled in the light of new information. Devotees of crime novels, by the way, will recognize that this type of behavior is not restricted to Morse – creating situations like this is part of the novelist's skill!

Time to reflect

Let's pause for a moment to take stock. Koestler's Law told us that creativity is about finding new patterns of existing component parts, but didn't tell us what the patterns or parts were in a business context. The next stage of the argument was my assertion that the relevant patterns for business are called learning, knowledge and experience, and that a necessary condition for creativity in business is a willingness to unlearn. Finally, the puzzle illustrates how hard it can be to unlearn in practice. Let me summarize how all these concepts fit together.

To make this concrete, let me use another musical analogy. I want you to imagine for a moment that pianos, and all other musical instruments, do not exist. The Beatles happen to be in Hamburg and, by accident, tune their FM radio to a classical channel, and happen to hear Beethoven's Fifth Symphony. Having heard the symphony, how could they go about creating "She Loves You"? What they can't do is to stick a few notes on the end of the symphony – that just doesn't work.

What they have to do is in fact a two-part process:

- firstly, they have to break Beethoven's "Fifth" apart, to "discover" the notes; and

- secondly, they then have to recombine the now-discovered notes into the new pattern, that of "She Loves You."

As it happens, musical instruments do exist, so the first step is not necessary: the notes are available, free, bare, for any composer to recombine at will. But if musical instruments did not exist, this two-part process would be the only way to do it. Likewise, in literature, words are freely available to be recombined into novels, and in art, the colors are freely available to be recombined into paintings.

But this is not the case in life. Genes, the basic elements of heredity, which are formed from long sequences of nucleotides, are not free, but are strung together on chromosomes. And the chromosomes I inherited separately from each of my parents *break and then recombine* so that my parents' genes are mingled in the chromosomes I pass on to my children. That's what sex is all about.

In this respect, business is more like life than music: the "parts" that need to be recombined to form the new patterns of idea generation are not free, ready to form new patterns, like the notes on a piano. Rather, they are bundled together in complex patterns – patterns we call learning, knowledge and experience. And before a new pattern can be formed, before we can be creative, before we can generate new ideas, our existing patterns must be broken apart, so that the elemental parts can be set free, to recombine into new patterns – the patterns at the heart of true innovation.

Idea generation in business is therefore necessarily a two-part process: firstly, we must break apart our existing patterns of knowledge, learning and experience; we must be willing to unlearn. For only then is the stage set for the second part of the process – the generation of stunning new ideas.

Well, that's all great as a theory. But how do we actually *do* it? That's what the next chapter is all about ...

Smart things to think about

DREAMING ... AND DRUGS

Many people are very startled when they first come across the concept that new ideas are generated by a two-part process in which the first part is one of breaking apart existing learning, experience and knowledge. The very possibility that our thinking might in some way have to be "broken apart" is most upsetting.

In fact, there is a very common situation in which this happens quite naturally: every day, in fact – or rather every night. When dreaming. We have all experienced dreams, and we all know the strange manner in which images and sounds, faces and places, get transformed, mixed up, rearranged. Sometimes this is enjoyable, sometimes frightening ... and sometimes wonderfully creative, for there are many stories in which major discoveries have been made on awakening from a dream, just one example being the formulation, in 1869, by the Russian chemist Dmitri Mendeleyev (1834–1907), of the periodic table of the elements – the unifying concept underpinning much of chemistry.

Drugs too can affect the mind, sometimes beneficially from a medical point of view, sometimes disastrously from a personal and social point of view. Those who admit to having taken hallucinogenic and psychedelic drugs report all manner of bizarre consequences, some of which have led to artistic achievement, most notably the poem, *Kubla Kahn*, written by Samuel Taylor Coleridge (1772–1834) after an opium-induced sleep.

4
InnovAction!

Making idea generation deliberate and systematic

Idea generation is a two-part process: before you can generate new ideas, you must be willing to unlearn your existing ideas.

How, then, can you unlearn?

Paradoxically, the easiest way to unlearn is to rejoice in your learning! And *InnovAction!* is the name of the process which helps make this happen, and to use your unlearning as a springboard for generating stunning new ideas.

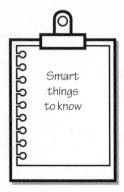

INNOVACTION!

InnovAction! is a six-step process to make idea generation deliberate and systematic.

1 Define the focus of attention

The first step is to define the area in which you wish to innovate – the focus of attention. In general, a narrower focus ("Let's invent some new games based on chess") is preferable to a wider one ("Let's invent a new game").

2 Define what you know

Having defined the focus of attention, document, as a series of bullet points, what you know about the topic, its characteristics and features, all the assumptions you make about it ("Chess is played by two players … "). You can do this alone, but if you are doing this as part of a group, do this step by yourself, in silence, without consulting colleagues.

3 Share

Now share your list with your colleagues, and compile an aggregate list of characteristics, features, and assumptions.

4 Ask "How might this be different?"

Choose one of the features from the list, and ask "How might this be different?"

5 Let it be

Then let the conversation go … you will be amazed by what happens.

6 Then choose another feature

When the discussion on the first feature starts to lose energy, go back to the list of features compiled in Step 3, choose another, and proceed with Steps 4 and 5. Cycle around Steps 4 and 5 for no more than three hours.

You will have noticed that I have referred to a "focus of attention" – a somewhat clumsy phrase – rather than "problem" or "issue." There's a reason for this.

There is a school of thought – a school whose motto is: "If it ain't broke, don't fix it," whose students believe that the only time you need innovation is when you have a "problem" to solve, an "issue" to address, a "burning platform" to escape from. Yes, problems, issues and burning platforms are indeed triggers for the need for innovation, but it might be that by the time you've noticed that, yes, we've gotta do something about this, by the time you've decided what to do, and by the time you actually pull the trigger, the only person you shoot is yourself, in the foot (if you're lucky), or in the head (if you're not). Because it's taken you so long to react, the other guy has shot first. Or, in the words of guru Gary:

Smart quotes

"Face it: out there in some garage, an entrepreneur is forging a bullet with your company's name on it. Once the bullet leaves the barrel, you won't be able to dodge it. You've got one option: you have to shoot first. You have to out-innovate the innovators, out-entrepreneur the entrepreneurs. Sound impossible for a decades-old incumbent? It is. Unless you're willing to challenge just about every assumption you have about how to drive innovation and wealth creation in your company."

Gary Hamel, "Bringing Silicon Valley Inside," *Harvard Business Review*, September–October 1999, p. 72.

And then there is a second school of thought – one that nurtures a spirit of "constructive restlessness," one that continuously searches for better ways of doing things.

SMART PEOPLE
TO HAVE ON
YOUR SIDE:

ROSABETH
MOSS KANTER

I borrowed the term "constructive restlessness" from Rosabeth Moss Kanter, a professor at Harvard Business School. She is a great advocate of the importance of innovation, one of the founders of, and most thoughtful contributors to, the field of managing change, and the author of many notable articles and books, including *The Change Masters: Corporate Entrepreneurs at Work*, and *When Giants Learn to Dance*. "Constructive restlessness" is almost a contradiction-in-terms, but it is from this apparent contradiction that it gets its power. "Restlessness" refers to a state of mind that is never satisfied by the *status quo*, always asking probing questions, never complacent. If this attitude is displayed by someone in power, it is often a disguised form of criticism of the past: "what a mess I have to clear up as result of the incompetence of my predecessor"; if displayed by those lower down, it can be seen as disruptive terrorism. That's where the "constructive" comes in, for it flags that neither of these are the case: the restless spirit is seeking to build a better future, not to score a point over the allegedly incompetent past; there is no hint of disruption or terrorism, for the intent is to deliver genuine improvement. To me, it captures most succinctly that attitude of mind most appropriate to asking *InnovAction!*'s magic question "How might this be different?"

People who attend this school don't wait until there is a problem to solve, an issue to address, or a burning platform to escape from. These people are ever alert to new opportunities, ever creating their own future. They're the ones who shoot first. They're the ones who are smart. Their motto? *Meliorem modum bananam aperire scio*: I know a better way of opening a banana!

SMART THINGS
TO DO

THERE'S ALWAYS ANOTHER WAY . . .

By this stage in the book, you must be really hungry. So why not treat yourself to a nice, fresh banana?

I'll bet you opened it by holding the "pointy" end, breaking it back at the stalk. So find another banana, and this time, hold it by the stalk (a natural enough thing to do, after all, for this is a form of handle). Then, with the nails of the middle finger and thumb of your free hand, pinch the "pointy end," quite gently, until it splits. Carefully peel the skin back, neatly nipping off that nasty black bit at the end of the banana (you'll find that it sticks to the inside of the skin). Then, as they say in the US, enjoy.

Well, I expect you didn't know you could peel a banana that way. And it's a way that always works very easily, even for unripe bananas, so there's an end to all that undignified tugging at the stalk-end when an unripe banana doesn't readily split.

There is, in fact, a very good reason why a banana always splits easily from the "pointy" end. Nature designed it that way. When a banana is on a banana plant, it is attached by the stalk. So the only way to release the seed is by splitting, naturally, at the "pointy" end.

So why don't we open bananas at the "pointy" end? Two reasons. Firstly, that's how our mothers taught us (the learning trap strikes again!). And secondly, opening a banana at the stalk-end generally works. We do not have a banana-opening problem. We do not suffer from a banana-opening crisis. We are not adrift on a banana-opening burning platform, forcing us to find another way.

But that doesn't mean that another way isn't there ... just waiting to be discovered ...

InnovAction! in action – chess

The best way to see how this works is by example. So let's define our focus of attention as the invention of new games based on chess. That's Step 1.

Step 2 is to define what you know, as a series of bullet points. You might have done this at the start of Chapter 3; if you didn't, here is a typical list:

- There are two players.
- The game is played on a board.
- The board is flat.
- The board is a big square …
- … made up of 64 smaller squares …
- … in an 8 × 8 array.
- The smaller squares are in two alternate colors …
- … usually black and white.
- The pieces form two teams of different colors …
- … usually black and white.
- There are a total of 32 players on the board at the start …
- … 16 on each side.
- Each side's team comprises eight pawns, two castles, two knights, two bishops, one king and one queen.
- These pieces are positioned in specific locations, in two rows, at the start of the game – pawns in the front row, the others in the back row (castles in the corners, then knights, then bishops, then king and queen, the queen being on a square of the same color).
- Players can move only one piece at a time.
- Players take alternate turns.
- Each piece has a specific pattern of movement – the castles in straight lines, the bishops diagonally …
- All pieces can move only across vacant squares, with the exception of the knight, which can jump over intervening pieces.
- Any one square can be occupied by only one piece at any one time.
- If a player moves a piece onto a square occupied by an opponent's piece, the opponent's piece is removed from the board, thereby depleting the opponent's forces.
- The objective of the game is to capture the opponent's king: this is known as checkmate.
- If a player is in a position to capture the opponent's king at the next move, that player must warn the opponent by declaring "check."
- With a single exception, a piece maintains it's identity throughout the game – a knight is always a knight. The sole exception applies to a pawn which reaches the opponent's back row, when it can become a queen.
- Pawns can move only forwards.
- It is an intellectual game.
- It is a game of strategy.
- You usually play it seated at a table, sitting down.
- The game is often played with a time limit on each move.
- It can be played by men as well as women.
- It is played all over the world.
- It is boring to watch.

This list is by no means comprehensive – you have probably thought of some additional or different points, which is jolly good, because that illustrates Step 3 – Share! Given the same task of describing a given topic (in this case, chess) different people usually come up with different lists. The purpose of the share step is therefore to gather together each individual's observations into a longer, richer, more comprehensive list that represents the group's collective, rather than any one individual's specific, knowledge.

Step 4 is to choose any feature on this list and say, "How might this be different?" So let's choose the first item: there are two players. How might this be different?

Your first thought is probably: "It can't. Chess is played by two players, and that's that." Well, that is that for chess-as-we-know-it-today. But it doesn't have to be like that, for if we can imagine a world in which there are a different number of players, then we have invented something different from chess-as-we-know-it-today. And if it's different, it might be new …

So, how might this be different? If there aren't two players, there might be … well, only one. Only one? How on earth would only one player play chess? Mmmm. Perhaps by playing chess against oneself. Or perhaps by playing a form of solitaire – you lay your pieces out as normal on your side of the board, and the objective is to move all your pieces to the symmetrically opposite positions on the other side of the board in the minimum number of moves. And perhaps you could make this more difficult by introducing rules like "no more than three pieces can be on any one row at any one time," or whatever.

"That's pretty dull," I hear you say. Well, you could well be right. But at the moment, that's not the point. Statements like "That's pretty dull" are evaluative put-downs, and have no place in idea generation. Remember the

Innovation Target? Evaluation, the white zone, is separate from idea generation, and premature evaluation is a cardinal sin. In idea generation, an idea is an idea; there are no stupid ideas, only ideas.

But having only one player is only one answer to "How might this be different?" There are many others ...

Let's try, for example, four. How could you organize a game of chess with four players? Well ... in lots of ways.

One is to have four players playing separately – for example, by having teams along all four sides of the board. The standard board doesn't have enough room, so why not play on a bigger board – say, 12×12 – but with standard 16-piece teams lined up in two rows in the central portion of each of the four sides? So that combines two "How might this be different?" questions – we've changed the number of players, and also the size of the board. Now that's getting quite different, and leads to all sorts of additional strategies: do some players form alliances against one or more others?

Another way of organizing four players is as two teams of two. How might this be organized? In lots of ways ...

The first is like doubles tennis – each player plays one move at a time in a specific sequence: team A, player 1; then team B, player 1; then team A, player 2; then team B, player 2, and so on.

This itself has (at least) two different ways of being played – the players on any given team are allowed to consult on each move, or maybe they aren't. And not being allowed to consult becomes more fun if the left arm of one of the team is strapped to the right arm of the other – like the way the legs are linked in a three-legged race – and they have to use that arm to move the pieces!

Another way of organizing the game might be for the two player 1s on each team to play against each other in the normal way not for just a single move, but for the first five (or six, or ten …) moves, then handing over to the player 2s for the next five (or six, or ten …) moves, rather more like tag wrestling than doubles tennis. You could allow the players on each team to consult, or not; and if not, do the non-playing players observe the moves the playing players are making, or not? If they don't, they have to pick up a game, several moves in, sight unseen, and continue, later handing back to their partners, who also take up a more evolved game sight unseen. If two-player chess is a test of intellectual individuality, then four-player chess played in this way would be a fantastic test of intellectual teamwork. That, for sure, is not dull!

You see how things are developing … and we've only just started. What if there were 32 players? What if 3? That's what Step 5 – Let it be – is all about. If you let it be, and let the conversation run, it leads to the most amazing places.

Well, that was fun, but I feel I'm running out of steam on asking, "How might this be different?" for the feature "There are two players." So let's invoke Step 6 – Then choose another feature.

Let's take the feature that, with the exception of the pawn, a piece always maintains its identity throughout the game – a knight is always a knight. How might this be different? Well, that's a strange one! Why on earth should a knight change into anything else? No reason at all, and no reason why not either – the fact that a knight is always a knight just happens to be a rule of chess-as-we-know-it-today. So how might a knight change into something else?

One way, perhaps, would be for a piece to take the identity of any piece it captures; a second, for a piece to land on a "magic" square. One of the features of chess is that all the squares on the board are identical (aha! that one wasn't in the list!) but suppose one (or more) squares is "magic" in that, if you land on it, something "magic" happens – like the board of *Scrabble*. For example, you might draw a card (like the "Community Chest" in *Monopoly*) which might say "If you're a knight, you are now a bishop," or even "Your piece is forfeit." Alternatively, you might throw a dice, and depending on what number you throw, your piece changes in a specific way. Now there's an idea ... suppose the piece itself is a dice! Instead of having pieces like we do now, suppose that each piece is a cube, with pictures of the familiar pieces on each of the six faces. The pieces could start in the normal positions, with the normal piece-picture on the top. But when a piece lands on a "magic" square, you roll the piece itself, and it becomes whatever it becomes. The dice, of course, doesn't have to be a cube, and it doesn't have to have different pictures on each face: one dice, which starts as a knight, might have knight pictures on four of the six sides, a pawn on a fifth, and a skull and cross bones (you lose!) on the sixth. The possibilities are endless ...

InnovAction! in action revisited

Let's look at what happened there, exploring why ***InnovAction!*** works, and how it all fits in with last chapter's discussion of Koestler's Law, patterns, component parts, learning and unlearning.

Step 1 – Define the focus of interest

This is all about pragmatism. Since Step 2 is to write down everything you know about the focus of interest, if this is too broad, this is an impossible task. If, for example, we had chosen "let's invent a new game," this is so diffuse and diverse, the list of bullet points would have been both endless and structureless.

Step 2 – Define what you know

This is the start of the unlearning process. But the starting point is what you know, not what you don't know. So rejoice in your learning, for your learning is a springboard to idea generation – you've just seen it work.

An important part of the process is to express your learning as a series of simple, distinct bullet points – so "The game is played on a board," "The board is flat," "The board is overall a big square," ... rather than the more complex "The game is played on a flat, square board comprised of 64 smaller squares, of two alternating colors, in an 8 × 8 array." To explain the reason for this, let's remember the puzzle of pages 106–112. By defining what we know as a series of simple, distinct bullet points, we are taking our understanding of something which is quite complex, and beginning to disaggregate it into the component parts. The metaphor is that chess-as-we-know-it-today is a complex pattern, akin to the "brick" as a complete shape.

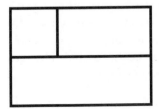

The individual bullet points help to delineate the individual component parts, and the more simple and distinct the individual bullet points, the closer we are to identifying all the "parts" which comprise the existing "pattern" to which we ascribe the label "chess" (to use Koestler-style language).

Step 3 – Share

That was hard to simulate in the narrative, but I'm sure you understand the context. During Step 2, each individual in the group was writing down, by themselves, in silence and without consultation with colleagues, their own list of bullet points. During Step 3, the group shares, to derive a collective, aggregate list of bullet points.

You may be thinking that this is a dull thing to do, since, especially for something like chess, everyone would have the same list. In my experience – and I've done this literally hundreds of times, from exercises like chess to real issues like redesigning the interior layout of a retail store – the process is far from dull. And never, but never, do any two people have the same lists. Not even for something like chess. Certainly, many people will have some points the same ("the game is played on a board"), but each person will have at least one point that is different, fresh. Perhaps it's something personal – from time to time, for example, when I run the chess exercise, someone writes "the game is boring"; perhaps it's a matter of perspective, such as "you usually play it at a table, sitting down"; perhaps it's a matter of observation – it is extremely rare, for example, for people to write down "only one piece can occupy any one square at any one time" (did you think of that one?). Once the lists compiled by each individual reach about ten points, you may rest assured that no two lists will be identical.

Why is this? To explain this, let me go back to a different metaphor, the metaphor of the raindrops carving valleys. As we saw on page 101, learning can be likened to the action of rain carving valleys in a landscape: as we learn and experience life, each individual's mental "landscape" gets ever more richly carved. The point is that it is indeed each individual's landscape: mine is mine, yours is yours, and they will inevitably be different. For sure, there may be many points of similarity – or even identity if we have certain experiences, knowledge or learning in common – but there are inevitably some points of difference.

During Step 2, the task of compiling your own personal description of what you know about the focus of attention encourages you to zoom down whatever valley it is that is relevant, to stop at the bottom of the valley, pause, look around, and describe what you see. *And we all see different things.* Because your learning, knowledge and experience is different from mine, the shape of your landscape is different from mine, and its features will be different too.

The purpose of the share is therefore to gather together our collective view of the landscape, for this will be far richer than any one person's individual view. And by the time the share is complete, two things have happened.

Firstly, on the flip chart, there will be a comprehensive list of bullet points about the focus of attention, so that the complex pattern (in this case "chess") is thoroughly unbundled into its component parts. But secondly, something is happening in people's minds. The explicit identification of the separate bullet points eases the process of unlearning, for by breaking down a complex bundled pattern into an often large number of specific component parts, you are in a far stronger position to see how these now accessible building blocks can be recombined into new patterns. And the fact that different people identify different features causes you to think, "Why didn't I see that? Yes, that makes sense – but I'd never really noticed that in chess, any player can only make one move at a time. It's so obvious, too: but the truth is that it isn't on my list!" This breaks down the arrogance that only you can have all the ideas in this place, that you know it all. For sure, as a smart manager, you know a lot, and you have great ideas. But neither you, nor anyone else, has a monopoly on learning, knowledge, experience or ideas.

Step 4 – How might this be different?

It is here that, in Koestler's terms, the parts are being recombined into new patterns. Steps 2 and 3 have set the scene by unbundling the existing patterns into their component parts, and in Steps 4 and 5, you discover all sorts of new patterns. And during this process, you are also incorporating "parts" from outside the immediate focus of interest: the idea of a "magic square" on a chess board, for example draws on any number of other games from snakes and ladders to *Scrabble*; the different ways of determining what happens when you land on the magic square draws on *Monopoly*, and the general use of dice. As you see, generating new ideas is indeed about recombining parts that already exist into new patterns – but the first step is to be willing to pull the existing pattern – in this case chess – apart, to disaggregate it into its component parts, to unlearn.

For, once this has been done, the process is amazingly simple, and extremely exciting and energizing. All you have to do is to take any feature you like, and ask, "How might this be different?" And once you get over the shock that, yes, it can be different, ideas begin to flow in a veritable torrent.

InnovAction! in action – the nine dots puzzle

NINE DOTS REVISITED

Use the **InnovAction!** process to solve a variant on the well-known nine dot puzzle. Your task is not to join all the dots with only four lines without taking your pencil off the page: it's to discover as many ways as possible of joining all the nine dots with just a single straight line!

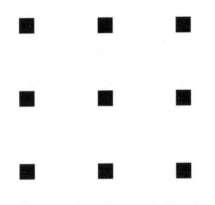

You probably know the version of the nine dot puzzle in which you have to join all nine dots with just four straight lines. But if you watch someone who hasn't seen the puzzle before, this is what they do: they pick up a pencil, and start drawing on the puzzle. They start at the top left, move to top right, down the right-hand side, across the bottom, then up to where they started. Damn! That one in the middle hasn't been caught! So the next time they start at top left, go diagonally through the middle ("Got it!"), down to bottom right, up the right-hand side, across the top (back to the starting point), and then, with their last line, down the left-hand side to bottom left. "Blast

– the one in the middle of the bottom row is still unjoined!!" Try as they might, there's always one dot that gets away. And the frustration mounts. Do it in one straight line? You must be crazy.

But smart managers who know about *InnovAction!* aren't crazy at all. In fact, to some of their more action-oriented colleagues, they can appear to be amazingly dull. Because they think before they leap. Given the nine dots problem, the smart manager starts in the same way – by picking up a pencil. But there the similarity ends, for the smart manager does something different with it. Rather than drawing on the puzzle, and trying to solve the problem randomly, by unsystematic trial and error, the smart manager (having already done Step 1 of the *InnovAction!* process by defining the focus of attention as solving the nine dots problem), goes into Step 2, and defines what she knows about the problem:

- There are nine dots.

- They are in a square array.

- There are three rows of three dots each.

- The dots are a couple of centimeters apart.

Mmm. That's all pretty obvious stuff. Anything else? If I was trying to explain the problem to someone on the other end of a telephone, how could I describe it, so they would really understand? Or if I was trying to explain it to a Martian, what would I say? Have I described the problem fully? So, what about:

- The whole pattern is written on a piece of paper.

- The dots in this case are in fact small squares, a few millimeters long, and a few millimeters wide.

The paper. There's something about the paper I haven't captured. What can it be? Oh yes ...

- The paper is a flat surface.

Indeed it is. Why hadn't I noticed that before? And while we're thinking about things like that, there's also the point that:

- The pencil I am using has a lead which is about – I'm not sure exactly – but somewhere around a millimeter thick.

And a rather more subtle one:

- The paper is a continuous surface.

Smart managers know that writing down what they know is neither trivial nor easy – sometimes it's very hard to spot such "obvious" features like the fact that the paper is flat. That's so obvious, it's not even worth writing down.

Isn't it? For as soon as you have written it down, your mind immediately starts thinking, "How might this be different?" – you just can't stop your mind from doing it! Indeed, one of the problems with Step 2 – defining what you know – is to have the discipline of *not* leaping straight to Step 4 too soon!

But sometimes you can't stop yourself – if the paper wasn't flat, what might it be? Folded, wavy, like corrugated cardboard. And if it was like corrugated cardboard, then the three rows of dots might be on adjacent ridges, with the folds between them. So all I have to do is to make the folds a bit deeper, so the ridges come together, and the three rows of dots merge into a single row, and then I can easily join them all, in a single stroke. Well, that's one solution! That was Step 5, wasn't it? I didn't even notice I was "letting it be" … it was so natural …

So let's go to Step 6 – choose another feature and challenge that. What about the last one, that "the paper is a continuous surface." That's both obvious and a bit obscure. What does it mean? It means all parts of the surface are connected directly to all other parts, with no gaps. How might this be different? Well, the surface might be discontinuous – whatever that means. What would a discontinuous surface look like? It would have disconnected bits, it would be cut up. Ah. Cut up. Why don't I cut out each of the nine dots, and put them in a nice neat line, one next to another? Then I can join them in one straight line. Obvious! That's a second way. Or I could put them diagonally against one another, and join them differently – so that could be a third way. Or I could stack them one on top of another, and join them by drilling down the center of all the dots with a very sharp pencil. That's a fourth way!

I think I'm running out of steam a bit now, so let's invoke Step 6 again, and choose a different feature. What about "the dots are a couple of centimeters apart"? How might this be different? Mmm. Well, they could be very far apart … that doesn't seem to be too interesting. What about the other extreme? They might be much closer together – touching in fact. Touching. A cluster of dots, all together. But if they were like that, all I need do is swipe them with a rather thicker stroke, like with a felt-tip pen. Easy. But in fact, the dots aren't touching, they're a couple of centimeters apart. So, what's the problem? I just need a super-wide felt-tip pen, something like a paint roller. Just one stroke will cover the lot. That's – what am I up to now? – a fifth way! Wow, I've discovered – so far – five different ways of joining all the dots with one straight line in a matter of minutes! That's amazing – I thought it was impossible!

And there's another interesting point here too – see that feature "The pencil I am using has a lead which is about – I'm not sure exactly – but somewhere around a millimeter thick"? If I'd have asked "How might this be different?" of that one, I probably would have discovered the paint roller solution by that route. Mmmm. Different starting points can lead to the same destination …

Wait a minute! I've just noticed a feature I haven't already written down:

- The paper is stationary (as well as stationery!!), and I move the pencil.

How might this be different? What if the pencil were still, and the paper were to move? Or rather, what if the pencil moved slowly in a straight line, and the paper were to rotate underneath it? If we got the timing and movements of the paper just right, the pencil would move only in a straight line, but the dots would end up all joined. In fact, you could imagine this as a sort of robotic operation – rather like the robots on a car assembly line. The robot arm could hold the pencil and move straight; meanwhile, and in synchrony, the mechanism holding the paper could be programmed to rotate the paper just so. That's a sixth way! And all six are so, so obvious … with hindsight. It's amazing what you *can't* see when you're trapped deep in that valley of learning! But once you get those raindrops on a "ridge," and start looking around a bit …

Some people, of course, would argue that folding the paper, cutting the paper, using a paint roller, rotating the paper, or whatever, are all against the rules. What rules? Who set the rules? No one has explicitly stated that you can't cut the paper. Maybe the so-called "rule" was simply something that was imposed in your own mind … by you.

How many "rules" are there in your business that are just the same? And can you imagine what might happen if they were "broken"?

Some more on chess

SMART THINGS TO DO

HOW MANY NEW CHESS GAMES CAN YOU DISCOVER?

Go back to the list of features of chess on page 122, and use some of the ones we haven't already discussed as the triggers for a series of "How might this be different?" questions. See how many new games you can discover in just twenty minutes.

The record is 157!

It's worth spending a little more time on the chess example as, so far, we've hardly scratched the surface.

Let's take another of the assumptions: the pieces are positioned in specific locations, in two rows, at the start of the game – pawns in the front row, the others in the back row (castles in the corners, then knights, then bishops, then king and queen, the queen being on a square of the same color). This is an extremely important feature of chess: before you start, you know the dispositions of both your own pieces, and your opponent's. As a result, chess experts can learn a whole series of opening moves, and these are written up in books and have exotic names such as *Giuocco Piano* and *The King's Indian Defence*.

How might this be different?

In a staggering number of ways!

A very simple one is to rearrange the back row: the pieces are still lined up in two rows with the pawns in front, but suppose the knights swapped places with the bishops? If that were to happen, then all the opening gambits in all of the books would have no value whatsoever – the play of the game would be entirely novel.

This leads to some intriguing possibilities. Assuming that we can rearrange the positions of the back row only (a very direct manifestation of Koestler's Law, for this is truly a new pattern of existing parts), then:

- An umpire could lay the pieces out on behalf of both players, symmetrically.

- An umpire could lay the pieces out on behalf of both players, asymmetrically.

- Each player could lay out his or her own pieces as he or she wishes, without the opponent seeing the positions until the game starts.

- Each player could lay out his or her *opponent's* pieces, with the final positions being seen only at the start of the game.

- The pieces are placed on the board one at a time, each player alternating, in full sight of the other player.

- The pieces are placed on the board one at a time, each player alternating, in full sight of the other player, but with each player positioning the opponent's pieces.

And that's only rearranging the back row!

The idea of laying the pieces out one at a time triggers some other ideas, for example:

- Each player starts off with a sum of money, and can buy pieces at different prices. There is enough money for a normal set, but, if the player wishes, two queens can be purchased, but only at the expense of not having, say, two bishops and a castle.

- Players place, say, twelve of the sixteen pieces on the board, and keep four in reserve. Play starts as normal, and the players can introduce the four reserve pieces at specific stages in the game, for example, when an opponent's piece is captured; or when one of one's own pieces is captured; or after a specific number of moves; or when one of one's own pieces lands on a magic square; or by purchase; or when a dice shows a six …

So far, we've kept to two rows of pieces, with the pawns in front, which is very similar to the layout of chess-as-we-know-it-today. What other dispositions might we have?

- What about in three rows, with gaps? Maybe we'd have to extend the board to, say, ten rows deep to provide a little extra space.

- What about dividing each player's sixteen pieces into two groups of eight, and positioning each of these two groups in any eight of the nine squares of the two three-by-three corner arrays on the appropriate side of the board? Alternatively, the two groups of eight could occupy diagonally opposite corners.

- What if, rather than laying out your pieces one at a time, or all together, you could lay them out, say, four at a time – and you are allowed to put them amongst your opponent's pieces?

- And then there is the possibility of laying them out anywhere on the board!

You get the idea. The possibilities are literally endless: and we've explored *only three* of the features of chess-as-we-know-it-today (two players, each piece maintains each identity, and the opening positions)!

Every single example I have described is real – they have all been generated in client workshops, during the course of a twenty-minute exercise. And they are just a tiny fraction of the total of new games that a whole host of people – from manufacturers to marketeers, from scientists to civil servants, from managing directors to secretaries – have suggested. And in celebration of the imagination and creativity of all these people, before I end our exploration of new games based on chess, let me cite just a few more examples:

- Change the objective – instead of just capturing the king, you have to capture the king *and* be in possession of a "special" square. (Pearson Television drama executives and story writers.)

- A game with sixteen players on each side: one player and fifteen advisers. (A group from the UK Ministry of Defence.)

- Gay chess – all the pieces are queens. (Lex Service senior executives.)

- Each player wears a blindfold, and has to remember the positions. (Engineers from the National Grid Company.)

- The board has a magic square which can accommodate two pieces at the same time. If the pieces are the king and queen of the same color, a pawn is born! Or a knight (a prince). Or a new piece – a princess, a piece that, like the queen, can move in any direction, but, being younger, can move only two squares at a time! (A group attending the conference, "The Marketing Forum," held on board the P&O ship *Aurora*, in September 2000.)

Wonderful. Just wonderful.

InnovAction! as a group process

InnovAction! is more fun in a group

InnovAction! is a process that can be used by an individual, working solo; the only stage that is inapplicable is Step 3 – Share. In my experience, however, *InnovAction!* works extremely powerfully in small groups. These sessions invariably benefit from the presence of a facilitator who is not directly involved with the process, and so can reassure people, coach them, keep the process moving, and deflect any unhelpful behaviors. I'll deal with how to design and facilitate *InnovAction!* sessions, and also with training, later; let me take a moment now to explore some of the interpersonal behaviors that often arise, and how they can be handled.

I'll assume that the focus of attention has already been agreed; that all the participants in the group already know each other; and that they have all had some training, and so know the basics of Koestler's Law, patterns, unlearning, and how *InnovAction!* works.

Step 2 – Define what you know

This is where each individual writes down, as a series of bullet points, the key features of the focus of attention. Most people find this very difficult, even after some practice. Some of the things that are going on in people's minds are:

- I don't know anything about this, so I can't write anything down.

- Why on earth should I bother to do this? It's a total waste of time!

- This is trivial.

- I can't write that down – it's obvious!

- I won't write that down – everyone else will already have it.

- How can I discover something that no one else is writing?

- I know so much about this, I don't know where to start.

- This is laborious – and it's taking a hell of a long time.

These are all normal, human thoughts, but they do get in the way. As soon as any individual spends more than a couple of minutes pondering on any of these, the interest dissipates, the fidgeting starts, there is suddenly an urgent desire to make a phone call, two individuals catch each other's eye and start chatting, and the process degrades from there. A facilitator can keep alert for this sort of thing, and nip it in the bud, but since all these anxieties start in an individual's mind, it's helpful if people know how to deal with these personally.

The *InnovAction!* process is designed to help people unlearn and, as a consequence, to discover new patterns. An essential prerequisite, clearly, is that there is some learning, knowledge and experience in the first place! The process will not work if an individual has absolutely no knowledge whatsoever which is relevant to the chosen focus of attention.

In any business context, however, the likelihood that this is the case is zero – absolutely zero. Any individual that has lived for more than ten years will inevitably have some relevant knowledge, however small. I frequently encounter this objection when I do the chess exercise – people often say they have no knowledge of chess. This has never been true: what people are really saying is "I don't know a lot about chess," "I have never played chess," "I am not a chess expert," "I think chess is a game for pointy-headed intellectuals, which I am not," or "I think chess is dull and boring." All these statements could well be true, but they are not the same thing as "I have no knowledge whatsoever." I have yet to discover someone who does not know that chess is a game played by two players, that it is played on a board, that the board is flat, that the board is a big square, that the big square is made up of a lot of little squares. As we have seen, even the knowledge that chess is played by two players can lead to some stunning new ideas.

The next two issues – "Why on earth should I bother to do this? It's a total waste of time!" and "This is trivial" – reflect either a lack of understanding of the process, or an unwillingness to follow it. The reason for bothering to do this is to tease out the component parts of your learning, knowledge and experience, as is required for unlearning. Yes, it is something of a bother. No, it is not a waste of time. No, it is not trivial.

The clutch of objections, "I can't write that down – it's obvious!" "I won't write that down – everyone else will already have it," and "How can I discover something that no one else is writing?" are manifestations of self-censorship, fuelled perhaps by a belief that by writing down "there are two players," other people might laugh, or perhaps by a competitive instinct that regards this exercise as some kind of win-lose game that I must win.

The facilitator can do a lot to help make the climate supportive, and after experiencing one or two **InnovAction!** sessions, people soon realize that nothing is "obvious," and that it doesn't matter if someone else has also identified the same feature. And anyway, it might not be exactly the same, and the difference might be critical. The competitive instinct is rather harder to deal with: some people try to be just too clever. But smart managers know that this isn't a game of how-can-I-be-seen-to-be-smarter-than-my-so-called-colleagues.

The last two issues – "I know so much about this, I don't know where to start," and "This is laborious – and it's taking a hell of a long time" – are much more valid. As we saw in Chapter 3 (see page 105), except in the most rudimentary start-ups, innovation in business *never* takes place on a green-field site: we've introduced new products before, we've designed new processes, we've evolved our organization structure, we've built good relationships, we have a strategy.

If we are applying the *InnovAction!* process to any of these real business contexts (as, in practice, we are), then our learning, knowledge and experience can fill books, and take forever! How on earth can I write it down in a series of bullet points? This is one of the reasons why a narrow focus of attention is preferable to a broad one, but even with a narrow focus, the issue "Where do I start?" is still valid, and yes, it does take time.

It helps to approach this in a structured way, and once you get going, you soon tap into rich veins. Clearly, any specific focus of attention will have different characteristics, but there are a number of themes, which apply broadly as suggested in the next box.

ASK QUESTIONS

Here is checklist of the kind of questions that you can ask to help you structure Step 2 of *InnovAction!* – Define what you know.

Products

What is it? What are its features? What are its benefits? How is it used? Who uses it? How is it manufactured? How is it distributed? How is it priced? How is it serviced and maintained?

Processes

What is it? What is the process map? Who is involved with the process? How does this process interact with related processes? What are the metrics of the process (throughput, elapsed times …)? What technology is used?

Organization

What are the formal structures? What are the informal structures? If a Martian landed, what would he see, hear, feel? What performance measures are associated with the structures? Who are the key players? What are their personal styles? How do they interact?

SMART THINGS
TO DO

When writing down the features of the situation-as-it-is-today, take care to bear two important things in mind:

- Write descriptions, not evaluations.

- Write what does happen, not what doesn't.

All too often, when describing, for example, a process – say, recruitment – people write down statements such as:

- We are far too slow in responding to initial enquiries.

- Our assessment panels involve too many people.

- Our salary structure is not competitive.

- We don't recruit people over 35.

- We are not systematic in taking up references.

These statements may (or perhaps may not) be true. In Step 2 of *InnovAction!* they are positively unhelpful for two reasons.

Firstly, all these statements are negative, self-flagellating, and generally downbeat. The atmosphere that *InnovAction!* seeks to create is positive, exciting, upbeat. To surround yourselves with flip charts of how bad you are casts a cloud of gloom over the proceedings, and inhibits the later stages of the process.

And secondly, statements like these invite an argument. Those responsible for, or involved in, the recruitment process are unlikely to feel good as this torrent of criticism is heaped over their heads in public, however genteelly expressed. At best, this creates an atmosphere of sullenness and silence; at worst, it provokes active defense, as those who own the process give you the fifteen reasons why it takes three weeks to respond to a letter, and why we can't yet handle e-mails because your department (that's code for "you") refused to accept that memos can be created electronically rather than on paper. This debate is antagonistic, builds entrenched positions, and will kill the remainder of the process.

So, far better to remember those two golden rules of being descriptive, not evaluative, and stating what does happen, not what doesn't:

- On average, we take three weeks to respond to an initial enquiry by letter, and we do not accept e-mails. Our best performance over the last three months was three days; our worst, seven weeks.

- Senior appointments go through an assessment panel comprised of seven people.

- According to a survey carried out last June, our median salaries were in the bottom quartile of our market.

- Our current target age range for middle management recruits is 28–35.

- A recent internal study of our last 20 recruits showed that references had been taken up on 15.

These are all statements of fact, and they need, of course, to be correct. They are also all statements of what actually happens. Nowhere is there an actual or implied value judgement of goodness or badness – this is just what happens. There is therefore no need for anyone to be gloomy or defensive – this is the way it is, as we all know.

Statements of this type are far more powerful in stimulating the question: "How might this be different?" – What do we have to do to handle e-mail applications? What if the assessment panel didn't have seven people on it? What if our salary structure were different? How might our recruitment age profile be different? What if we didn't bother to take up references at all?

All these questions are forward-looking and positive, and open up a constructive debate. That's exactly what you want.

Step 3 – Share

During Step 3, each participant in the group shares their list of bullet points. And I have seen some mighty dysfunctional groups – I'll never forget the amazing argument between two people when sharing their assumptions on chess:

"The squares on the board are chequered, black and white," one person said.

"No they're not!" shouted someone else.

"Eh?"

"The squares aren't black and white. They're red and white."

"No they're not. They're black and white."

Yes, two fully grown adult males continued in this vein for about ten minutes, as the rest of the group looked on, at first amused, then bemused, then bored, then angry.

The idea here is to share, not to argue. If one person's experience of chess is that the squares on the board are black and white, and another's is that they are red and white, then that's the way it is. There is no law saying everyone's experience must be exactly the same – in fact, it's the diversity that enriches the process. It's not a question of right versus wrong. It's much more a process of rejoicing in both ... and.

For, as we have already seen, this process is all about exploring each other's mental landscapes. Given any trigger – chess, recruitment, pricing policy – we all zoom down our valleys labelled chess, recruitment, pricing policy. And as we look around from the bottom of the valley, we all see different things. During the share, we have the opportunity to gain an understanding of what other people's mental landscapes look like, but only if we listen, and only if we encourage others to describe their landscapes as fully and richly as they can, without fear of being put down.

The language we use is critical.

INNOVACTION! STEP 3 – SHARE

During the share, the things people say, and the language they use, has an enormous impact. One of the most important things a smart manager can say is nothing at all: it's very hard to talk and listen at the same time. One of the main benefits of the share is for you to get an understanding of how your colleagues see the world, despite the drive for you to ensure that everyone else understands how you see the world. So smart managers listen, intently.

And when smart managers do say something, they say things like:

- "Tell me more about that," so inviting someone to explain their bullet point more fully.
- "My perception is [like this], and I'm intrigued that yours is [like that]. What do you have in mind?" when there are two descriptions of ostensibly the same thing.
- "Thanks for asking that – let me explain more fully . . ." when you are asked about one of your points.

These are all positive, open, encouraging statements, inviting a deeper and broader discussion. That way, you can get to know other people's mental landscapes, and they can get to know yours.

Peter Senge, in his best selling *The Fifth Discipline*, calls this process "dialog," as we describe our "mental models" – our explanations of how we see the world working. Mental models represent our fundamental beliefs, and strongly influence our behavior, but they are rarely articulated. This part of the *InnovAction!* process is an opportunity to do this safely.

Peter Senge is the Director of Organizational Learning at the Sloan School of Management at the Massachusetts Institute of Technology. He shot to fame with the publication in 1990 of the business best-seller *The Fifth Discipline: The Art And Practice of The Learning Organization*, which features on a list compiled by *Harvard Business Review* of the seminal business books of the last 75 years. The "fifth discipline" of the title is "systems thinking" (see pages 16, 17, 28 and 29), the other four being (very briefly) "personal mastery" (being very good at what you do), "mental models" (having a profound understanding of what you are doing), "shared vision" (in which the mental models of the individual members of a team are deeply and naturally shared), and "team learning" (the recognition that highly integrated teams can learn, and operate, far more effectively than the same number of individuals). Senge's thesis is that these five disciplines can and should work in harmony, and when they do, the organization can be immensely powerful, invigorating and productive, not only for the organization as a whole, but for its individuals too. Senge's two more recent books (with various co-authors), *The Fifth Discipline Fieldbook: Strategies and Tools for Building a Learning Organization* (1994) and *The Dance of Change: The Challenges to Sustaining Momentum in Learning Organizations* (1999) are well worth tracking down, and are very different in style from the usual sort of management text: both are a compendium of articles, case studies, thoughts and insights into all aspects of the five disciplines separately and collectively, which can be read on their own, or as part of the wider narrative.

SMART PEOPLE
TO HAVE ON
YOUR SIDE:

PETER SENGE

When the process works well, it is often startling ("Wow, I've never thought of that before"), and frequently illuminating ("Now I realize why he does things that way"). It also helps create a climate of unlearning, as we gain a deeper appreciation of other people's perspectives, and as I slowly begin to realize that I do not possess a monopoly on wisdom.

As regards the actual process of sharing, there are a number of different ways of doing it. One way that works well with me is for one person to record the points on a flip-chart by inviting each person in the group to state only one point, and to go round and round the group until all points are covered. The fact that each person can say only one point at a time stops long speeches, is a lot more active for the participants, and also avoids the situation in which the last person to speak has nothing new to say. It also forces everyone to contribute – no one can pass, at least for the first few rounds – and so keeps people's attention and interest. During this, the facilitator should encourage questions, so ensuring that each person's contributions are fully understood, and the facilitator must – repeat must – write down what is said. All too often, the facilitator writes down only what he or she agrees with, or thinks "sensible." The role of the facilitator is to record, not to censor.

Another method is for each person to write down each of their own bullet points on separate A5 index cards, or sticky Post-it notes. This relieves the facilitator of the need to write things down, for the process here is for the facilitator to invite each person, once again in sequence, to stick their point onto a piece of flip-chart paper, or onto the wall. The benefit of this is that as more points are added, they can be arranged and grouped into cohesive themes.

One last thought: you will often hear someone say "my next point has already been covered." Maybe. But maybe not quite. Encourage the person to say a bit more, just in case there is a particular, perhaps apparently minor, but nonetheless new or even slightly different, point.

Step 4 – "How might this be different?"

After the share, the next step is to choose a feature from the aggregate list, and ask: "How might this be different?"

HOW MIGHT THIS BE DIFFERENT?

In idea generation, "How might this be different?" is *the* killer question.

All new things must, by definition, be different; but not all different things are necessarily new. But they might be. So what a great place to start.

KILLER QUESTIONS

How do you know which of the many features on the aggregate list to start with? In fact, and in practice, you don't. For in asking: "How might this be different?" we are embarking on our journey into the unknown, we are taking the raindrop out of the valley, we are unwiring our hard-wired brains. And, by definition, you cannot know where this will lead. By the same token, you cannot reliably predict which trigger will point you in an "interesting" direction.

So my advice is not to worry about it. Have a brief discussion amongst the group to see if anyone has any particular views, and then choose a feature and go for it. If the "How might this be different?" discussion leads to interesting places, fine; if not, no matter, invoke Step 6 – "Then choose another feature," and start afresh again. For one of the benefits of *InnovAction!* is that, like in business, you are not starting with a blank sheet of paper, but with a wealth of material. With *InnovAction!*, you never get stuck. In my experience, *Innov-Action!* never comes close to exhausting the initial stock of triggers, but ends in a mixture of exhilaration and exhaustion, when, after about three hours, the group chooses to stop, having generated more ideas than they know what to do with! Indeed, the ideas come so thick and fast that it becomes impossible for the facilitator to write them all down. So it's helpful to have a pack of plain, unlined, ideally multi-colored, A5 index cards handy, so that whenever an idea pops into anyone's head, they can write it on a card, and then stick the card to a wall, alongside all the other cards. For legibility, use a felt-tip pen to capture the essence of the idea, and do be sure to sign each card so that whoever is writing-up the session afterwards knows who to refer to for clarification.

Smart things to think about

INNOVACTION! AND BRAINSTORMING

Everyone is familiar with brainstorming, and in many ways, **InnovAction!** and brainstorming are similar. Both encourage a spirit of free thinking and exploration, both work better in small groups rather than as an individual activity, and both require a climate in which the participants don't criticize one another, and avoid premature evaluation.

There is one major and fundamental difference. Typically, brainstorming starts with, literally, a blank sheet of paper, and the participants are invited to come up with whatever ideas they like.

Some people relish the freedom, but many, once the initial splurge of yesterday's problems has been exorcised, just dry up. The absence of a structure, and of a defined process, just doesn't help.

InnovAction!, in contrast, does not start with a blank sheet of paper. On the contrary, it starts with a very full sheet indeed – a sheet that reflects the group's collective learning, knowledge and experience. This list, combined with the question "How might this be different?", provide both structure and process. "How might this be different?" gives you a well-defined focus, concentrating your attention, and guiding your thoughts; the list of features provides a wealth of starting points and triggers, so that when one line of thought naturally peters out, you can start again somewhere else.

This, of course, reflects reality – innovation in business almost never takes place on a green-field site, with a blank sheet of paper. Rather, it takes place on a very brown, muddy, well-trodden site, with a wealth of learning, knowledge and experience on which to build.

Some people – fortunately in my experience only a very few – find the question "How might this be different?" extremely difficult to cope with: they just can't imagine anything other than the *status quo*, and even the possibility of there being four players in a chess game provokes the reaction "but they can't – chess has only two players." "Yes, we know that. But we're imagining a situation in which there are four players. How might that work?" "No idea. Can't imagine it. Just can't." Oh dear. The best thing you can do is to try to help them; the best thing they can do is – voluntarily – to find something else to do.

Others suffer from premature evaluation in all its various manifestations – "we've done that before, and it didn't work," "that's hardly new, is it?" "that's crazy" – and all the rest. You need a strong facilitator to stop this, but ideally, the groups should be self-policing.

Another problem is the slow start. Sometimes, when asking, "How might this be different?" of a particular feature, nothing much happens. The group looks at each other and gets nervous. It may be that this is truly a dead-end, but it may also just be a bit slow. Don't rush to invoke Step 6 – the choice of another trigger – but let things run: that's really what Step 5 – Let it be – is all about.

Step 5 – Let it be

For when you let it be, the conversation can be amazing. What happens is that one person says something, and that triggers a thought in someone else, and then a third person makes a contribution, until a fourth person suggests such a good idea that it stuns the group to silence. And then, the process starts again, in a different direction.

Alex Osborne might not be a familiar name, but you have probably heard of the advertising agency that bears his initial, BBD&O, which he helped found in 1919. Throughout his career, Osborne was intrigued by creativity, and was always searching for, and developing, tools, techniques and processes to help make innovation deliberate, systematic and safe. He soon recognized the importance of creating a non-judgemental environment, and that what at first sight might appear to be a wild idea could in fact contain the germ of a very practical one: "It is easier to tone down a wild idea than to think up a new one." Osborne was the originator of brainstorming, coining the term way back in 1939. His book *Applied Imagination: Principles and Procedures of Creative Problem-Solving*, was first published in 1953, and the most recent edition (1993) is still available.

Often, the "intermediate" ideas are "crazy," but no matter – if this is the path to something much more "sensible" so be it. This is the process of forming and reforming new patterns, of combining and recombining different parts, of getting the raindrops out of the valleys, of unwiring our hard-wired brains. And then quite suddenly, the raindrop falls into the valley of a stunning new idea.

InnovAction! of course is not a linear process – working inexorably from start to finish, step by step, in a perfectly logical, rational order. On the contrary, it is much more fluid – now moving forward, then backtracking, side-tracking, hitting blind alleys, reversing, now jumping. Rather than being linear, the process is more one of a stretched spring – the overall direction is from "here" to "there," but at times you might be heading backwards. And the fact that it isn't "logical" or "rational" does not imply that it is "illogical" or "irrational" – the former insinuating that it makes no sense, the latter that it is mad. To my mind, something that is not logical doesn't have to be illogical: I think there is a third state that I call "non-logical" – something that is neither logical, nor illogical, just different; obeying a different, but nonetheless sensible, set of rules, but rules which are different from those of pure logic. The fact that logic exists does not imply that logic is the only possible mode of thought – a point made vigorously by de Bono in many of his books (see, for example, *I Am Right, You Are Wrong* and *Water Logic*). Likewise, the process is non-rational rather than irrational. In fact, the logic and rationality of **InnovAction!** lie not in the process itself, but in the foundations of the process – the importance of Koestler's Law and the significance of patterns, the recognition of the need to unlearn. That's all supremely logical and makes a lot of sense; it is profoundly rational and in no way mad. How wonderful that a non-logical, non-rational process can be built on such logical, rational foundations!

THE POWER OF THE *BBC*

InnovAction! is a process you can carry out by yourself, but – like some other human activities – it's a lot more effective, and more fun, with others. Somehow, something magic happens when brains are connected together. This is the power of the *BBC* – the *brain bank connectivity*.

Let's assume that an individual brain has a creative power of one unit. Two brains, operating individually, therefore have a total creative power of two units. But if the two brains are connected, if the two people are communicating meaningfully and co-operatively, then there is an additional contribution to their collective creativity attributable to the linkage between the brains. The total creative power of the two linked brains – the *BBC* – is therefore two (for each of the two brains individually), plus (let's say) a further one for the linkage: that's a total of three.

Now consider what happens with three connected brains A, B and C. There are three individual brains, but there are now *four* different linkages (A and B, A and C, B and C, and the threesome A and B and C). The total *BBC* is now seven. Something very interesting is happening, for the number of *linkages between the brains* is getting bigger faster than the number of individual brains themselves. In fact, for a total of *n* brains, assuming that each separate link has a creative power equal to that of an individual brain, and that all linkages are of equal strength, there is a formula for the *BBC*:

Smart
things to
think about

For n linked brains, the $BBC = 2^n - 1$

So, for two brains, $n = 2$, the $BBC = 2^2 - 1$, namely, 3; likewise, for 3 brains, $n = 3$, the $BBC = 2^3 - 1$, namely, 7. For an *InnovAction!* group of 8 brains, the BBC is 255! This number is vastly greater than just 8, the BBC of the same eight people working individually in silos, by themselves.

I'm sure we could debate for a long time whether or not the linkage between two brains has a creative power equal to that of an individual brain, or whether all linkages are of equal strength. Well, I don't mind about that. If the power of the linkage is a different number, or if not all linkages are of equal strength, then that merely alters the arithmetic to an equation of the type:

$$BBC = n + \alpha \, [2^n - (n + 1)]$$

in which "α" is some fudge factor which expresses the creative power of a link relative to that of an individual brain.

The main point is this. The term 2^n increases very fast with n, and very quickly dominates the equation for the BBC, even for relatively small (positive and non-zero) values of the fudge factor "α." That means that the creative power of a group is potentially vastly greater than that of the same number of individuals. But only if the brains are connected. Only if people are talking. And, more importantly, listening.

Harnessing the power of the BBC is, to my mind, *the* major opportunity, and *the* major challenge, for any knowledge-based industry.

In practice, of course, it doesn't necessarily have to work that way. If the fudge factor "α" is a negative number, then the BBC gets *smaller* as the number of brains increases. This happens when people become disconnected, when connections that used to exist get broken, and when brains that used to be active in creating and building the business get sidetracked. Next time you experience a "merger," you'll probably see this taking place before your very eyes.

InnovAction! in action – mineral water

MINERAL WATER

You and your colleagues have just taken over a company that manufactures and distributes mineral water. Use the **InnovAction!** process to discover as many new products, based on mineral water, as you can.

Allow five minutes for writing down your bullet points (aim for about 20), then another ten for a share if you are doing this as a group, and no more than 20 minutes for idea generation.

Unless you happen to be a keen chess player, the chess example is just an abstract exercise. This is one of the reasons it tends to work so well – it isn't anyone's problem, so no one gets defensive about it. There's a second reason too – absolutely everything about chess is arbitrary! There is no fundamental reason why the board is 8×8 – it just is. Yes, it works quite well at that size, but there is no fundamental human law that says that it must be. So, when you ask: "How might this be different?" there is nothing – absolutely nothing – that stops any of chess's rules, features, conventions being different in any way. As soon as this penny drops, the ideas flow like water.

The result of changing the size of the board (or whatever) may or may not result in a more interesting game than chess-as-it-is-today, but that is a question of evaluation, not idea generation. And whilst we're on the subject of evaluation, I'd better let you know that, although every new game I've described (and a huge number I haven't) was created originally during one of my client workshops – they've all been discovered before!!

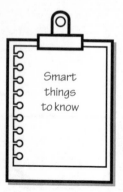
THE ENCYCLOPEDIA OF CHESS VARIANTS

Yes, that was a surprise to me too!

One day, I was talking about the chess exercise to Graham Lee, a teacher at Oakham School, who happens to be something of a chess expert. He then said, "Have you seen a book called *The Encyclopedia of Chess Variants*?" "No. What's that?" "It's a book about different games based on standard chess – you might enjoy it." So I tracked it down: it's written by David Pritchard and published by Games & Puzzles Publications.

What a book! Here is a quotation from the Introduction: "How many chess variants are there? At least 40,000 ..." That makes the record I mentioned of 157 look pretty thin. The *Encylopedia* describes about 1450 different games, each with its own name, from *Abdication Chess* (with a 9 × 9 board, and an extra piece called a duke) to *Zugzwang Chess* (where you are not obliged to move if you don't want to, unless you're in check).

The fact that all these games have been thought of before is neither here nor there, and certainly not an indictment of the **InnovAction!** process. Chess, after all, has been played around the world for well over a thousand years, and it would be amazing if no one else had ever thought of rearranging the starting position (the game which keeps a row of pawns, but allows for different patterns in the back row, is known as *Baseline Chess*), or of having more than two players (such as *Double Bughouse Chess*, which is played by four players, in two teams of two, on two boards, simultaneously). The fact that ordinary business people, without knowing much about chess, and certainly not of the existence of any chess variants, can discover so many different games so quickly demonstrates the power of the process, and builds confidence that yes, you can do it. And if you can do it for chess, you can do it for your business too.

If it turns out, during the evaluation, that a particular new product, say, is already on the market, then so be it. Far better to have the idea in the first place than no ideas at all. To me, what is new to you is innovation – even if you subsequently discover someone else has thought of it before.

The exercise on mineral water is closer to the business world, and it may be that you are in this, or a related, business. As we move closer to your business, the process becomes more difficult, because there are more vested interests, and there may be external reasons – such as legislation or regulation – why the question "How might this be different?" offers precious little scope. Nonetheless, the process still works.

So, here are just a few features of mineral water, all, once again, actual examples from my client workshops:

- It comes in glass or plastic bottles.
- It is still or fizzy.
- There are different tastes.
- It is clean, and disease free.
- It is healthy.
- You drink it.
- It contains minerals.
- The bottle is stylish.
- It often has a "designer" name.
- Bottles are of different sizes.
- There is a screw top or cap.
- The bottle is often colored.
- It is a natural product.
- You drink it cold.
- You usually drink it by itself.
- The source is usually in a remote mountain location.
- It is convenient to use.
- The bottles are full of water.
- You own a bottling plant.
- The bottle has a label.
- It comes from springs.
- It has bubbles.
- There is a strong national image – often French or Italian.
- It quenches thirst.
- You drink it in restaurants and bars.
- You can use it as a mixer.
- It is a marketing triumph.
- It is exclusive.
- It is expensive.
- It is a luxury.
- It has snob value.

It is rare, by the way, for people to write down "you drink it" or "you drink it cold," without some prompting. It's so obvious, that you don't notice it …

… but when you ask "How might this be different?" it so happens that these two rather banal features lead to some very interesting places indeed.

If "you" don't drink it, who else might? Or what else might? Pets, maybe. What about bottled water, marketed specifically for pets? You can picture the television ad in your mind, with the voice over "... with minerals specially selected to ensure your cat has the glossiest possible fur – and none of that nasty chlorine that the water company has to put in tap water to kill the bugs!" Maybe the water could be sold as a twin-pack with the pet food.

And if you don't "drink" it, what else might you do with it? Mmm. What else do I do with water? Well ... lots of things. I wash in it ... that leads to all sorts of individual targeted products: special water for your teeth, your hair, your oh-so-soft, hand-wash-only clothes. Your baby – yes, babies are special, who wants nasty hard tap water on that soft skin? And talking of soft skin, what about your face? Or the faces of, say, teenage girls? Yes, why don't we market water specially for teenage girls to wash their faces with, ("we don't have to put chlorine in our water to kill the bugs – we don't have any bugs in the first place"). This means we could position it not as water, but as a cosmetic, displaying it on the supermarket shelves with high quality soaps and shampoos, maybe, and charging a premium price accordingly.

Another thing I do with water is cook, so maybe there's a market for selling water to be used for cooking, say, organic vegetables, or as a twin-pack with cup-a-soups or whatever.

And what about the feature "We drink it cold"? How might this be different? Well ... if it isn't cold, it's hot. There doesn't seem to be much mileage in selling hot water – it would be difficult and expensive to keep hot. Maybe this one's a dead end. But wait a minute ... don't we drink huge quantities of hot water? Not as hot water, of course, but as tea and coffee. And where does the water we use come from? From the tap of course... But why? Why can't we market bottled water, specially for use in tea and coffee? We can sell it cold, just as we do now, but for *use* hot. And we could sell the special kettle too! That's a huge market! And the features about special minerals, no chlorine, health and so on can all form part of the marketing image. After all, if people buy bottled water to drink cold when they don't actually need it (we all used to drink tap water once upon a time – in fact, not so long ago!), why can't we market water for use hot?

Water with organic vegetables, water with soup, water with tea, water with coffee … what else do we have water with?

Well, whisky for one. Lots of people drink whisky with water, don't they? And what sort of water do people use? Mmm. From the tap… But that's crazy. Nuts. Don't many of the whisky companies, especially the fancier ones, make a fuss about the Highland river water, unique to their product? And people dilute it with stuff from the tap? Why don't the distilleries market twin packs of malt whisky, plus a bottle of authentic Highland river water, so that, when you drink whisky and water, you use the right water?

And another, rather different accompaniment, is an aspirin. Or any pill, for that matter. There you are, after work, in a crowded underground train heading for a main-line station. You've had a hard day, and your head is thumping. Before you dash for your commuter cattle truck, you rush into the pharmacy for a packet of aspirin. And what do they sell you? A packet of aspirin. Just a packet of aspirin. What are you supposed to take it with? No one likes gulping pills down straight. Why doesn't the aspirin come as a twin-pack with a small bottle of water … your brand mineral water?

And all those come from just two features – "You drink it" and "You drink it cold" – and letting it be. And those were the most obvious features too …

Different ways of being different

That oh-so-simple question "How might this be different?" is the centerpiece of the *InnovAction!* process. After defining what you know in terms of a long list of bullet points, and sharing your list with those of your colleagues, the individual pieces of your collective, complex, bundled patterns of learning, knowledge and experience become teased apart, and "How might this be different?" triggers the formation of new patterns. When doing this, it is helpful if the group contains as diverse a community as possible, even perhaps including "outsiders" such as customers, suppliers, and technical experts. They have an entirely different perspective, and can contribute many different "parts," so that, when the new patterns begin to be formed, the stock of "parts" which you can recombine is as wide as possible.

"How might this be different?" acts as a mental springboard, taking you from what you know to what might be different. As we have already seen, what might be different is not necessarily what might be new, but it is one hell of a good place to start. For the converse is manifestly true: what is new is necessarily different. So, by taking you away from the familiar towards the different, we are definitely heading in the right direction. And even if we subsequently discover that what was new to us isn't necessarily new in a more global sense, then no matter: our confidence that perhaps we can discover something genuinely new next time is enhanced, and maybe we can find some feature of our "not-so-new" idea that we can tweak to make it genuinely new. Remember, all western music is composed of just 12 basic notes, and many, many pieces start with, and a huge number contain, the sequence doh-me-soh. And remember too that there's more than one restaurant in town. As Gary Hamel points out, the key to strategy is being *different* – significantly so:

Smart quotes

"In a nonlinear world, only nonlinear ideas will create new wealth. Most companies long ago reached the point of diminishing returns in their incremental improvement programs. Continuous improvement is an industrial-age concept, and while it is better than no improvement at all, it is marginal value in the age of revolution. Radical, nonlinear innovation is the only way to escape the ruthless hypercompetition that has been hammering down margins in industry after industry. Nonlinear innovation

> requires a company to escape the shackles of precedent and imagine entirely novel solutions to customer needs."
>
> Gary Hamel, *Leading the Revolution*, Harvard Business School Press, 2000, p. 13

So, anything that helps you discover something that is, firstly, different from what you do now, and, hopefully, different from what your competitors are doing, must help.

The question "How might this be different?" clearly does this in a very direct way. What makes the question so powerful, of course, is the wealth of material to which it can be applied: that long, long list of features of the world-as-we-know-it-today that we compiled so laboriously! But having compiled it, what a storehouse! What a set of springboards to jump from! As the chess example made abundantly clear, it is far, far easier to discover differences in an individual feature than it is to grapple with the whole. And although the "How might this be different?" exploration might start with a single feature, it easily and naturally expands to embrace progressively more.

"How might this be different?" can be asked in a non-specific sense, inviting the team to explore in a general way, following any line of thought that comes to mind. But it can also be asked in a number of more focused ways, which generally fall into four categories dealing with:

- size and scale;

- sequence and flow;

- roles and responsibilities; and

- function and purpose.

This classification is about emphasis rather than scientific rigor: the boundaries are soft, and as with all exploration, both physical and mental, you can start off in one direction, but soon find yourself heading in another …

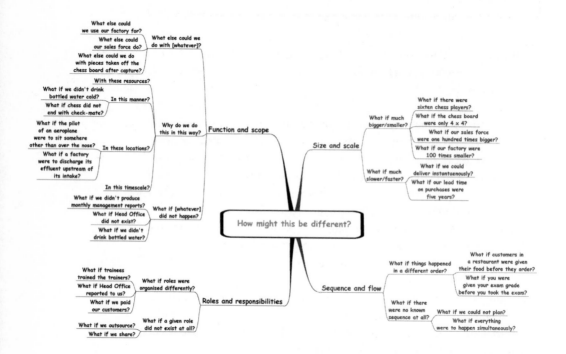

This mind map captures the main ways in which *InnovAction!*'s magic question "How might this be different?" can be asked. The list is not exhaustive … but it's not a bad start! The main questions are illustrated with some concrete examples, some of which relate directly to the text, but some not …

Size and scale

Many aspects of business life are associated with measurable characteristics of size and scale, and many of the bullet points on the aggregate list of features-of-the-world-as-it-is-today can be measured or counted. The "How might this be different?" question can focus on these, encouraging you to stretch your imagination to how the world might work if the size or scale of various specific component parts were enlarged or diminished.

"What if we played chess with more than two players?" is a simple (but, as we saw, very powerful) example of this; two more general – and more challenging – ones are "What if the sales forces were only one tenth of the current size?" and "What if our factory were a hundred times bigger?" As with all "How might this be different?" questions, the purpose of the question is not to stand as an idea in its own right; rather it is to act as a springboard to help you escape from your prison of experience, to get those raindrops out of your valleys.

And once you can escape from the valleys of familiarity, you can discover some very interesting places indeed. Here, for example, is a (somewhat paraphrased) conversation that actually took place in one of my workshops:

"What if the factory capacity were a hundred times bigger?"

"Well ... we'd have to sell a hell of a lot more of our product."

"And that means a huge advertising campaign."

"And a very different logistics capability."

"Wait a minute, though ... increasing our capacity doesn't mean that we have to make more of our existing product."

"Mmmm. I don't follow you. What do you have in mind?"

"Well … maybe we could make different products …"

"But why do we have to make our products? Why couldn't we make our competitor's products and cannibalize their market with look-alikes?"

"Look-alikes? What sort of look-alikes?"

"You know, similar products, but not quite the same!"

"Do you mean like own-label brands?"

"Yes, that's just what I had in mind – although I didn't realize it at the time!"

"But our major competitor doesn't make own-label brands."

"Hey – that gives me a fantastic idea. Why don't we use our existing spare factory capacity to manufacture competitor look-alikes, to sell to the super-markets as their own label brands?"

"Wow, that's a new one!"

"Yes, and it's a multiple whammy. We increase our throughput, we fill our spare capacity, and we increase our factory utilization. We also add to our sales volume and revenue, and if we get the pricing right, we'll increase our profits as well. And we'll be opening a new channel – we're pretty sniffy about own-label too. But the really smart thing is that we cannibalize not our own products, but our competitor's! How can we lose?"

"But won't the competitors retaliate?"

"They might, but it will take them some time to spot what's going on …"

"Mmm. Wow. That's some idea. Why don't we devote some quality time to thinking it right through?"

"Yes!"

I've paraphrased only a little, but what doesn't come through from my dialog is the speed at which it took place, or the number of different people contributing – there were about ten in this group. The idea is a potential blockbuster, and it's a great example of letting it be, as well as of the *BBC* – brain bank connectivity. The conversation started in a pretty stilted manner, covering the familiar and predictable ground of advertising and logistics, and it might have stopped there. But it didn't – the group let it be. Then someone suggested making different products, and someone else piggybacked on this to suggest not any-old different product, but the competitor's products. That then led to the idea of own-label manufacture, not of our products, but of our competitor's. That then led to the final idea of manufacturing competitor look-alike own-label products using existing surplus capacity. And that can happen with today's factories – but we got there by imagining what might happen if the capacity were dramatically increased. As I've already said, the power of "How might this be different?" is not in the immediate answer to the question, but to where it might lead. And the result is always just a new pattern formed from the existing parts. But what a new pattern!

Sequence and flow

All business processes have a sequence and a flow, and so a second generic form of the magic "How might this be different?" question is to imagine significantly different sequences and flows.

In most restaurants, for example, the usual sequence, briefly, is (starting at the time you have been seated): you are given a menu, you choose the food, you order the food, you are then served the food, you eat the food, the plates are taken away, you ask for the bill, you pay the bill, you leave.

What if you were served the food before you ordered? Crazy! How would the restaurant know what you wanted? Well, maybe the restaurant doesn't offer any choice, so everybody gets whatever the chef is making. But maybe the restaurant does know what you want. Eh? How would the restaurant know what you wanted before you go there? Easy – because you've been there before, maybe many times. Indeed, every time you've been there, the restaurant has produced an itemized bill, specifying exactly what you ate. But what does the restaurant do with that information? Probably the same as you do with the bill – throw it away (assuming you're not keeping it to claim against tax, that is!). Yes, the restaurant will keep a record of the sales value (for their accounting), but they probably throw away the detail. Oh dear. What a waste. My local Italian restaurant really should know that I just love fresh asparagus. And if they were to phone me early in the week and say, "Hey, Mr Sherwood, we have a great order of the most fantastic asparagus coming in next Saturday morning. Can we book a table for you and your wife for 8.30 that evening?" there's quite a chance that I'd say "Yes, what a good idea!" So I and my wife have a nice meal, and the restaurant pre-books my table and takes control of the booking process – rather than waiting for me to call them, they call me … Now that idea is not, repeat not, crazy. That's what customer relationship management means for a restaurant. And they have all the information they need – they've been collecting it for years. Or have they? Once again, it's all about new patterns of existing component parts …

Roles and responsibilities

The last example started by invoking a change in sequence – "What if you were served the food before you ordered?" – and, among other things, ended up with a change in role: instead of a situation in which I phone the restaurant to book a table, they are proactive in contacting me to book a table on my behalf, and our roles have been reversed.

Roles and responsibilities are always a major feature of processes, organizations and relationships, and so focusing "How might this be different?" on the roles and responsibilities of the various actors on the chosen stage can be a very powerful way of generating new ideas. A question that always stimulates a good discussion, after the initial shock has passed, invites you to explore a world in which roles are reversed – "What if head office reported to us?" is always fun, and teases out all sorts of issues about how the hierarchy does, or does not, add value; for another example, let me describe an episode that took place in a workshop with the Child Safety Division of Britax International. Just by way of background, Britax is a manufacturing company, and the Child Safety Division makes a range of prams, push chairs, and child safety seats for cars. The child safety seats come in three sizes – a cradle for babies, a well-padded small chair for toddlers, and a larger chair for young children. Their major sales channel is through specialist or general retailers in markets such as Europe, the United States and Australia, and there are only a handful of other major manufacturers in the global market. One special feature of this market, though, is the power not of the major competitors, but of the car boot sale. Child safety seats are in essence indestructible, and so when the infant grows out of the cradle, what does the parent do with the seat?

One of the bullet points in describing the market was the obvious (but, as ever with such obvious points, rarely stated) "Our customers pay our retailers." This is all about process and role and so, "How might this be different?" led to a role reversal expressed by "What if we were to pay the customer?"

The discussion started, of course, with all the expected comments about that being the fastest way to bankruptcy that anyone had ever thought of, but the group let it be. If we were to pay the customer, how could we do this? After all, the customer we are talking about – usually the mother of the recently born child – doesn't deal with us, she buys the seat at the retailer. In general, we don't know who the customer is, so there is no way of paying her.

Why don't we know who she is? Because we don't have any way of capturing her name and address. Why not? Well ... we just don't. But if we could capture the end-consumer's name and address, we could then send her a check. But if we captured her name and address, we could send her things other than just a check ... things like a card for the baby's first birthday ... things like offers on new fabric covers for the seat (you know what happens to those ...) things like vouchers for the next seat in the range ...

But won't this direct contact with the customer upset the retailers? Mmm. Good point. It might. But we could still capture the name and address, and instead of reimbursing the customer direct from us, we could arrange for this to take place through the retailer. That would mean that the customer would have to come back to the shop. Hey – that gives me an idea! Suppose we sent the mum a voucher for the toddler seat, inviting the mum to redeem the voucher at their local retailer for a discount, where she could also leave the now-unwanted baby cradle! That means we make a follow-on sale of the toddler seat, as well as withdrawing the cradle from the car boot sale market! If cars can be traded-in, why not child safety seats? And the same could of course apply to the upgrade from the toddler seat to the top-of-the-range model! Instead of having a series of one-off sales, we could build a relationship with the mum, so that the sale of the baby cradle locks in the sale of the two upgrades too. And all this can take place even under the current pricing policy where (thank goodness!) the customer still pays us!

By letting it be, and by imagining a world in which the relationship between the manufacturer and customer was reversed, we took our raindrops out of the familiar valley of current experience, up onto a neighboring, very strange ridge ("We pay our customers? That's nuts!"), tottered around a bit, but eventually fell into a very real valley indeed – the valley of how we can build a new and very different relationship with our customers.

As with the restaurant example, customer relationship management is not "new" in any fundamental, global sense. And people have been trading in cars for years. But no matter. These particular ideas, and the business model they imply, were all new to Britax, and also to their particular market. So it works for them. No need to be snooty about "originality." As Koestler's Law states: *the more familiar the parts, the more striking the new whole.*

Function and purpose

This category is the broadest, for it probes to the heart of function (what actually happens) and purpose (to what end). "How might this be different?" can lead in all sorts of directions, as triggered by questions such as:

- What else could we do with ... ?

- Why do we do this in this way?

- What if [whatever] didn't happen at all?

This last form of question – a negation which postulates a world in which a particular feature is not present, or does not take place – usually creates the most apparently strange contexts, but often the most rewarding ones too. Questions such as "What if there were no Head Office?" and "What if we stopped preparing annual budgets?" challenge the most fundamental organizational beliefs, the most fiercely held prejudices. They really do jolt the raindrops out of the deepest valleys – they are true "raindrop-shakers."

MY WORST MOMENT

I was once running a workshop with a senior team of bankers. It felt a bit like that scene towards the end of the film *Mary Poppins*, in which (the appropriately named) Mr Banks, the father of the children for whom Mary Poppins is the nanny, is addressing the board of a bank, a board populated by geriatric, whiskered, Victorians. In my case, the individuals were not especially geriatric, nor particularly whiskered, nor obviously Victorian ... but the atmosphere was pretty similar. I'd done my best to make things lively, and we managed to complete a session of capturing the key features of banking-as-we-know-it-today without too much of an undertone of why are we doing this, I have better things to do with my time, young man.

The time came to ask, "How might this be different?" and so I alighted on the feature, "We pay interest on savings accounts."

"Let's go for that one," I said. "Let's imagine what would happen if interest rates were zero."

Dead silence. Stony stares at me; meaningful glances at one another.

"You do realize, Mr Sherwood, that interest rates are the fundamental cornerstone of the banking business?"

"Yes, I do appreciate that. But I'm not suggesting that interest rates should or will go to zero. I'm just suggesting this as a way of exploring a very different world, as a means of getting the raindrops out of the valleys."

Even deader silence. Try as I might, I couldn't get any discussion going at all, and I have never been invited back to that bank since.

I contrast that wretched experience with what happened at another bank, where the penny dropped very quickly that, if they didn't give interest on savings accounts, depositors would have to be motivated in a different way to leave their money in the bank. This led to a discussion of the benefit of offering security and safety, and of the possibility of offering other forms of reward to depositors. One suggestion was for benefits in kind, for example, an account targeted at children between the ages of about 8 and 15. If you put your money with us, you don't get any interest, but just before your birthday, we give you a voucher for the local bicycle shop (or, these days, PlayStation shop!). That captures the customer while they're young, offers something of real value to them, gives them the benefit of a discount by virtue of the bank's buying power, and helps build a stronger relationship between the bank and local traders. A win-win game all around ... and, as ever, something that can be done even while we are paying interest on the regular savings accounts held by their parents.

Another idea – to appeal to the parents – was a lottery account. If you have a balance of at least, say, £100 in a particular form of account, then you don't receive interest, but all the account numbers are put into a lottery every month, and one account wins the total interest amount. From a cost point of view, this is no more expensive to the bank than paying interest on each individual account. But if this type of account can attract a large number of new customers, all of whom give the bank their names and addresses, then perhaps the benefit to the bank is more in exploiting this new database than in holding lots more small deposits ...

This second bank had no problem at all in exploring a world in which interest rates are zero, and found some very interesting new landmarks. But that first bank ...

Another example. In a discussion of management processes, one particular bullet point is always on the list: "We have annual budgets." How might this be different? Well, let's imagine a world in which we just didn't budget: let's explore what might happen if we wished budgets away.

It is at this point that the financial control community have apoplexy, but, as usual, let me reassure them that I am not suggesting this as a specific idea to be implemented; rather, I am using it as a springboard to a different world, a world which it might be worth exploring for a short while.

What would such a world look like? Well, I agree, that one version of this world is a total loss of financial control and commercial doom. But this is not the only possibility. The world might also contain features such as the absence of a rush to spend whatever might be left in the kitty as the financial year comes to an end (if you happen to be in a government department); a world in which much more time is spent on managing the business rather than on crunching numbers; a world in which the political game is very different too. And a world in which things happen very differently in period 10, when you are looking at period 9's management accounts only to discover (yet again) that sales are below budget. And because sales are below budget, we have to do something to meet the period 12 profit target. But since we're now in period 10, the range of things we can actually do is pretty limited – so we'll cut the marketing budget, stop training, fly economy not business class, and cut those IT projects at head office. As it happens, the marketing department, the trainers, and the IT department had seen this one coming a long time ago, because they've learnt all the tricks. So their original budgets already contained some deliberate fat in periods 10, 11 and 12; fat that they strenuously argued for when the budget was negotiated a year or more ago; fat that they knew would be cut out so that cuts could be seen to be taking place; but fat that in fact could be cut out without damaging anything really important. The only people who will actually suffer are those suckers who planned long-haul flights late in the year. What kind of crazy would plan to fly long-haul in the last quarter of the year? People as naïve as that deserve what they get.

You might regard all these things as the normal hurly-burly of organizational life. But you might also think that some of these behaviors aren't so helpful, and that it might be worth devoting some quality time to exploring how these dysfunctional behaviors might be changed, even in a world where there are annual budgets.

Why are budgets annual? What business has a natural rhythm of exactly twelve months? Is this the only way to ensure that publicly uttered commitments can be met? Surely there must be another way …

One other way might be to replace a static, annual budget by a rolling process, harmonized with the natural rhythm of the business: say, a three-month firm sales forecast and production schedule, with the next three months more uncertain, and the next six softer still. Do I hear you say "That's nuts, that can't work!"? Can't it? Why not? And what problems might need to be solved to make it work?

And whilst we're on the subject of budgets, and different ways of doing things, there is an interesting event that takes place annually in the UK. Every winter, during late January and early February, the press usually carries headlines such as "More Hospital Bed Closures!! Old Age Pensioners Denied Emergency Treatment!!" The closure of hospital wards in the UK's National Health Service is something of an annual ritual, and, to my mind, is directly caused by the budgeting system.

Let me explain. The Health Service, as a government-owned body, conforms to the government's budgeting cycle, with a financial year beginning in April and ending the following March. In essence, each hospital receives a bag of cash (I simplify somewhat) every April that has to last until the following March. Real life being what it is, come January, the originally full bag of cash is pretty depleted. And since the Health Service cannot take any measures to increase its revenue, the only thing that can be done is to cut costs. Regrettably, hospitals don't have a marketing budget in the first place, so they can't cut that one; also, they don't do that many flights. So training and IT go the usual way, but no one notices that. What is noticed is the only other lever the Health Service can pull to cut costs in the short term. And that's to stop treating patients – after all, it's those nasty patients who consume all those expensive drugs, who eat the food, who have those costly operations. If we stop treating patients, all those variable costs don't get incurred, so we can conserve that precious cash. So wards get closed, and beds kept empty. And then it gets into the newspapers.

How might this be different? Let's take the feature "we budget annually, April to March." Let's not be so dramatic as to imagine we stop budgeting altogether; this time, let's take a gentler approach by asking "Suppose we didn't budget from April to March, but over a different part of the year – from, say, October to September. What would happen then?" Real life being what it is, we'll probably still run out of money in period 9. But in this world, period 9 is in June, not December. So we won't be faced with ward closures at the height of the miserable British winter, when there is often an epidemic of influenza, and old people suffer pneumonia … We may still have to close wards, but the damage won't be anything like as severe …

Questions such as "What if we didn't do budgets (or whatever) at all?" are usually the most dramatic examples of "How might this be different?" for they usually represent the most direct attack on the *status quo*. As a consequence, they can be singularly powerful, shaking people out of complacency, a supine acceptance of the-way-things-are-now. Why are things like they are? Do they have to be? Why? How different might they be?

InnovAction! and lateral thinking

Everyone has heard of lateral thinking and, as its originator, Edward de Bono, not infrequently points out, the phrase is now to be found in the Oxford English Dictionary, and so is officially part of the English language.

De Bono coined the term in his book *Lateral Thinking for Management*, first published in 1967; as with all innovations, lateral thinking is itself a new pattern formed from existing parts, not least of which is the name – in *The Act of Creation*, published in 1964, Arthur Koestler refers to a process which he calls "thinking aside."

Lateral thinking, thinking aside, **InnovAction!**; all are names for particular processes which share a common objective – to provide a mechanism to aid the process of unlearning, and for the discovery of new patterns; all have their own distinctive methods.

Central to lateral thinking is a new word, "po," invented by de Bono and standing for "provocative operation." To see how this is used, let's take one of de Bono's own examples, which he expresses as "Po: planes land upside-down" (see *Serious Creativity*, HarperCollins Business, paperback edition 1996, p. 156).

In everyday language, this means "As a way of provoking new thoughts, let's consider what happens if planes land upside down." If this were to happen, as well as having all the drinks spill, and the passengers feeling odd, the pilot, though ostensibly upside down, would have a good view of the ground when the plane is landing. This makes a lot of sense, and I'm sure we'd all agree that it is a "good thing" for aircraft pilots to have as good a view of the ground as possible when landing. And, come to think of it, the pilot of a plane the size of a jumbo jet couldn't be sitting in a more unhelpful place when landing, perched on top of a hugely bulbous nose-cone, with a perfect view of the sky above, but a 100 percent obscured view of the ground below. Aha – what a great idea! Have pilots sitting, the right way up of course, in a capsule underneath the plane (rather like the bomb-aimer's place in a World War II bomber), so that the plane still flies the right way up, but the pilot can now see what is going on as the plane lands. Alternatively, have two positions for the pilot, one on top for general flying, the other underneath for take-off and landing; or, at the very least, have a video camera which projects an image of the ground into the cockpit. Any of these ideas has got to make more sense, be cheaper, and be easier to engineer, than the solution developed by the designers of the Concorde supersonic plane. Their way of making sure the pilot can see the ground on landing is to have the entire nose assembly of the aircraft dip down. A video camera has to be cheaper.

Po, the provocative operation, provokes and shocks our thinking to consider the unthinkable – what happens if planes land upside down? And if we reflect on this, and – my language this time – let it be, then our raindrops, wrenched out of their valley by being po'd, discover the bright new valley of innovation.

Many of the examples cited in de Bono's various books are dramatic and startling. One notable one is "Po: a factory is downstream of itself" (see *Po: Beyond Yes and No,* Penguin, 1990, p. 95). This translates to: "As a way of stimulating your thinking, consider what might happen if a factory, which is situated by a river and uses the river water for its manufacturing process, is sited downstream of itself." When I first read this one, it made my brain hurt, but once I got my mind around it, I was able to follow de Bono's explanation that one consequence of this would be that the factory is obliged to take its own effluent into its intake pipes. At first sight, this is not a good thing, for the "downstream" factory is being polluted by its "upstream" ghost. It can become a good thing, however, if the "upstream" ghost cleans its own effluent before discharging it into the river.

This suggests that a regulator, or government agency concerned about the environment, could take the very simple measure of introducing a law to force all river-sited factories to discharge their effluent upstream of their intake pipes. The factory as a whole is sited in a perfectly normal way, all that's different is the relative siting of the intake (downstream) and effluent (upstream) pipes. Once again, a somewhat bizarre "po" has forced the raindrops out of the valley (almost literally in this case), and some exploratory thought has discovered a valid and practical new idea.

There is no doubt that de Bono has written a lot of very good stuff, and he has been an enormously successful evangelist. But the difficulty I had when reading many of his books was the question "Where does 'po' come from, daddy?" – de Bono seemed to me to be producing the various "pos" like rabbits from a hat. Each of them had a wonderful story, but I was left with thinking that it probably was as hard to discover the right "po" as it was to have a good new idea in the first place. Maybe I didn't read de Bono's books carefully enough, but it seemed to me that rather than solving the problem of how to generate new ideas systematically and safely, "po" just pushed the problem back one stage from discovering a new idea to discovering the right "po."

And that's the key difference, I believe, between *InnovAction!* and lateral thinking. *InnovAction!* has a very specific and well-defined starting point – what you know, as expressed in that now-familiar list of bullet points. It isn't a blank sheet of paper, and it isn't arbitrary. It isn't magic, and it isn't luck. It's what you know. Once you've got that list of bullet points, you can then ask "How might this be different?" and springboard from there, as we have now seen with the very many examples in this chapter.

InnovAction!'s "How might this be different?" is, in fact, doing much the same job as de Bono's "po," for the exploration process from there is very similar. But whereas de Bono is not – to my mind anyway – very clear on where the "pos" come from, I am crystal clear where "How might this be different?" comes from – it comes from your learning.

Indeed, if we go back to the two de Bono examples, we can see how the two processes converge. De Bono's "Po: planes land upside down" would map onto the list of bullet points describing planes-as-they-are-today as the feature "planes land the right way up" – one of those obvious-but-true descriptions of the way-things-are-today that are so hard to notice. How might this be different? Well, they might land upside-down, and we go from there. A bit further down (or, more likely up) the list of bullet points in *InnovAction!*, though, you are quite likely to find "the pilot sits in a cockpit above the nose-cone." How might this be different? Well ... he might sit somewhere else ... actually in the nose-cone, or right at the front, or underneath perhaps. And maybe the "good idea" is discovered rather more directly.

Likewise, if we take "Po: a factory is downstream of itself," then the list of bullet points of riverside-factories-as-we-know-them-today might include (if we had been thorough enough) "effluent is usually discharged downstream." How might this be different? What if the effluent were discharged upstream? Aha. As we have now seen many times, the richer and more perceptive list of features of the world-as-it-is-today, the more likely you are to find that special differentiating feature.

So, smart managers should definitely read de Bono, especially *Lateral Thinking for Managers*, and *Serious Creativity*: then take a view as to which process you prefer, or indeed, mix and match the pieces as you like. As Koestler said (again!), it's all about new patterns of existing components.

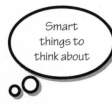

Smart
things to
think about

GETTING THE LEVEL OF DETAIL IN THE DESCRIPTIONS RIGHT

Fundamental to the *InnovAction!* process is the list of bullet points describing the world-as-it-is-now. Every innovation manifests itself as a change in one or more of the features of its predecessors, and so the richer your list of features of the *status quo*, the more likely it is that it is you, rather than your competitors, who will discover the next new idea.

Much of this is about careful observation, noticing detail, and paying attention, often to the blindingly obvious. As we have seen in the text, if you do not explicitly notice that you drink bottled water, you might miss the possibilities of using it as a cosmetic; if you happened not to spot the fact that the paper on which the nine dots puzzle is drawn is flat, drawing a single straight line through all of them is that much harder; if you fail to observe that most riverside factories expel their effluent downstream of their intake, you might not discover the environmentally friendly policy of switching them about.

Writing the bullet points describing the world-as-it-is-now therefore warrants considerable care and thoroughness, and, in general, the finer the level of detail, the better.

Springboards and retro-fits

Talking of mixing and matching, this is a good time to declare that *Innov-Action!* and lateral thinking are not the only two techniques in the smart manager's idea-generation toolkit. If you come across some of the other books on the subject, you will find that there are literally hundreds on offer: the sister Capstone publication, *The Ultimate Book of Business Creativity*, by Ros Jay, lists thirty-six, neatly in alphabetical order, from "The 7 × 7 Technique" to "Verbal Checklist." *101 Ways to Generate Great Ideas*, by Timothy Foster claims 101; and *Techniques of Structured Problem Solving* by Arthur VanGundy catalogues no fewer than 250! This appears to be a bewildering array. Are they really all different?

In my view, they are not. All, certainly, have the same objective – to provide some structure to guide you through the process of unlearning, to ease the process of finding the "parts" you need to recombine to generate new ideas. The mechanisms to do this appear to be very different, and many of them are presented as "black boxes" – a set of apparently arbitrary rules of thumb that might work under certain conditions, if you're lucky, and maybe gifted with a vivid imagination too.

I hope I haven't presented *InnovAction!* in this – to my mind unhelpful – way. Much of the purpose of this chapter, and the last one too, has been to present a rigorous, meaningful and intelligible intellectual framework to provide you with a deep understanding of what you are seeking to do in idea generation, and why the *InnovAction!* process actually works. So, if you agree with me that Koestler's Law is not only profoundly true, but offers a deep insight into the process of idea generation; if you recognize that the "patterns" which are relevant in business are called learning, knowledge and experience; if you agree that the key problem is then one of unlearning; and if you agree that innovation in business never, just never, takes place on a perfectly green-field site, then the *InnovAction!* process is self-evident. It must work, and you can see why it must work. And you can apply it to any situation you care to, from new product development, through process redesign, to new organization structures, new forms of relationships, breakthrough strategies, and – ultimately – to a new habitual way of thinking for you.

InnovAction! is constrained by two features. The first is the thoroughness of the list of bullet points you compile concerning your knowledge of the focus-of-attention-as-it-is-today. As we have already seen, if you didn't happen to notice, and then write down, that chess is played by two players, you might have missed the fertile territory of four-man tag chess; if you didn't happen to notice, and then write down, that we drink mineral water cold, you might have missed the potential gold mine of water sold for use in tea and coffee; if you didn't happen to notice, and then write down, the fact that your factory makes your own products, you might have missed the possibility that it might be able to make own-label lookalikes of your competitors' products. And given that you, and your colleagues, have an immense amount of learning, knowledge and experience, how on earth can you ensure that you are capturing the right bits, and being as thorough as possible? Not easy, especially when you remember that many of the "parts" you need – particularly the technological ones – for tomorrow's innovations exist not in your organization, but in the outside world. Maybe you can keep lists of the key assumptions of your business on wall charts, in full view of every-one, with a huge sign saying "How might this be different?" Maybe that's what knowledge management systems really should do ...

The second constraint on *InnovAction!* is closer to home – your personal, and your organization's collective, imagination. So you've got a list of bullet points a mile long, as comprehensive as can be. You've asked "How might this be different?" and you're sitting there, mouth open, brain frozen. You can't, just can't, no matter how hard you try, imagine how "this" could pos-sibly be different from the-way-it-is-now. What on earth do you do?

Well, don't give up – like all personal skills, *InnovAction!* requires practice. The first time a child gets on a two-wheeled bicycle, he falls off. Always. From the child's point of view, he has every right to say, "Daddy, you misled me. This cannot work. My own experience tells me so." Left to his own devices, as he tends his grazed knees, the child needs to be very brave to get on the bike a second time and try again. But dad is around, and he encour-ages, soothes, and says, "Let's try again. I'll hold the saddle a bit longer this time." That's what dads are for. And mums too.

It's also helpful to conduct *InnovAction!* sessions in a small, supportive group. Everyone's brain freezes from time to time, but it is much less likely that everyone's brains will freeze synchronously. Remember the power of the *BBC* – quite soon, someone will say something that triggers your brain to thaw. And once the ideas begin to flow ...

One of the great benefits of *InnovAction!* is that it has an anchored starting point – a starting point firmly embedded in your knowledge, learning and experience. And you have an enormous amount of this. So, if "How might this be different?" doesn't seem to be leading anywhere in particular for a given item after a sensible try, drop it and choose another, and another, and another again. In my experience – with the sole exception of those bugaboo bankers I mentioned a while ago – the process works, and works well.

Because you are starting from what you know, the *InnovAction!* process acts as a springboard, catapulting you from what you know to what you might know. I contrast this process to a very different form of process, a process that I call "retro-fit."

An example of a retro-fit method for idea generation is the "random word" process, which works like this:

• Choose a focus of attention.

• Choose a genuinely random word, perhaps by opening a dictionary, perhaps by looking in a newspaper.

• Compile a list of words generated by word association from the trigger word.

• Then see if any of the words on the list suggest a new idea related to the focus of attention.

<table>
<tr><td>

SMART THINGS
TO DO

</td><td>

RANDOM WORDS

You have an opportunity to enter the restaurant business, but you want to create something rather different.

Choose as your random word "mirror."

Compile a list of at least 30 words triggered by "mirror," and see what ideas you can generate!

</td></tr>
</table>

When you do this, you don't have to link all your words back to the original trigger – in fact, the list may be a whole sequence of random words which have nothing to do with each other at all. Most people, however, use one word as a bridge to another in all sorts of ways – mirrors are for looking into, so that suggests "look," "reflect," "see"; "see" sounds like "sea," so that can lead to "ship," "boat," "float"; this might trigger a rhyme with "goat" leading to names of animals ... The list can evolve in a myriad of ways, especially if done in a small group.

Here, for example, is my list starting from "mirror":

• look	• famous	• clean
• reflect	• infamous	• wash
• see	• criminal	• washing powder
• sea	• notorious	• supermarket
• ship	• Ingrid Bergman	• trolley
• boat	• Casablanca	• bus
• float	• Africa	• train
• goat	• Zulu	• teach
• elephant	• Z Cars	• educate
• big	• television	• student
• huge	• film	• school-boy
• giant	• theatre	• short trousers
• friendly	• theatricality	• short skirts
• happy	• showmanship	• knees
• celebration	• soap opera	• legs
• celebrity	• soap	• diamonds

You can see how my mind is working (any psychiatrists reading this, please don't despair!): the flow through animals led to big things; a few days ago, I had a conversation about Roald Dahl's book *The Big Friendly Giant*; wasn't there a Hitchcock film called *Notorious*, which starred Ingrid Bergman? Z Cars was a long-running police series on BBC television in the sixties; and somewhere in my mind is the name – a prohibition era gangster, I think – "Legs" Diamond. Also, the process isn't linear – when I put down "soap opera," my mind had drifted back to "television."

So, does this list trigger any thoughts about – ah, yes, that was it – restaurants?

Well, let's take "Legs" Diamond. He was (I think) a gangster. So what about a chain of pizza restaurants, themed on Chicago in the twenties? The waiters could be dressed up as hoods, and the waitresses as speakeasy girls; the pizzas could have names like "Al Capone Special," "Nitti Gritty" and "Elliot Ness Monster"; there could be screens (see the trigger "television"?) around the restaurant showing clips of gangster movies like *White Heat*, *The Roaring Twenties*, *Some Like it Hot*, *The Sting* ... For a touch of theatre (another word on the list), you could even imagine a fake police raid (that's there too, implicit in Z Cars) from time to time to liven things up! And what about *Pizza Nostra* as the name of the chain?

There's another theme running through the list, as a sort of undercurrent, of celebrity and show. What about a restaurant which does not have small tables for couples and foursomes, but has big, round tables, seating about twelve? You wouldn't go to a restaurant like that to have an intimate conversation with a loved one – you'd be seated with strangers. But what if those strangers were people you actually wanted to meet – celebrities? Can you imagine a restaurant which advertised "Book now to meet next month's celebrity guests" – maybe there would be four or five tables, each with a celebrity from entertainment, maybe a sports star, a journalist, a novelist, whatever? Every month, the restaurant could line up a different list of celebrities, and – provided the celebrities wouldn't object to being "on show" for the evening in this kind of context (some celebrities might love it) – that would draw the crowds.

Speaking of celebrities, there is one celebrity in a restaurant who is often overlooked – the chef. What about a restaurant that advertises "Celebrity chef of the month"? What I have in mind here is a bit like pop stars and opera singers who go on tour. One of the benefits of this is that a much wider population sees the star live, and the star earns quite a tidy sum too. What about someone acting as an impresario, orchestrating tours of the leading chefs, so that diners in New York, London, Paris, Copenhagen can enjoy the food of the world's master chefs in their own city?

Now the concept of people traveling (the chefs to the restaurants around the world, in that case), combined with the word, television, triggers another thought. Let's wrap that together with "celebration" and "happy." It so happens I'm writing this a couple of days before my younger son's eleventh birthday, and one of the treats he really enjoys is a celebratory birthday meal at a restaurant. For occasions like birthdays and anniversaries, you don't want a table just for two, because it's really nice to have family and friends together. But one reason they often can't be together is because they live a long way away – overseas, perhaps.

So what about a network of restaurants, around the world, with web-cameras and TV screens, linked by the Internet – a sort of social video conferencing? That way I could celebrate with family and friends in all sorts of locations at the same time. It's not quite as good as all being together in the same place, but it's a lot better than not being together at all. Who will be the first to open a chain of e-restaurants?

Going back to the list, let me pick up "supermarket" and "trolley." Sometimes I find shopping fun, sometimes it's a chore. Many supermarkets have a coffee shop where you can take a break, and rest those tired feet. But I haven't ever experienced a coffee shop where I can sit down, and then someone says to me "Welcome to our supermarket. Please enjoy our complimentary cappuccino and croissant/tea and muffin/whatever. My name is Amanda, and I am your personal shopper. Please give me your shopping list, and I will wheel the trolley around and collect everything you need. I'll be back in about twenty minutes so you can check everything is OK, and our electronic trolley will automatically total everything up. When you're happy, you can pay me, here at your table, by credit card/loyalty card/cash/whatever, and then I'll wheel the trolley to your car." That's a different sort of restaurant too.

You get the idea: the list of words produced from the original random trigger acts as a seed for new ideas.

How does this work? Well, if we go back to our landscape, raindrop-in-the-valley metaphor, our focus of attention (restaurants, in the case) takes us down our mental valley labeled "restaurants." The random word – and it really doesn't matter what it is (if you remember, I chose mirror, because I happened to be looking into one whilst I was thinking about this) – pitches your mind into a totally different place, nothing whatsoever to do with the focus of attention. It's as if you threw a ball as far as possible in your mental landscape, and it happens to roll into a distant, unrelated valley such as "mirror."

Then, as you stand in the distant valley ("mirror"), the word association process invites you to look around, and see what other "valleys" you can identify, in whatever direction you happen to scan. And, very quickly, your mind goes from valley to valley, skirting ridges, noticing peaks, helter-skelter through your mental landscape. And if you do this in a small group, everyone is going in different directions, and it becomes quite impossible for a facilitator to write it all down!

After a few minutes of this, and a list of say, thirty to fifty words, you will find that you have scanned a huge amount of your mental landscape, totally freely, to the extent that you can often forget what the original focus of attention was!

The next stage is to "stand" in these distant valleys, and "look back" towards the focus of attention, and see if anything pops into your mind. In this way, the random word process is "retro-fitting" possible trial solutions (solutions associated with concepts such as supermarkets or celebrities) to the original question "What themes can I generate for a new restaurant format?" This is in contrast to the *InnovAction!* process, in which you start from everything you know about restaurants, and use this as a springboard to new ideas.

RETRO-FITS

Using lists of random words is only one of a number of "retro-fit" techniques, which all share the common feature of projecting you from the "home" valley to a distant "valley," setting you the challenge of retro-fitting a path between the two. Some more "retro-fit" techniques are:

Simile, metaphor and analogy

This is an enhancement of the use of random words, introducing more rigor into the process that takes place after the list of random words has been compiled. Once you have the list, use it to ask questions such as (with reference to the list on page 185 in the context of developing a new type of restaurant): "In what ways is a restaurant like a theatre?" (simile), "How can a restaurant be happy?" (metaphor), "What do short trousers and restaurants have in common?" (analogy). In each case, you are forcing the search for some kind of relationship between two apparently distant concepts.

Proverbs

Write down a list of proverbs, sayings or clichés ("Look before you leap," "A bird in the hand is worth two in the bush," and so on), and see if these trigger any ideas. "There's no place like home," for example, could well stimulate new ideas concerning the design of an office layout.

And for those of you with vivid imaginations ...

Role-play

In this, you imagine how someone else might tackle the problem. How might St Francis of Assisi tackle it? Or Albert Einstein? Or Napoleon? Margaret Thatcher? A magician? A medical doctor? Attila the Hun?

> ### *Journeying*
>
> Imagine now that you are going on a journey, from whatever starting point you choose, to a real or imaginary destination. Describe in detail what you see, hear, feel; describe the weather, the people you journey with and meet, the adventures that happen along the way. Do any of these images trigger any ideas?

A very important point is that springboards and retro-fits are not mutually exclusive – the same ideas are potentially accessible from both starting points, and can be discovered working either "forwards" or "backwards." "I go to a restaurant with my family" is a likely bullet point on the restaurants-as-we-know-them-today list; "How might this be different?" – well, I might go with strangers. Why would I do that? Mmm. If the stranger was someone interesting – a celebrity, even – then that might be fun. Theming the restaurant around meeting celebrities follows very naturally from there. Likewise, the idea of the visiting chef comes very quickly to mind from the feature "A restaurant usually has only one key chef." You might like to think of how the others might arise in a similar way.

InnovAction! which springboards from what you know to what you might know, can certainly result in ideas which are very similar to those generated by a process such as random words, which encourages you to retro-fit from a series of possible trial solutions back to the original issue. Although the results can be the same, the processes are very different: *InnovAction!* starts on the very solid ground of the known, and moves you to the unknown; the use of random words pitches you directly into the unknown, and then encourages you to work backwards from a variety of different potential possibilities.

In my experience, some people just love the "retro-fit" techniques, and are amazingly good at using them. I don't have the data to prove it, but I suspect that these are the people who perceive themselves to be "creative," and who are regarded by their colleagues as such. It's no accident that the random word technique is beloved by advertising agencies – it is a very powerful method for creating metaphors, and much advertising is based on explicit or implicit metaphor. It is also the stock-in-trade of comedians, and we all marvel at those who can make great jokes by bringing together seemingly distant concepts.

DRAMA, HUMOR AND INTELLECTUAL CREATIVITY

As I have already noted, Arthur Koestler's *The Act of Creation* is not in any sense a business book – it is much more a book on philosophy.

A major theme running through the book is Koestler's belief that drama, humor and intellectual creativity are fundamentally very similar, and share a basis of the discovery of new patterns of existing component parts. The difference between these three activities, he asserts, is attributable to our emotional engagement. Great drama is great because it draws our emotions in – we empathize with the characters in a play, we see ourselves, we feel what they feel. In contrast, humor relies on emotional detachment and separation – much humor, as we all know, is in fact rather cruel. Intellectual creativity is emotionally neutral – we are neither engaged nor disengaged; we are objectively trying to solve a problem.

Smart things to think about

It is also my experience, however, that quite a large community find retrofits very difficult indeed. How on earth can I think of some link between an arbitrary list of words-that-are-all-over-the-place and a restaurant? Actually, I've not the remotest idea how Attila the Hun would do it. I'm sorry, but this process just doesn't work for me. My imagination just can't handle it.

It's very unusual, however, to find people for whom *InnovAction!* does not work. Everyone can bring some knowledge to the table, and everyone can ask "How might this be different?" This question, for sure, does demand some imagination, and – like those awful bankers again – there are some whose imaginations are so limited that they get stuck. But these people are very few – most people, and especially those who do not perceive themselves as creative, can get a lot out of *InnovAction!* because its starting point is so well-anchored in their everyday experience.

Smart managers, of course, have a portfolio of tools and techniques in the kitbag, and know which to use when. In the case of idea generation, the selection is determined by the learning styles and characteristics of the group. Retro-fits appeal to inherently creative people, are generally more wacky, but can be difficult to use by more "ordinary" people; *InnovAction!*, as a springboard, is thorough, systematic, duller to some, but a safer bet for the majority.

Well, it's been a long chapter, so thanks for reading this far! I trust, however, that it hasn't been a struggle – rather, I hope that you've found it energizing, exciting, exhilarating. What – other than a couple of things that, yes, do come to mind – can be more ecstatic than discovering a new idea?

But, somewhere in your mind, I know that there is a little voice saying "Well, it's all very well to play party games such as inventing new variants of chess. And those bottled water examples, though quite cute, had a very strong feel of 'here's one I invented earlier'. What happens when you try this stuff with a real, solid business problem – one that's been around for ages, and that no one has cracked? Is this all no more than a very good sales job, snake oil in book covers? Does this *InnovAction!* business actually work for real?"

I understand that, and it's right for smart managers to ask tough questions. So, now you understand the process, the next few pages are a series of mini case studies entitled *"InnovAction! in action."* These all feature cameos of real examples – cases taken from *InnovAction!* workshops run with real clients on real problems. None of the material was in any sense pre-scripted or prepared earlier, everything that you will read actually happened. And I haven't over-embellished for dramatic effect: I am telling it like it was. There is no distortion, no invention of after-the-fact rationalizations: everything is true. My descriptions differ from a verbatim transcript in only two respects.

Firstly, time: the workshops from which the cameos have been drawn took place over times varying from three hours to two days. You will of course read through them in a matter of minutes; in practice, the discussions took place over a longer period.

And secondly, atmosphere. Maybe a more skilful writer that I could capture the atmosphere; I know I haven't done it justice. The buzz, the energy, the noise, the laughter, the stunned silence when a truly sensational idea is suggested – I can only ask you to imagine all this as you read on.

INNOVACTION! IN ACTION

Yorkshire Electricity – Cost-effective IT

An issue faced by many companies is to ensure the cost-effectiveness of its information technology function. This was the theme of a very productive workshop run with Yorkshire Electricity, one of the UK's privatized utilities. Amongst the (very long) list of bullet points describing the world-as-it-is-now were these two:

- We develop new computer applications for the business, and we also support the applications after they are implemented.
- We are a cost center within the business.

"How can we be more cost-effective in providing support to live applications?" was selected as a "focus of attention" for the *InnovAction!* process, and this was combined with asking, "How might this be different?" of the point "We are a cost center within the business."

If we aren't a cost center within the business, what else might we be? Well … we might be a profit center (this led to a number of ideas about how the IT department might generate revenue); or we might be a separate business altogether, with the utility business as a client (leading to ideas about a buy-out); alternatively, we might be owned by someone else. Who might that be? Perhaps it might be another organization that specializes in service … such as a company that helps motorists who have broken down at the roadside … such as the UK organizations the AA or the RAC.

This led the group to compile a list of bullet points about how the AA and the RAC provide their service, including:

- There is a one-off annual fee.
- There is a price list, offering different levels of service for different levels of fee.

- Service levels are published.
- Failed service levels attract penalties.
- The service provider sometimes sub-contracts work to local garages.
- Membership is held on a database.
- The person is covered, not the car.

This comparison triggered a number of ideas:

- *Pricing*. There were a number of ideas about changing the internal transfer pricing structure so that different prices correspond to different levels of service, so providing users with a good understanding of the true costs of different types of IT support, but without becoming bureaucratic.
- *Service levels*. There are already a series of service-level agreements, but these were formulated some time ago. In the spirit of "constructive restlessness," the group agreed it would be very helpful to look through these to ensure that they are fully fit-for-purpose, including the possibility of penalties.
- *Sub-contracting*. Could we use local sub-contactors, especially to support locations distant from the center?
- *Customer databases*. Amongst their large user community, there is a wide diversity in IT skills, and some users require much more support than others. Perhaps those who use the support service much more often should be charged more; or perhaps they should be invited to tailored training programs, so they can be more confident in their use of IT systems.
- *The person not the car*. This led to a discussion about how the support service could be tailored much more personally to each user, and then one person in the group proposed the raindrop-shaker: "What if each user had their own personal support consultant?" One way of doing this might be to recruit a lot more people ... so that each consultant would sit alongside each user ... but you don't have to do it that way ... what about a "virtual" consultant, providing the "help" service on-screen – just like a tailored version of the on-screen helpers provided with Microsoft products, but fully knowledgeable about the business's applications, and even the user him or herself ...

INNOVACTION! IN ACTION

Oakham School – An innovative teaching and learning environment

"Chaos!"

"A riot!"

"It'll be like *Lord of the Flies!*"

"Mayhem!"

I'd seen these words on a flipchart from across the room, so I wandered over to eavesdrop the conversation. I was in a conference center with a group of teachers and trustees from Oakham School, in Rutland, England's smallest county. The school teaches about 1000 children – 500 boys, 500 girls; 500 boarders, 500 day pupils – aged between 11 and 18, and has a reputation as one of the most forward-thinking schools in the UK. For some months, the school had been in discussions with a charity, concerning the possibility of funding a new building, and this had given the Headmaster, Tony Little, the idea that it might become a center for innovative learning and teaching.

Oakham School was founded in 1584, and a moment's thought will convince you that, fundamentally, teaching has changed little since those days in which the pupils sat at the foot of a master – possibly at that time a monk – and sought to remember his words of wisdom. Yes, the technology has evolved somewhat – the increasing use of print saved a lot of manual labor, and whiteboards and overhead projectors have replaced blackboards and chalk. But the process is probably sufficiently similar that a pupil time traveler, teleported from Oakham in 1584 to Oakham in 2000, would probably recognize where he had landed.

At the top of the list of the bullet points describing "the classroom experience," the selected focus of attention, was "there is a teacher." How might this be different? Well, suppose there is no teacher … and you arrive at the words I quoted at the start of this box.

"Wait a moment, folks," said John Fern, a historian. "Our kids really aren't that irresponsible. They often carry out lots of tasks without minute-to-minute supervision."

"Yes, they do a lot of project work, which they really enjoy. Let's make this a bit more concrete. Suppose we take something we do already – like preparing a debate. And let's suppose further that we were to give the kids a whole day to use the new building to do just that. But with no teachers inside the building at the same time. How would we organize that?"

"There would have to be some really good preparation, so the kids had a series of well-defined and appropriate tasks."

"And were organized in teams to do them … "

" … maybe with some people directly working on the specific task of preparing the debate, but maybe others doing research, or preparing materials, or even making a record of the process itself … "

"And if anyone did need some help, maybe there could be a web-camera or something, so that we could be contacted. That way, we're not actually in the building, but the kids aren't cut off if they really do need help."

"That makes our primary role as teachers one of helping the kids plan and prepare for the day, rather than in supervising the day itself."

"And that would go a long way towards our objectives, of making everything that happens in the new building contribute to the kids' creativity, oral communication, teamwork and initiative."

"But how would we allocate the building for a whole day? All our timetabling is driven by 40-minute teaching periods."

"Yes, that's true today, but why should that constrain everything? It would be quite unrealistic to expect the kids to carry out something as complex as this in just 40 minutes. Why don't we blow up the rule 'the timetable is king', and just timetable the new building differently?"

"But which department would the new building come under?"

"Maybe that's another rule we should blow up. Yes, today we have the biology rooms, the maths rooms, the modern languages rooms – petty fiefdoms we all jealously protect. So why don't we make the new building a resource for the whole school, so that the building as a whole, and all the space within it, isn't 'owned' by any one department? Wouldn't that really encourage interdisciplinary working and learning?"

"You know, you give me an idea. What stops us from blowing up the rules about timetables and ownership even in our existing buildings? Yes, it will be great to have a new building to do all sorts of whizzy new things in, but if we want to create an innovative teaching environment, maybe some of the ideas we've just discussed could apply right now … "

INNOVACTION! IN ACTION

Nestlé UK – What if we didn't eat chocolate?

One of the most exhilarating workshops I have been involved in was with a division of the world's largest food company, Nestlé: the unit that manufactures and markets the UK's most popular confectionery brand, *Kit Kat*, as well as other leaders such as *Smarties*, *After Eight* and *Aero*. Much of the workshop was spent on developing ideas for new brands, but unfortunately I can't talk about these here for they are all confidential – except for one, which arose from the chess exercise. One of the bullet points said "the pieces are made of wood or plastic." How might this be different? They could be made of chocolate!

What I can talk about, though, is a discussion resulting from a real raindrop-shaker. One of the assumptions about chocolate is, of course, that "we eat it," so, in the spirit of "How might this be different?" we asked "What if we didn't eat it? What else might we do with it?"

To help this, the group compiled a list of bullet points detailing the features of chocolate, other than that luscious taste, which included:

- Chocolate is fragrant.
- Chocolate is rich in energy.
- Chocolate melts at around 35°C, close to body temperature.
- The melting point depends on the mix of ingredients.
- Chocolate can absorb water from it surroundings.
- Chocolate is a "non-Newtonian fluid" (!) in that it does not flow like other fluids such as water.
- Solid chocolate is quite strong.
- Chocolate is easy to mould.

If chocolate isn't used for eating, its use would need to derive from these other properties, for example:

- **Fragrance**. Chocolate could be used as the basis for perfumed soaps, shampoos, air fresheners, scented paper, in candles ...
- **Energy**. Could chocolate be used as an energy source, such as a fuel for burning, or maybe instead of petrol in cars?
- **Melting**. If chocolate turns from a solid to a liquid at a specific temperature, could it be used in safety devices like fire sprinklers or fire alarms? Also, if chocolate melts, and then re-solidifies, it often shows a white "bloom," so providing evidence that melting has taken place. Could this be used as a quality indicator? For example, suppose there is a large shipment of chocolate, associated with, say, five "special" bars which melt at different temperatures. If, on arrival at the destination, all of these are solid, but two have the white "bloom," this would indicate that the shipment had been exposed to a particular temperature.
- **Water absorption**. How about using chocolate as an active ingredient in skin creams and face packs?
- **Special fluid properties**. One of these is that, when solid chocolate is subject to a sharp blow, it can extrude through small holes. This suggests that chocolate could act as a shock absorber. Imagine, for example, that there was a solid lump of chocolate behind the bumpers of a car. On impact, the chocolate would absorb the shock, and extrude through appropriately designed apertures.
- **Strength**. Use chocolate as a construction material in cold climates! For example, at Jukkasjärvi in Swedish Lapland, there is a hotel completely made from ice, which melts every May. So why not build one made of chocolate?
- **Easy to mould**. This suggests using chocolate as a mould for other materials – this would work well since chocolate can form a very precise shape.

Well ... I'm sure we'll all continue to eat a lot of *Kit Kat*, so it's most unlikely Nestlé will ever need to invoke these ideas – but it's amazing what ideas a group can come up with in the right environment, and once they get comfortable with getting the raindrops out of the valleys!

INNOVACTION! IN ACTION

Pearson Television – Television game shows

You might have thought that the chess game example was a long way from the business world. There are, however, two types of business for which this truly is the heartland. One of course is the industry which manufactures games such as *Monopoly* and *Scrabble*; the other is the television industry, for TV game shows are a very big business indeed, all around the world.

One of the biggest producers of these is Pearson Television – their titles include *The Price is Right*, *Sale of the Century* and *Greed*. As with chess, game shows are formulated around very clearly defined formats: these are just a very few of the features, as usual, in no particular order, for *The Price is Right*:

- Contestants are chosen live.
- Contestants are pre-screened.
- The host is enthusiastic.
- Anyone can play.
- The audience guesses too.
- The host doesn't know the prices.
- There is a "showcase" game.
- Contestants guess prices.
- The audience helps the contestants.
- The contestants can see the goods.
- Contestants are dressed smart casual.
- Contestants are individuals.
- The show lasts half an hour.
- Prizes are always different.
- The winner is the closest to the right price, without going over.
- The host makes the contestants feel comfortable and safe.
- Contestants can hear and see the studio audiences' reactions.
- The TV viewers can see the prizes.
- The key motivation is something for nothing.
- The star prize is worth many thousands of pounds.
- The game does not require literacy.

When the Pearson TV team asked "How might this be different?" this led to all sorts of intriguing places, for example:

- What if contestants were not individuals?
- What if the focus were on a feature other than price?
- What if the price has to be quoted in a different currency?
- What if contestants were not in the studio?
- What if TV viewers could not see the prizes?
- What if contestants were given a week to answer?
- What if there were no host?
- What if the contestant cannot hear the audience?
- What if the item you had to guess about were not goods or
- services?
- What if the host behaved badly?

At the time these lists were compiled, one of these was just becoming evident: the central feature of the BBC's top game show, *The Weakest Link* is the singularly aggressive behavior of the UK host, Anne Robinson. Another was implemented a few months later: on New Year's Day 2001 in the UK, the contestants on *Who Wants to be a Millionaire?* were couples, rather than individuals – both partners had to agree on the answer!

There's still lots of scope though … the concept of a contestant who cannot hear the audience leads to the "soundproof box," enticing the studio audience to engage in even more bizarre antics to offer advice; the idea of viewers not being able to see the prize leads to the possibility of a game where the audience can't see the prize, but might have other clues to guess the price, or to the thought that the contestant doesn't see the prize, but maybe is given an unusual view of part of it, or perhaps a silhouette, and so has to guess what the object is as well as its price.

If the contestants aren't in the studio, then the event could take place on location, leading to crossovers with programs such as *Antiques Road Show*, or a reality game show – what would happen if it took place, for example, on the forecourt of a second-hand-car dealer?

And what about the idea that the focus is on something other than price? What might that be? How old an antique is; how big a jewel is; how heavy a casket, full of banknotes, is ... And what about taking the concept of guessing a feature (as in *The Price is Right*), and combining this with the prize from *Blind Date*? What would happen if the objects on *The Price is Right* were not consumer goods, but good-looking members of the opposite sex? What features would you have to guess right to win the prize?

5
How to be Wise

Evaluation is all about taking wise decisions

Once the *InnovAction!* process gets motoring, ideas get generated in their tens and hundreds. A two-day idea-generation workshop can easily produce three or four hundred new ideas, even if many members of the group have never used the method before. During the workshop, as the energy level rises, people write their ideas on brightly colored A5 index cards, which are then stuck on the wall and, every now and again, the group clusters the cards together according to various themes. As participants read the cards, more ideas come to mind, and more cards go up.

Some of the cards are likely to refer less to ideas than to questions, or to actions that should appear on someone's "to do" list, but that will still leave a huge number of cards identifying, at the very least, the germ of a new idea.

What on earth do you do with all this stuff?

That's what wise evaluation is all about – how to select those ideas that the organization wishes to take through development and implementation.

EVALUATION IS A DECISION-MAKING PROCESS

Evaluation is about taking decisions – decisions as to which ideas to progress, which to shelve. And decisions are made by people – people who are subject to all the normal human pressures of politics, ambition, drive, fear, doubt. The objective of designing a process for wise evaluation is to ensure, as far as possible, that these natural human frailties do not get in the way.

As we saw when we discussed the Innovation Target (see page 31), when you decide to take an idea into development and implementation, you are doing two main things.

Firstly, you are committing resources – real resources that have costs, and that could be deployed elsewhere. A wise organization therefore wishes to be confident that committing those scarce resources to do "this" rather than "that" is commercially and organizationally the best choice. The ideal here is the "due diligence" test: imagine that in five years' time, some outside consultants do a study on your decision-making process – a situation that often arises in the public sector. If the consultants' report says: "Given the information available at the time, the team took the best decision possible," then you have passed the due diligence test. For sure, as time evolves, new information comes to light and new opportunities arise. But real business decisions have to be taken today, on the basis of today's information. So your aspiration should be to take the best possible decision in the light of the information available. That way, you and your colleagues can be confident that those resources are being committed wisely.

But however robust your decision making, you cannot foretell the future, and the idea might just not work out as you had hoped. For the second thing you are doing when you commit to development and implementation is to take a risk – things might just turn out differently. In taking your decision, you can't wish the risks away, or pretend they don't exist. What you can do, though, is to get as much insight as possible into the nature of those risks, and devise strategies to avoid them, or reduce their impact should they come to pass.

Wise evaluation – the subject of this chapter – is therefore all about providing a framework to help you and your organization make the best possible decision, so you can allocate scarce resources to best effect, in the light of as full an understanding of the risks as possible.

REFRESH YOUR MEMORY

Go back and take a look at pages 23–30, which set out the most important principles of wise evaluation. I'm not going to repeat them here, for the rest of this chapter will build on them.

SMART THINGS TO DO

Evaluation as a business process

The heart of wise evaluation is to select the "good" ideas from the "less good" ones in a timely and cost-effective manner, without creating a situation in which the originators of ideas – especially of those not selected – get demotivated, and say, "There's no point in suggesting ideas in this place – no one ever listens." Idea evaluation is in fact a business process, and can be designed and managed as such, as suggested in the next box.

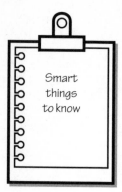

Smart
things
to know

THE SIX PRINCIPLES OF WISE EVALUATION

Transparency

The manner in which evaluation takes place should be open, accessible, fair and intelligible. This avoids charges of nepotism or favoritism.

Completeness

The information used to support the evaluation decision must be robust, thorough and complete, so that nothing of relevance can be inadvertently – or deliberately – overlooked.

Balance

No idea is perfect no idea is all bad. Wise evaluation ensures that ideas are assessed in a balanced way – in the light of their benefits, their resource requirements, and their risks – in a spirit of constructive enquiry as opposed to adversarial hostility. This, together with completeness, ensures full professionalism.

Speed

Set performance measures as to the maximum amount of time that an idea, once formulated, can be "pending evaluation." What about one week for ideas that can be evaluated locally (within the department), one month for ideas that cross significant boundaries, and a maximum of three months for ideas that require much consultation?

Feedback

Don't keep the originators of ideas in purgatory. Make sure that the results of all evaluation decisions are fed back quickly to the originators, with explanations.

Pragmatism

Ideas are of all shapes, sizes and qualities, so don't impose a single monolithic process, applied in the same way to all ideas.

The Evaluation Sieve and the Evaluation Grid

Some people envisage the evaluation process as a funnel (see for example, p. 102 of *The Age of Innovation* by Felix Janszen), but to me, this metaphor conjures up images of squeezing together, as things put in the "wide" end of the funnel get forced together before extrusion through the "narrow" end. Personally, I don't see the evaluation process quite like this: the metaphor I prefer is that of a series of sieves, with different mesh sizes.

Smart things to think about

EVALUATION AS A SIEVE

Imagine you have a pile of gravel, and your task is to separate out the different grades of stone sizes. One way of doing this is to use a series of sieves of progressively finer mesh sizes. The first sieve has a very coarse mesh, and when you put a shovel-full of gravel on the sieve, and then shake it, all but the very biggest stones go through. The stones left in the sieve are the biggest, and they can be put in a neat pile. If the material that went through the first sieve is then shovelled into a second sieve, of a slightly less coarse mesh size, then the stuff staying in this second sieve is "size 2." This process can continue through as many sieves as you like, and the gravel gets separated by size.

Idea evaluation can be thought of similarly, with two main "sieves," which differ not in physical mesh size, but as regards the questions asked:

- Sieve 1 – "If this idea is implemented in full, what business benefit does it bring?"
- Sieve 2 – "What resources are required to deliver this benefit?"

There is also a third, subsidiary, sieve:

- Sieve 3 – "How radical is this idea?"

The action of the first sieve is to separate ideas according to the likely benefit. I'm a great believer in simplicity, so initially, I use just three categories – "high," "low" and "don't know." The second sieve separates according to the likely level of cost, and once again, the three categories I've just mentioned are a pragmatic start. The third sieve separates ideas according to the likely degree of risk, in that a radical idea is probably more risky than an incremental idea.

Smart things to think about

INCREMENTAL IDEAS, RADICAL IDEAS AND BLOCKBUSTERS

"We only want blockbuster ideas – ideas that are really radical!"

You've probably heard that – I certainly have, especially when a client is briefing me on what they want from an idea-generation workshop. And when I hear it, I know I have a problem on my hands – or rather two problems, one of understanding, the other of expectations.

We had an initial discussion of this issue on pages 58–62, before our exploration of the **InnovAction!** process, so let me take matters further, in the light of our deeper insight. Let me deal firstly with the question of understanding – or, more accurately, misunderstanding. To me, the concepts of "blockbuster" and "radical" are very different. Yet they are often confused, and co-mingled. To me a "blockbuster" is an idea which meets with exceptional commercial or business success. Blockbusters can therefore be identified only after they have been implemented – we all hope for blockbusters in advance, but we can never actually know we have one until there is real, tangible experience of customer take-up (for a new product), or internal success (for a new process).

This is very different from the concept of "radical." To me, whether or not an idea is radical is a question of the features of the idea itself, and the degree to which these features are similar to, or different from, its antecedents and predecessors. If the new idea differs in only a few respects from its antecedents, then it is incremental; if in many, then it becomes increasingly radical. Whether or not an idea is radical is therefore a property of the idea itself, and the degree of "radicalness" can be assessed by comparing its features with those of the *status quo* as soon as the idea is well formulated, long before the idea comes to fruition. This comparison of features is, of course, facilitated by the **InnovAction!** process, especially if the process was used to identify the features of the *status quo* in the first place.

There is no law that I know of which states "all blockbusters are radical," nor one the other way round: "all radical ideas are blockbusters." Many blockbusters are, in fact, much more incremental than radical – sometimes ideas can be too radical in that the simultaneous change of a large number of features might be too much for the market to accept. "Radical" is a property of the idea; "blockbuster" is a term that can be applied only after the event, to describe how successful the idea is in practice. The two concepts are different, and should not be confused.

And since many incremental ideas can be enormously successful – I have already mentioned the example of *Who Wants to be a Millionaire?* (see page 61) – I always try to set the expectation that success for an **InnovAction!** workshop is ideas of all sorts, the incremental being just as potentially valuable as the radical.

In principle, three sieves, each with three separation categories, give 27 possible combinations; in practice, not all of these require attention, for the purpose of the sieving process is to guide us as to where we should devote scarce resources of attention, analysis and ultimately investment.

A very pragmatic, and relatively quick, process is therefore to take a batch of ideas, and apply the first two sieves, assessing each idea as regards benefits (high, low, don't know) and resources (high, low, don't know). Then, separate out those ideas with a don't know, and plot those remaining on a simple two-by-two "Evaluation Grid":

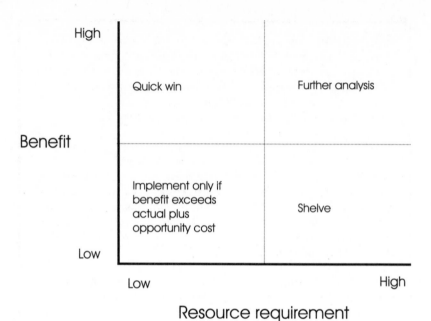

Ideas offering high benefit for low resources are archetypal "quick wins" – especially if they are incremental rather than radical – and should be authorized for implementation at once. Likewise, ideas offering low benefit for high resources should be shelved. But they shouldn't be lost, for circumstances might change – new technologies might become available which might radically reduce the resource requirement, or perhaps market conditions might change improving the benefit. At least once a year, and maybe twice, you should look through the list of shelved ideas to see if any should be re-assessed – a formal process for doing this will be discussed in the next chapter (see page 279).

Ideas offering low benefit for low resources might be worthwhile if the total net benefit package is sufficiently positive, if the risk profile is safe, and when the effort of introducing the idea does not distract people from more valuable tasks. Many ideas in this quadrant, however, will be shelved.

That leaves the most interesting quadrant – high benefit and high resource. These ideas are demanding, requiring high resources, but the effort of making these ideas happen might be a very good investment, for the benefits might be even higher. At present, we don't have enough information to take a decision, so these ideas warrant a more detailed analysis.

But what about the ideas that were associated with a "don't know" for either benefits or resource requirements, and so don't appear on the grid? This is a question of being pragmatic about how much effort is likely to be required to find out sufficient information to enable them to be plotted. There are no hard-and-fast rules here: if you consider that the effort is worth it, do it, and then plot the ideas on the grid accordingly; but if you have a good number of ideas in the "quick win" and "further analysis" quadrants, you may feel that you have enough to do to progress these. Once again, don't lose any ideas, but keep them for further review in due course.

Balanced evaluation

Any idea in the top right-hand quadrant of the evaluation grid – one that requires high resources, but potentially delivers high benefit – is very likely to require further analysis before a decision can be taken to run with it, or shelve it. A powerful tool for doing this is a development of some concepts originally proposed by Edward de Bono in his books *Six Thinking Hats* and *Six Action Shoes*.

Our objective is to design an evaluation process which meets the criteria shown in the box on page 208 by being robust, open, complete, fair and, most importantly, balanced. Edward de Bono suggested that these ideals can be achieved by examining an idea from a number of different perspectives, as represented by the wearing of six differently colored hats. I think it's useful to add a seventh (the purple one), too, and I summarize the roles of each hat, as I now use them, in the next box. Those familiar with de Bono's work will notice that my usage of the black and green hats is a little different from the usages originally proposed by de Bono: de Bono also tends to position his method as one of idea generation, whereas my method is firmly one of evaluation. Also, as you will see, the questions I associate with each hat are a natural extension of the three "sieve" questions, and so my form of the hats process builds on the work you will already have done in compiling the Evaluation Grid.

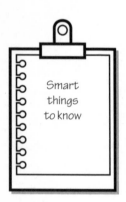

Smart
things
to know

BALANCED EVALUATION

To evaluate an idea in a complete, fair and balanced way, we need to examine the idea from a number of perspectives:

Benefits – yellow hat

What benefits will arise as a result of successfully implementing the idea? Who are the beneficiaries? What is the likely quantum of benefit? How long will it take for the benefits to come to fruition?

Issues to be managed – black hat

What issues need to be managed to bring the idea to success? Which issues are potentially "showstoppers," and how can these be circumvented? What are the risks? And how can these risks be identified and managed?

Constituencies and feelings – red hat

What *constituencies* (groups of people and individuals) will be affected by the idea, both when it is implemented, and also during implementation? What is their likely reaction *to the idea*? What can be done to manage these feelings to best effect?

Data – white hat

What data do we need to take an informed decision? What are the *sources of the data*, and how reliable are they? How do we handle uncertainty in the data?

Solutions – green hat

What solutions can we identify to the problems identified by the black, *red and white hats*? How can these problems be overcome?

Actions – purple hat

What actions should we take in the light of our analysis so far? Do we have enough information to take a decision? Or is it appropriate to continue this analysis further?

Process – blue hat

How do we orchestrate this process itself?

At first sight, the questions associated with the hats might appear clumsy and unnecessary – surely it's obvious when an idea is good or bad. Furthermore, the metaphor of the colored hats might be perceived as overly theatrical and trivial. Before you rush to judgement, pause for a while and try it.

As we saw in Chapter 2 (see pages 27–29), many organizations do not formally evaluate ideas until a business case is tabled. But long before resources are committed to creating a business case for any particular idea, all sorts of informal evaluative processes have been invoked to eliminate the ideas that never come close to being the subject of business cases. How does this take place? In many organizations, it is either a question of power (only the boss's ideas get any daylight), or a modern-day equivalent of the medieval process of trial by ordeal – by definition, any idea (other than one of mine) is wrong, and the burden of proof is on the originator of the idea to prove it is "right," against all opposition. Those who believe in the tough, macho, survival-of-the-fittest school of management will consider this the best way to operate; my view is that it is wasteful, and decidedly unsmart. So often the macho school encourages shooting from the hip and jerking from the knee. The smart school, in contrast, encourages thinking from the head – and the head is the place where you put your hat.

The essence of the hats process is balance – rather than saying "you must prove your idea against all opposition," and so setting up an adversarial conflict, the hats process says "let's collectively examine the idea as richly as possible before we take an important decision." The process is therefore one of examination, exploration and enquiry, and the standpoint is one of determining how to make the idea a success, rather than proving it will be a failure.

The metaphor of the hats is a mechanism to reinforce the nature of the process, and to help keep participants well-focused. While we are wearing the yellow hat, we must focus on the benefits of the idea, and so must not drift off down other avenues; while we are wearing the red hat, we are exploring people's feelings. Yes, you can be theatrical, and wear colored hats, or sit in colored chairs, to emphasize the roles, but you don't have to: part of the role of the individual wearing the blue hat – the chairperson – is to remind people of the roles and to keep the discussion on track.

The benefits – yellow hat

The yellow hat is all about benefits – what is good about the idea – and you should wear the yellow hat first. In many organizations this is startling, for the most natural start to most discussions about ideas is to discover as many reasons as possible why they won't work. So to wear the yellow hat first introduces a spirit of optimism right at the start. In fact, you will already have been wearing the yellow hat when you asked the first "sieve" question, so you will already have some good information – the purpose of asking this question again is to take matters to a much more substantial depth.

Smart things to think about

WHO BENEFITS?

Wearing the yellow hat can often be good fun – most people get a buzz from thinking about benefits. When I am running groups wearing the yellow hat, I watch the bullet points appear on the flip chart, and after a page or two have been compiled, I ask them to note, by each benefit, who it is that is the beneficiary. As they go down the list, "us," "the company," "we do" begins to appear item by item.

"That's great," I say. "This idea clearly offers lots of benefits to you. But is there anyone else out there who might benefit too?"

"What do you mean?"

"Nothing much … I was just wondering if there are any people, other than yourselves and your company, who might benefit, that's all."

"Who do you mean?"

My preference at that stage is to shrug my shoulders and lift my eyebrows, hoping that someone in the group will get the point. So I pause, and – inwardly – pray.

"Maybe he's talking about people like our customers," says someone else, to my intense relief.

"And maybe our suppliers too ... and perhaps people in the local community ..."

"What good suggestions," I chip in. "Why don't you spend a few moments thinking about people like customers, suppliers, the community, and maybe other constituencies too. Does your idea have any benefits to them too?"

And a few more pages of flip-chart are filled with benefits to others, benefits that they hadn't thought of, or noticed, until I prompted the thought. We all tend to be very self-centered, and inevitably we identify the benefits to "us."

It happens like that every time. But if you're alert to this, it won't happen to you. And, as a result, you'll identify a much richer package of benefits.

Issues to be managed – black hat

The stance taken by the black hat is expressed by the question: "What issues need to be managed to bring the idea to success?" These words are carefully chosen, for the starting point is the assumption that the idea can indeed be brought to success. In making this happen, however, a number of issues have to be managed along the way, and the purpose of the question is to identify what all those issues – and problems – are. Logically, of course, this enquiry is very similar to that initiated by "Let's have a really good time and find as many reasons as possible why Andrew's idea won't work," "This idea is stupid because ... " and "Why haven't you thought of ... ?" – these too identify any number of problems and road blocks.

There are, however, two major differences. The first refers to completeness. The question: "What issues need to be managed to bring this idea to success?" is seeking to identify all the problems likely to be encountered, so as to provide as comprehensive a picture as possible of what needs to be done, what resources need to be deployed, and what risks need to be managed. The more adversarial questions do not have completeness as an objective: rather, they are seeking to strike a killer blow – as soon as I can deliver a knockout punch, the fight is over. Such an adversarial frame of mind never examines all the likely problems, for the goal is that single devastating blow. If in fact the idea survives this assault, and a decision is made to go ahead, what usually happens is that all sorts of "unexpected" problems arise subsequently. Were they "unexpected"? Or was the original analysis weak?

The second difference between the two approaches is that of the viewpoint. The adversarial viewpoint takes the stance that the idea is bound to be a failure – all we need to do it to prove it to be so. This is very different from the stance of the question: "What issues need to be managed to bring the idea to success?" Here we are imagining that the idea can work successfully, and that the task on hand is to be mature and insightful in identifying in advance all the things that might go wrong. By doing this we can anticipate, and hence solve, the problems and manage the risks. This viewpoint is constructive and positive, rather than destructive and adversarial, and the difference between these stances is both profound and important.

As with the yellow hat, you won't be starting this process cold: much good information will be available from the work you did in answering the second and third "sieve" questions.

Smart things to think about

IT'S ALL ABOUT LANGUAGE

Those of us who enjoy a spirit of advocacy just love the game in which, if I can prove you wrong, then this proves me right. Logically of course this is flawed, for the demonstration that one point of view is "wrong" is not evidence that any other point of view is necessarily "right" - both could be equally "wrong" or inappropriate. But we have all seen examples of this game being played throughout our organizational lives.

An important aspect of this game is our choice of language - we choose our words carefully, so as to maximize our chances of winning. I am a great believer that you can learn much about an organization's culture just by listening carefully to the words used in meetings and conversations.

Language is especially important as regards the use of the black hat. The role, as we now know, is to identify, comprehensively, all the issues that need to be managed to bring the idea to success. Accordingly, the emotional standpoint of the black hatter is positive rather than negative, constructive rather than destructive. The black hatter is also politically neutral: neither an advocate nor an opponent; neither in cahoots with the idea's author, nor a hired assassin. When wearing the black hat, you should therefore try to avoid emotionally- and politically-charged language such as, "the problem with this idea is that ... "; "this idea won't work because ... " as well as the familiar put-downs "we tried that before and it didn't work ... "; "that may be OK for the competition, but we do things differently ... " and the rest.

Far better to use phrases like, "To make this idea work, we're going to have to ... "; and "The learning we had from our most recent experience with something like this was ... " Questions such as "How can we avoid/solve/address [whatever]?"; "What did we/others learn last time we did this?"; and "What other risks will we have to manage?" are good too.

Feelings and emotions – red hat

The red hat is also seeking out problems, but from a rather different angle – the very personal angle of individuals and constituencies. The implementation of any new idea will inevitably affect people and, at the end of the day, the success of the implementation is totally dependent on how people react to the idea and feel about the idea. This, of course, is particularly true of ideas associated with changes in processes, organization and relationships. How many times have you heard: "That idea didn't really work" or "That new process wasn't as big a success as we had hoped," or whatever? What, fundamentally, is the basis of these statements? Sometimes the problem is technical – the technical aspects of the idea just didn't work. But in my experience this is rare: far more likely, people – either as individuals or as groups – didn't end up behaving as the advocates of the idea wanted them to. Why not? Because, for whatever reason, they didn't want to, maybe because they didn't like the idea, or as a result of how the implementation of the idea was managed. We all know how to play organizational terrorist when we want to, and some of us are very good at it.

There is, of course, no law saying that everyone must like every new idea and buy in to it. Some ideas will inevitably cause some individuals or groups to be upset, perhaps because the change itself is perceived as an unnecessary upheaval, perhaps because as a result of the idea they are genuinely disadvantaged.

The purpose of the red hat is to identify, as comprehensively as possible, what these reactions might be like. In some ways, this overlaps with the black hat view, for these all represent issues to be managed. In many organizations, however, it is rare to consider people's feelings explicitly – in many macho cultures, it is taboo to think about feelings and emotions, for only wimps have feelings in the first place, and there are no wimps around here, are there? Well, I've been in some pretty macho cultures, and my observation is that the feelings *are* there – they are just not shown. The fact that the feelings exist still implies that people will respond in a variety of ways when their feelings are stimulated by the emotions that every human being experiences – fear, anxiety, approval, excitement, enthusiasm, whatever. It may be counter-cultural to let feelings be seen explicitly, but the resulting behaviors – blocking, defensiveness, evasion, political maneuvering, support, endorsement, alliances, deals and all the rest – are usually evident in abundance.

The smart manager recognizes this, and knows the importance of managing all these issues. The benefit of the red hat is therefore making it explicit that, yes, people do have feelings, even if they don't show them overtly, and that it is wise to anticipate those feelings and so devise strategies to overcome any resulting problems. The smart manager fully appreciates that a thorough red hat analysis can be instrumental in managing change effectively, and in making change stick.

Smart things to think about

FEELINGS MATTER

Partners in professional firms often have a high degree of independence and freedom, and this was particularly true when I was a partner in "old" Deloitte – that is, before its merger in 1990 with Coopers & Lybrand.

One aspect of this was the conduct of meetings. If the matter being discussed did not take my fancy, I could detach myself from the conversation – I would think about other things, doodle, look out of the window, make sure I avoided eye contact with others. I was not in any sense actively destructive, but I certainly was not on board. When the meeting was over, I could leave the table and did not feel bound by any agreements reached – I could go away and do my own thing. Sometimes, my detachment was driven by "intellectual" dissatisfaction, in which I could marshal cogent arguments as to why I was not in agreement, but more often, it was driven by emotion – I simply did not like the idea, felt threatened by it, or whatever. My actions would be driven more by emotion than by reason.

A smart meeting chairperson, of course, did not let that happen. She would notice my distraction, and deliberately involve me in the conversation – "Dennis, what do think about that idea?" or even "Dennis, how do you feel about that idea?" would shake me out of my personal reverie, and oblige me to respond. I would not lie, and would articulate my dissatisfaction, causing me to reflect in my own mind as to the true nature of the discomfort. And usually, matters got resolved sensibly.

I don't feel any particular guilt in documenting this type of behavior – I suspect we have all had similar experiences. Feelings matter. And it is foolish to pretend they don't.

Data – white hat

Most business decisions are better informed by reference to the appropriate data, and the role of the white hat is to identify what data is relevant. The data is usually required to quantify issues determined by the other hats, for example:

- As regards benefits:
    How much revenue will be generated by the new product? What will the volumes be? What are the costs? And the margins?
    How much money will be saved by introducing the new process?

- As regards issues to be managed:
    How much will the change program cost?
    What are the legal and regulatory issues?
    What do we know about competitor activity in this area?

- As regards feelings and emotions:
    How might we design a staff survey to find out their opinions?
    How can we learn more about what our customers might think about this?

Questions of this type all have quantifiable or factual answers. Some will be established facts (such as those relating to legislation); some will draw on historic data (existing costs, for example); some will require forecasts (future revenue streams); some will relate to surveys (especially as regards feelings). All, however, are manageable, and all will contribute to the wisdom of the final decision.

In a more general sense, two white hat questions relevant to a new product are:

- How will it be used?

- What does it look like?

These questions can be answered in terms of a written description, and maybe a drawing or two. Far, far better however, is a model, a prototype, something real. The closer an idea can come to reality, the easier it is to appreciate it, and to become enthusiastic about it. Making an idea real, in whatever ways are possible, is therefore an important contribution to the evaluation decision.

Smart things to think about

BLACK DISGUISED AS WHITE

The white hat seeks data, but the head wearing the white hat might have black thoughts in mind. It all depends on language, on tone of voice and on body language.

I once worked with someone who smiled with his teeth, not his eyes. This confused me for a while, but not for long. Whenever, with a "smile" he asked, "How much is that likely to cost?" he was not making a factual enquiry, seeking to understand some data – he was making a highly emotionally-charged statement. The emphasis on "that," the raised eyebrows, the knowing looks around the room to his political colleagues – all these signaled his disgust with the idea, and his contempt of the idea's originator.

On paper, though, the words constitute a legitimate white hat question; in actual use, the question is not a white hat question at all. Nor is the intended meaning a legitimate black hat question, for the black hat stance is one of assuming the idea can be made a success, and then discovering what we need to manage to make it so. The emotional stance for the black hat is positive and constructive, as well as realistic and feet-on-the-ground too; it isn't negative, miserable, destructive.

Smart managers are alert to malicious black masquerading as white, and never stoop to using this naïve ploy themselves.

Solutions – green hat

Many of the issues identified by the black and red hats will be problems of greater or lesser significance. Often, these problems can be perceived as overwhelming, and so the role of the green hat is to allow some time and space for identifying solutions.

The key question asked by the green hat is therefore "How can this problem be overcome?" and the emotional stance is that this is, in principle, possible. Usually, the process invoked to answer this question is one of idea generation, and you can very successfully use *InnovAction!* to identify and challenge all the assumptions in the normal way. The point to note here is that *InnovAction!* is not being used to generate new ideas in general, but rather to identify new ideas very much focused on solving a specific problem, which itself has been identified in the context of exploring a "bigger" idea.

As an example, suppose the idea being analyzed using the "hats" process is to develop a new product, and that the black hat has identified that an issue to be managed is the need to go to full 24-hour, three-shift working. It is also likely that the red hat analysis will have identified that "our staff won't like the disruption of three-shift working." This could be seen as an overwhelming problem, a true blocker. But the job of the green hat is to tease out solutions to the problem such as a new incentive package, revised agreements with unions, recruiting from different sources (such as students), or sharing staff with neighboring businesses – even competitors. There is no law saying that any of these potential solutions will work, or will be cost-effective, but their exploration keeps the matter open, and – you never know – you might come up with a very good solution.

Smart
things to
think about

GREEN HATS IN ACTION

The problems identified by the black and red hats can often appear to be overwhelming. But there are always solutions. Two of the most imaginative solutions I have ever come across relate to the D-day landings in Normandy in June 1944.

Some of the most obvious requirements about an invasion are that the landing site should be accessible, and at or close to a major port, to allow supplies – especially of men, equipment, munitions, food, fuel oil – to be brought ashore as soon as possible to support the invading army.

After the disaster of the Dieppe raid in 1942, the Allied armies learnt how strongly defended France's Channel Ports were, despite their proximity. As a result, the Allies examined the possibility of landing in Normandy. Amongst an enormous number of issues to be managed were:

- How do we solve the problem of there being no port, at which we can land supplies safely?
- How do we solve the problem of getting fuel oil on shore quickly?

Either one of these appears to be a showstopper; together, the situation seems to be absolutely impossible. But then the green hatters had their say, and came up with two incredible solutions:

- the Mulberry Harbours – harbours constructed of massive concrete blocks, floated across the channel, and positioned as jetties and breakwaters at the invasion beaches themselves; and
- PLUTO – the pipeline under the ocean – which piped fuel oil right across the Channel from the English South Coast.

What amazing solutions to overwhelming problems! For sure, our business problems are never anything like this serious, or on this scale. But there is always a solution out there somewhere ...

Actions – purple hat

The role of the purple hat is to ask: "What next?" The overall purpose of evaluation, remember, is to lead to a decision as to whether or not an idea is to be taken into development and implementation, and the role of the hats process is to structure the gathering of supporting evidence so that this decision can be taken wisely. One of the benefits of using the hats is that the process can be as modest or as extensive as is appropriate – it is quite possible to carry out a hats analysis in an hour or so; you can also use the hats framework as the basis for a fully documented business case or feasibility study, which might take months. To devote months of effort, however, costs money, and so the role of the purple hat throughout the process is to ask, from time to time, "What do we do next? Do we have sufficient information to take a decision, or is it worth continuing this analysis to a deeper level?"

Smart things to think about

MAKING DECISIONS

As I have stressed many times throughout this chapter, the ultimate objective of evaluation is to take a decision – do we proceed with this idea or not? Decisions are taken by people exercising judgement, not by systems following algorithms. The whole purpose of the hats process for balanced evaluation is to provide the decision-making body – an individual, or a small group – with appropriate, balanced, comprehensive information on which that judgement can be based. But at the end of the day the decision is taken by people, and the decision is based on human judgement.

Orchestration – blue hat

The final hat is the blue one – as worn by the person chairing or orchestrating the process. The role here is quite straightforward: to determine how the process overall will be used, and to keep it on track. In my experience, this is usually very easy to do. The process itself is simple, and it is extremely rare for anyone to object to either its underlying motive – balance and wisdom, or its method – to examine an idea from a multiplicity of angles. What I find amazing is the willingness with which people "play the game" – even the most died-in-the-wool black hatters, who have never been heard to say a good word about anything for the last umpteen years (I'm sure you've met him!), will amaze both themselves and everyone else that, when they are asked to put on a yellow hat ("just for once"), they do so, and at last say something positive. It works. It really does.

Evaluation in practice

BUSINESS CASES

Take a look at your business's guidelines for producing business cases and feasibility studies – perhaps you can find a recent example of the finished article, or maybe you have access to some guidelines. Compare the structure of your document to a structure derived from the key questions of the "hats" process:

- What are the benefits?
- What are the issues to manage?
- How will people feel?
- What data do we need to take a balanced judgement?
- What solutions are there to the problems identified?
- What do we do next?

If you do this, you will probably find that there is a lot on the benefits – business cases are always written by advocates, and advocates always stress the benefits. You will also find stacks of data, from market projections to detailed analyses of costs, from NPVs to IRRs. In good business cases, you will also find at least some analysis of risk. But – in my experience – the risk analysis is often relatively shallow, and there is rarely an explicit analysis of feelings and emotions.

One of the strengths of the hats framework is that it can be beneficially used at all stages in the evaluation process, from the initial idea right through to the full business case; the difference lies in the depth of the analysis, not the breadth.

A GOOD IDEA THAT BACKFIRED

Many businesses actively seek to encourage everyone throughout the organization to have ideas, and to put them forward safely. This benevolent thought often translates into a suggestion scheme, whereby individuals are invited to submit suggestions, either by putting a slip of paper in the box in the staff canteen or, these days, by e-mailing the Innovation Center.

What might happen next?

Well, people are motivated and excited (good), and feel empowered (even better), and put lots and lots of ideas into the scheme (which was the scheme's objective, so this is great). This flood of input comes to the central team of two people, who have been asked to look through the ideas, and select the "good" ones. The two people in question also have a day job to do, and so take some time to look through the suggestions, which continue to come in daily. This processing delay means it takes some time before any decisions can be taken, and before there is any feedback to the originators. Before too long, there is a rumor on the shop floor "Don't bother suggesting anything – nothing ever happens, and no one ever tells us what's going on!" and the scheme is discredited from below.

But worse happens from above. When the team of two look through the suggestions to produce the short list to refer to senior management, senior management take the view that short-listed items are "trivial," "impractical," and "not appropriate at this time," thereby confirming their view that only they can have any good ideas.

And so the well-intentioned suggestion scheme slowly slides into oblivion, and the cynics congratulate themselves that, once again, they were right.

This anecdote is real, and many organizations have started off with the best of intentions, only to be disappointed. With, admittedly, some degree of hindsight, let's do a quick hats analysis of this particular way of encouraging people to suggest new ideas. So, the proposition we are evaluating is:

"We intend to introduce a suggestion scheme in which individuals are encouraged to put forward new ideas. Individuals will write their ideas on a form, and submit them either on paper or by e-mail to the Innovation Center. The ideas will be sorted, feedback will be given, and the best ideas will be taken to a committee of senior managers for approval. We will also reward the best ideas."

<table>
<tr><td>

SMART THINGS
TO DO

</td><td>

EVALUATION IN PRACTICE

Think about this proposition for a few moments, and do a quick yellow, black, red, and white hat analysis. Then choose two or three of the most difficult-looking problems, and put on the green hat for a few moments to see if you can come up with some solutions.

</td></tr>
</table>

Here is my list of benefits:

- The scheme will result in more new ideas than we had otherwise.

- Some of these ideas might have significant business impact.

- The scheme will encourage people throughout the organization.

- The scheme sends all the right messages about the importance of innovation in our business, and how everyone can contribute.

- People throughout the business will feel pleased with a more positive climate.

- Those who get rewards will feel good.

And here are some issues to be managed:

- How can we design a process so that ideas are handled quickly, both in terms of selection and evaluation, and also in providing feedback?

- How can we ensure that the feedback is constructive, and that those whose ideas are rejected don't get discouraged themselves, and don't discourage others?

- How will we manage a situation in which, after an initial splurge of suggestions, things might just dry up?

- How will the Innovation Centre judge which ideas are "good"?

- Will that judgement align with that of the senior management panel?

- What if the senior people don't like the ideas selected by the Innovation Centre?

- How will we judge who gets a reward?

- What form will the reward take?

These are some red hat issues:

- The workforce might feel:
    good because of the encouragement;
    good because they can suggest ideas in a much more direct way then hitherto;
    discouraged if they get slow feedback;
    let down and misled if they get no feedback;
    disappointed if one of their own ideas is rejected;
    elated if one of their own ideas wins an award;
    jealous if one of someone else's ideas does …
    … and maybe suspicious and critical of the criteria by which awards are determined;
    under threat if they believe that the number and perceived quality of the ideas they personally suggest are being used in some way as a measure of their personal performance …
    … and maybe confused if they feel they haven't been trained in how to generate ideas.

- The staff at the Innovation Center might feel:
    good because this raises the profile of innovation in general, and their role in particular;
    stressed if they are inundated with a large number of ideas quickly;
    disappointed if the flow of ideas is modest;
    under threat if their performance is measured by the number of ideas …
    … and angry if their performance is measured by the perceived quality of the ideas, which, by definition, are not theirs, but other people's;
    good if the senior management panel endorses the ideas they put forward …
    … but under threat if they don't; and
    unfairly treated if the workforce blame them for anything they don't like.

- And the senior managers might feel:
    skeptical, especially if "we've tried that before" …
    … alternatively, excited by the prospect of empowering everyone to come up with new ideas;
    very pleased if at least some of the ideas they are given to review are perceived as "good" …
    … alternatively, frustrated or angry if they believe that the ideas they are given to review are "trivial," and that all the time and money devoted to the scheme has been wasted.

The white hat might identify the need:

- to assess the volume of ideas likely to be generated, and how this might evolve over time;

- to determine the criteria for judging, at the Innovation Center, what constitutes a "good" idea, and agreeing those criteria with the senior managers; and

- to determine the criteria for judging which ideas are to win an award, and how that judgement may be seen to be taken fairly.

This analysis took about twenty minutes to think through and note down, and, even for such a simple-looking idea, it does identify quite a few points that aren't so simple. Central to the whole concept is the question of what constitutes a "good" idea – what might appear to be a good idea to the idea's originator might be judged trivial by a panel of senior managers. If this happens just occasionally, then there is unlikely to be a problem; on the other hand, if this happens to most of the suggestions, then the whole concept very quickly becomes discredited.

Time for the green hat. What ideas can we generate to address the problem of inadvertently stimulating a whole host of "trivial" ideas? One way of doing this is to use the *InnovAction!* process on the core of the idea itself, two particular features of which are:

- the proposal focuses on the suggestion of ideas; and

- the proposal encourages individuals to suggest ideas.

How might these be different?

Well ... suppose the proposal were to encourage not the suggestion of a "raw" idea, but the suggestion of an idea which has been through at least an initial evaluation process. So, instead of just suggesting an idea by itself, the material that is put forward is accompanied by an initial hats analysis. That way, the originator is obliged to think beyond the raw idea, and consider the benefits, the issues, the feelings, the data. The originator can then take a much more balanced view, and submit only those ideas which have been taken at least one step beyond the initial suggestion.

This richer concept can be taken further by considering how "the proposal encourages individuals to suggest ideas" might be different. Suppose the concept was one in which teams, rather than individuals, were encouraged to come up with ideas. How might this work?

Well, suppose that an individual has a bright idea. Rather than putting that idea straight into the suggestion box, the idea originator is encouraged to convene a small group of, say, three or four people they feel comfortable with. The role of this small group is to carry out an initial hats analysis, on the basis of which they take a collective decision whether or not they feel the idea is strong enough to put forward to the more formal process. If they collectively decide it isn't, the matter is dropped there; if they decide it is, they fill out a brief set of forms, one describing the idea in as a whole, and then one page each for benefits, issues, feelings, data, any other related ideas, and recommended actions. This pack is then submitted to the Innovation Center (or wherever), and it is this pack that is reviewed.

What are the benefits of this, enriched, process relative to its predecessor?

Several. Idea generation continues to be encouraged, but a much more rigorous process is encouraged at source. This will result in fewer ideas being passed through (so reducing the workload at the Innovation Center), but those ideas that are passed through are likely to be of much better quality, since they will have had some initial analysis. This initial analysis is carried out locally, in safety. Because this first level of evaluation is being carried out by the originator, and some people the originator trusts, if in fact the local team decide not to progress the idea, the originator is much less likely to feel aggrieved or damaged. The process has been conducted "in private" rather than "in public," so there should be much less of a concern that the originator is being "judged"; furthermore, the process is being carried out quickly and locally, not slowly and remotely. And most importantly, because the originator is sharing the initial idea with other people, it is most likely that the idea itself will become enriched as a result of the contributions of others.

There are, however, two important issues to be managed to make this work. The first is that people need to be trained in both idea generation and idea evaluation, so they can generate new ideas, and apply the hats process, with confidence. Secondly, people must be allowed the time to convene the local groups to carry out the evaluation, and this time must be allowed for in budgets, in work practices, and in performance measures.

How much training is required? How much will this cost? And how can we estimate the time to be allowed for the local groups? This is all good white hat stuff, and needs to be assessed. And, not forgetting the red hat, the most likely reaction of local management is to resent the time being taken, possibly at short notice, to convene the local evaluation groups. This then leads to the green hat idea that maybe this can be incorporated into normal working practices, so it is not seen to be something special. Many organizations – especially in manufacturing – already have mechanisms such as quality circles or continuous improvement teams, so why not dovetail this process alongside these very similar initiatives?

> Smart things to think about

WHAT ACTION WOULD YOU TAKE?

You have now read about two alternative ways of introducing a staff suggestion scheme: one in which individuals are encouraged to put ideas straight into the suggestion box; the other in which individuals are encouraged to discuss their ideas with a local team, then do an initial hats analysis, and only when the local team are confident do they submit the idea into the formal process.

Which of these two would you choose to adopt? Or, if neither, how would you design an even better process?

This invites you to wear the purple hat, and take action. Which did you choose? Why? As you will have noticed, the text of the last few pages has been an iterative hats-style exploration on the basic idea of a suggestion scheme. What started as a bright idea – "let's have a suggestion scheme" – was constructively examined using the hats, and enriched to encourage local teams rather than individuals, and to have as its output not just a "raw" idea, but an idea that has been subject to some initial, rigorous analysis. So, if you feel that this process added value to your own thinking, why not use it for real?

6
The Unlearning
Organization

Innovation is all about culture

So, we now know how to generate stunning ideas, and how to evaluate them wisely too. The next step is to make them happen – to take the ideas we have decided to progress through the two outer zones of the Innovation Target, the zones of development and implementation. As we have already discussed (see page 31), although idea generation and evaluation can be activities carried out by individuals or small groups, development and implementation usually require resources to be mobilized on a far greater scale. Making innovation happen is therefore an organizational activity, rather than an individual or a group one, and, as a consequence, is highly dependent on organizational culture.

The purpose of this chapter is therefore to explore the cultural issues underpinning innovation. Much of this will relate to the stages of development and implementation specifically, but there will be much that relates to idea generation and evaluation too – all of which, I trust, will be totally consistent with the cultural themes underpinning the previous chapters.

Our goal is to explore how to build an organization which is fundamentally innovative, in which creativity and innovation are deeply rooted core competencies, in which creativity and innovation are a natural part of the "way we do things around here." As we have seen, since creativity and innovation in business never take place on a green-field site, before we can learn to do new things, we have to unlearn the old ones. The organization I am describing is therefore not so much a "learning organization," but rather an evolution of that concept – an *"un*learning organization."

How, then, can we build an unlearning organization?

That's what this final chapter is all about, and our starting point is to examine just what it is that enables us to recognize an innovative organization, and distinguish it from an uninnovative one ...

Innovative and uninnovative organizations

Smart
things to
think about

INNOVATIVE AND UNINNOVATIVE ORGANIZATIONS

Imagine you are visiting an organization famous for its innovation and creativity. What would you see, sense, feel, hear?

And then imagine you are visiting another organization, with a reputation for being singularly uninnovative. What would you see, sense, feel, hear?

What do you think are the key characteristics which distinguish them?

I often do this as an exercise in my client workshops, with one group doing the first question, and another the second.

The following boxes show the kinds of responses that usually arise.

Characteristics of an innovative organization ...

- Lively
- Open
- Noisy
- Laughter
- Flat-structured
- "Yes ! Yes ! Yes !"
- Lots of light
- Plenty of space
- Lots of personal touches
- A communal area where people can chat
- Young
- White-boards
- Pictures
- Excitement
- Variety of dress
- A balance between the numbers of men and women
- Flexitime
- Time is allowed for innovation
- Exploring
- Lots of waste-paper baskets
- People treated as individuals to be developed
- No manuals
- Delegation
- Flexibility
- Respect
- Trust
- Sharing
- Success
- Lots of books, magazines
- Lots of contact with the world outside
- Individuals, not clones
- Energy
- Healthily skeptical
- Decisive leadership
- Friendly
- Listening
- Risk-taking
- Untidy
- No offices
- Fun
- Learning
- Unlearning too
- Provocative
- Willing followership
- Enthusiastic
- Questioning
- Knowledge is seen as a shared resource
- Lots of computers
- Rules can be challenged
- Happy
- Serendipity rules OK !
- Supportive
- Teams, not individuals
- Entrepreneurial
- Informal
- Training
- Payment by results

- Sterile
- Closed
- Hierarchy
- Old
- Silent
- Dull
- Lots of walls
- People treated as costs to be controlled
- Clones, not individuals
- Payment by toeing the line
- Boring
- Old-fashioned
- "Where's the business case?"
- Risk averse
- Fear
- Impersonal
- Humorless
- Minimum contact with the outside world
- We know it all
- Emotions not allowed
- Don't argue with the boss
- Judgemental
- Quick to evaluate
- Little natural light
- Long corridors
- Politics
- Safe, if you conform
- Training at a minimum
- Lots of paper, but almost neurotically tidy
- Knowledge seen as a source of internal competitive advantage
- Nothing ever questioned
- 9–5
- Time only for the day job
- Individual success takes priority over teams
- Advocacy, not debate
- Logic, not intuition
- I'm right, you're wrong
- Highly status conscious
- "It's not worth my job to risk that"
- Answers, not questions
- Talking, not listening
- Lots of rules
- Precedent rules OK!
- More men than women
- White shirts
- Efficient
- Procedures, procedures, procedures
- Hard-working
- Mistakes to be avoided at all costs
- "No! No! No!"
- Junior staff "know their place"
- Secretive
- Telling, not asking
- Regimented
- "We tried that once – it didn't work"
- Uniform
- Seniority wins over merit
- Narrow
- Complacent
- Bureaucratic
- Slow

You will recognize most of the items, agree with some, and maybe disagree with others. Some items might also seem to be paradoxical – amongst the descriptions of the innovative organization, you will see both "teams, not individuals" and "individuals, not clones." Can both of these be true of the same organization? A moment's reflection will show that, yes, they can: "teams, not individuals" means a culture in which people take a team view, rather than a parochial, personal one; "individuals, not clones" is a culture in which individuals are respected for their individuality, and are not expected to toe the boss's line thoughtlessly. In a vibrant, innovative organization, both these features can indeed co-exist.

These lists are taken directly from my workshops, and so represent stereotypes. In practice, of course, matters are more complex and less black and white; nonetheless, these lists do highlight two deep truths:

- Firstly, they verify that we *can* recognize an innovative organization, and distinguish it from an uninnovative one, from a whole host of features and signals that we can observe from almost the very first minute we step through the front door.

- Secondly, a moment's reflection will show that each of the items on both of these lists is an aspect of organizational culture, interpersonal behavior, or management style.

This second point is particularly important. For who is it that determines the organizational culture, the interpersonal behaviors and the management style? The general answer must be "we determine them ourselves," and the more senior you are, the more influence on the culture you are likely to have. The fact that all these features are indeed aspects of organizational culture, interpersonal behavior and management style implies that it is in our personal and collective power *deliberately to make* our organization innovative, if we wish to.

But this will not happen by itself: to change the organizational culture from being uninnovative to becoming innovative requires specific, deliberate action. Any manager, seeking a quiet life, will surely choose to build an uninnovative organization, for this is far easier to manage – everyone knows their place, everyone follows orders. Managing an innovative organization is a far more complex and demanding task for, by definition, in an innovative organization people have their own minds. Furthermore, without deliberate and continuous attention, organizations tend to revert of their own account to a relatively uninnovative state, for this is the thoughtless default in which everything happens as it happened in the past.

NO, IT'S NOT A 1960S HIPPY PARADISE

Discussions of innovative and uninnovative organizations sometimes makes uninnovative organizations appear to be like a Victorian workhouse, and innovative ones like a 1960s hippy paradise. Of course, real life is rather more complex.

Firstly, uninnovative organizations are not necessarily unsuccessful. Rather, success is totally dependent on the future being a seamless continuation of the past. In certain circumstances – some government departments, perhaps, and for industries not subject to substantial change – this works. My personal opinion, though, is that the assumption that the future will be a continuation of the past is, these days, an extremely high-risk approach – even for a government department.

Secondly, innovative organizations are not totally rule-free environments in which everyone can do whatever they like. Innovative organizations have any number of rules and procedures – as required for the smooth running of any community. What distinguishes the rules and procedures in an innovative and uninnovative organization is their status: in an uninnovative organization, a rule is a rule is a rule, and no one, but no one, can challenge one. In an innovative organization, by contrast, a rule is accepted as a rule provided that it continues to be fit-for-purpose. An innovative organization encourages its rules and procedures to be constructively challenged and, if as a result of the challenge, the rule is confirmed to be fit-for-purpose it is maintained; if not, it is changed or dispensed with. This is in no way giving license to arbitrary change-for-change's sake; rather, it is a mature recognition that no rule can be valid indefinitely, and that all rules should be subject to periodic scrutiny. This, of course, is the essence of Rosabeth Moss Kanter's concept of "constructive restlessness" (see pages 119 and 120).

Yes, it is true that creating and managing an innovative organization is more demanding than supervising compliance in an uninnovative one. But it *is* quite possible, and so the purpose of this chapter is to explore how this can be done.

What distinguishes an innovative organization from an uninnovative one?

Let's delve more deeply into those lists, and see if we can determine some patterns, and some general principles. In fact, this is exactly what was recently done by James Christiansen, who spent three years researching just this issue, publishing his findings in two highly informative books, *Competitive Innovation Management*, and *Building the Innovative Organization*, from which I learnt a great deal.

It would make life easy if the difference between innovative and uninnovative organizations could be boiled down to one or two key factors along the lines: "Innovative organizations do X and Y, and uninnovative organizations don't. So, if you want to become an innovative organization, all you have to do is fix X and Y, and everything will be fine." Unfortunately – and as I'm sure you expect – life is more complex than that. As hinted at by

In 1997, James Christiansen received a PhD from INSEAD for his thesis entitled *Managing Efforts to Improve Innovation Performance: The Role of the General Manager*. His research entailed a comprehensive study of how innovation happens in eight companies in five different industries, supported by additional research in twelve more companies from eight further industries. Two of the companies studied – 3M and Eastman Chemical – are role models of innovation best practice, so this provided Christensen with one end of the spectrum; some of the other companies find innovation more of a struggle, so Christiansen saw the other end of the spectrum too. His two books, *Competitive Innovation Management: Techniques to Improve Innovation Performance* and *Building the Innovative Organization: Management Systems that Encourage Innovation* present his very thorough findings, and are a good read. Christiansen is now with McKinsey & Company, and is also a visiting research fellow at INSEAD.

the lists of attributes of the innovative and uninnovative organizations we just looked at, the difference between the two types of organization isn't attributable to just a few characteristics, rather:

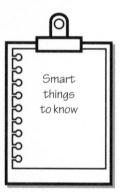

Smart
things
to know

HOW TO MAKE INNOVATION HAPPEN:

To make innovation happen, you need two big things, and lots of little things.

Let's take a look at just what is involved.

What are the "two big things"?

If you want to make innovation happen in your organization, the two big things you need are:

- firstly, the will to do it; and

- secondly, some financial "headroom."

The will to do it is, in a word, all about leadership. To make innovation happen within your organization, some things will have to change: maybe it's the reward system, perhaps it's the way budgets are allocated; maybe the criteria for promotion, perhaps the overall attitude to risk. Whatever it is that needs to be changed, introducing the change, pushing it through – and making it stick – all demand every ounce of all the familiar characteristics of leadership: being able to paint and articulate a compelling vision of how much better the future will be by having moved from "here" to "there"; building the right political consensus; keeping things going when they get tough. This is all hard work, and we all have a day job to do. So don't embark down this road if you don't have the will to see it through. Far better not to start, than to start and fail.

The second "big thing" I call financial "headroom." An absolute certainty about making innovation happen within an organization is that it is going to cost money and demand people's time. At the very least, money will be needed to finance activities such as training, feasibility studies and idea development, and time needs to be spent on idea generation, evaluation, development and implementation. Much of this time and money will have no immediately "provable" return, for, as we have seen at length, the early stages of innovation are exploratory, whilst the later stages of development and implementation are always subject to the risk that, at the end of the day, the new idea will not prove to be as powerful as we had all hoped.

All this money and time has to come from somewhere. And that "somewhere" is of course the same pot which is funding the advertising budget, the new head office building, the e-business project and the replacement of the factory machinery. And that pot might be very small, especially if the business is in trouble. One of the unfortunate truths in business life is that some organizations wake up to the fact that innovation is critical to business success far too late, asking the question "How can we become more innovative?" just at the time when they can't afford to do anything about it.

Smart things to think about

HOW MUCH SHOULD YOU SPEND ON INNOVATION?

I am often asked "How much should our innovation budget be?" My initial answer is usually along the lines: "If you sincerely believe, as I do, that innovation is the ultimate competitive advantage, then you should budget as much as you can afford, and put in place a number of processes to ensure that the money and time are spent wisely."

In practice, there are two ways of establishing what the budget might be, bottom-up and top-down. The bottom-up approach is to identify all the activities – training, travel, meetings, feasibility studies, market trials, prototyping, whatever – that are likely to consume time and money, estimate the quantum for each of them, and add all the numbers up. The alternative is to work top-down, and ask the question "How much can we afford to spend?" This is in essence a question of looking at the overall budget, and asking the directors to come to consensus about how much of that can be spent on an activity which is unlikely to give a return in the current year, and, at worst, might give no directly traceable return at all. This highly polarized approach certainly tests the will to do it! But, if the will is there, this can result in the agreement of a figure, which can then be used to allocate against various individual activities.

In my experience, organizations that are in the earlier stages of becoming innovative benefit more from the top-down approach: it is quicker, more pragmatic, and achieves the objective of ensuring that at least some funds – however big or small – are earmarked for innovation. As the organization gains more experience, and people begin to see that there is a return on the expenditure – as shown by an improved flow of ideas and their corresponding visible results – then innovation becomes progressively more well established as "the way we do things around here," and so becomes embedded in the normal budgeting process.

Ideally, of course, the will to do it and the budgetary approval come from the very top, for it is at the very top that power converges to a single person or a small group. If he, she, or they collectively have the will, they too have the power to allocate funds and to make it happen. In practice, however, the will and the funds do not have to come from the very top – a lot can be done from a local top, such as at business unit or even departmental level. It is of course harder to do things locally, for "to get away with it" you need at best the protection of your immediate boss, or at worst an agreement of benign non-interference – if your boss actively intervenes to stop it happening, then it won't.

So, let's assume that these "big things" are in place ...

What about the "lots of little things"?

The "lots of little things" are all alluded to in the lists of characteristics of innovative and uninnovative organizations presented on pages 239 and 240, but these lists are unstructured. Let me make things clearer.

Take, for example, the item in the "innovative" list: "People treated as individuals to be developed," which can be contrasted with the corresponding item on the "uninnovative" list: "People treated as costs to be controlled." Both organizations have personnel policies – the difference is the nature of those policies, and the way the policies are applied. Likewise, contrast "Payment by results" with "Payment by toeing the line": both organizations have policies regarding remuneration and reward – what is different is the way these policies are formulated and put into practice.

The "lots of little things" therefore refer to a host of policies and procedures, all of which will be familiar to any organization: policies and procedures relating to nine broad themes:

- the role of senior management;

- budgets;

- performance measures;

- reward and recognition;

- project funding;

- training;

- managing projects;

- managing the pipeline of ideas; and

- embedding innovation into the day job.

In an innovative organization, all the detail underlying these main themes has been deliberately designed to encourage, support and reward innovation, so that all aspects of the business are consistent and pointing in the same direction. In an uninnovative organization, it is rare that the detail has been designed deliberately to prevent innovation, for few people are sufficiently malicious and powerful to achieve that. Much more common is a situation in which various aspects of the detail are inconsistent and pointing in different directions – not because a malevolent force designed them like that, but rather because different policies evolved at different times. Well-intentioned efforts to become more innovative therefore become frustrated because the myriad of detailed policies are inconsistent.

An example. Suppose you have a great idea about how your business unit might collaborate with another in the group to develop a new product.

You go to the boss of your business unit, and you are puzzled that he is lukewarm. Is he deliberately trying to kill innovation? Perhaps he is. But suppose that his performance measures reward him for his business unit's profits, and that his bonus depends primarily on this – a totally normal situation in most businesses. Your proposal might be a jolly good idea, but since it crosses business unit boundaries, the benefit of the idea does not accrue to your (and your boss's) business unit exclusively. And if your boss has the choice between backing your project, and another, which in a wider sense might be less exciting, but which delivers benefits to your business unit exclusively, which would you expect the boss to choose? Your boss is behaving totally rationally by supporting the other project and rejecting yours. The issue is not that your boss is deliberately trying to kill your idea – rather, there is a (probably inadvertent) conflict between the performance measures applied to your boss, and the fact that your idea happens to cross organizational boundaries.

A moment's thought, of course, will show that it is most unlikely that this organization will ever discover anything useful about how different business units might collaborate, for it is in no one's interests to do this. In a general sense, this might be considered a "bad thing" – although many would argue that this is neither a good thing nor a bad thing, it's just the way things are when you give managers clearly-defined local objectives.

But things don't have to be that way – they can be designed differently. In relation to this example, suppose you can approach the Group directly for the funding of your idea – and approach them in a way which does not look like you are going behind your boss's back. Group, in fact, might have money available specifically for funding projects which cross organizational boundaries, for they realize that such projects will not get funding within their local business units. This gives the best of both worlds – local business unit bosses can maximize the profits of their units as well as supporting innovation locally, whilst Group provides funds for cross-business unit innovation.

This solution, of course, won't just happen by itself: it has to be thought of, and implemented – an example of both process and organizational innovation: process innovation in creating the mechanism whereby Group can allocate funds, and organizational innovation in making it safe for people working in any business unit to have direct access to Group. It is simply a question of making different aspects of business policies and procedures mutually consistent and supportive of innovation.

Nor is this solution "rocket science": it is a very straight-forward approach. But that doesn't stop it being powerful, for there are many businesses today that suffer from the problem of being unable to sponsor cross-business innovation.

The rest of this chapter will therefore look at some of the detail underpinning the nine themes mentioned on page 248, and, so as to set your expectations correctly, what follows is not, by any means, rocket science – rather, it is all "common sense." Also, there are quite a lot of checklists, which I summarize on the following two mind maps.

Funding

£

Who holds the funds?
How many sources of funds are there?
How close is the funding to the idea?
What information is required
to support the funding decision?
How quickly is the funding decision made?
Who decides?
What are the decision criteria?

Role of senior
management

Funding
Resource allocation
Promotion and reward
Story-telling
Managing cross-boundary
conflict
Mentoring
Reviewing
Protection

Lots of
'little' things...

Rewards and
recognition

What?
Monetary
Promotion
On the job
Becoming a hero

How?
Individual or team?
Who decides?
What are the criteria?
What about 'failure'?

Budgets

For what?
Training
Communication
Knowledge transfer
Idea generation
Idea evaluation
Idea development
Rewards

How determined?
Power-play
Top-down
Bottom-up
Driven by
strategy

And what about?
Uncertainty
Risk
Serendipity

Performance
measures

Of innovation

Inputs
Number of
people trained
Time spent on
idea generation...

Outputs
Number of ideas
Commercial
value of ideas

In general
Short vs long-term
Individual vs group
Consistency
Sharing
Risk

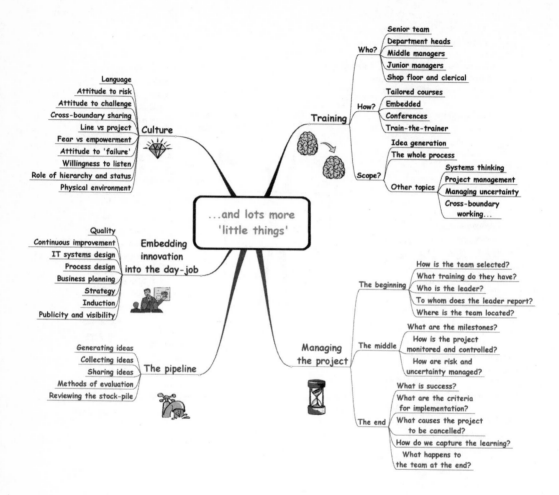

Culture
- Language
- Attitude to risk
- Attitude to challenge
- Cross-boundary sharing
- Line vs project
- Fear vs empowerment
- Attitude to 'failure'
- Willingness to listen
- Role of hierarchy and status
- Physical environment

Training
- Who?
  - Senior team
  - Department heads
  - Middle managers
  - Junior managers
  - Shop floor and clerical
- How?
  - Tailored courses
  - Embedded
  - Conferences
  - Train-the-trainer
- Scope?
  - Idea generation
  - The whole process
  - Other topics
    - Systems thinking
    - Project management
    - Managing uncertainty
    - Cross-boundary working...

...and lots more 'little things'

Embedding innovation into the day-job
- Quality
- Continuous improvement
- IT systems design
- Process design
- Business planning
- Strategy
- Induction
- Publicity and visibility

The pipeline
- Generating ideas
- Collecting ideas
- Sharing ideas
- Methods of evaluation
- Reviewing the stock-pile

Managing the project
- The beginning
  - How is the team selected?
  - What training do they have?
  - Who is the leader?
  - To whom does the leader report?
  - Where is the team located?
- The middle
  - What are the milestones?
  - How is the project monitored and controlled?
  - How are risk and uncertainty managed?
- The end
  - What is success?
  - What are the criteria for implementation?
  - What causes the project to be cancelled?
  - How do we capture the learning?
  - What happens to the team at the end?

The role of senior management

Senior management have an enormously important role in determining whether or not an organization is truly innovative – largely because they have the power to make things happen, or to block things they don't like. In many organizations, managers are promoted on their ability to get things done, and to deliver successful results on time, within budget. As we saw in our discussion of the Innovation Target (see page 44), these are the skills associated with the outer implementation zone, rather than the innermost zone of idea generation. Senior people who are strongly task-oriented and results-driven can often be intolerant of the more open-ended, exploratory, and ambiguous style associated with that magic question "How might this be different?" As I related with the story of Mark Selway (see page 54), however, this does not necessarily mean that innovation is stifled: most senior managers are intelligent, and can understand the intellectual framework of patterns, Koestler's Law, the need for unlearning, and all the rest. They may not like it personally, but if they can be moved from the lower left-hand quadrant of the diagram shown on page 52 to the upper left-hand quadrant (and maybe even the upper right-hand one!) then they are usually wise enough to "let it be" for others. This does, of course, require that they are initially open-minded enough to allow themselves to attend a "master class" (as we saw on page 48, smart managers would never dream of suggesting their bosses require training!), but if they are unwilling to do even that, then innovation is unlikely to get much airtime. Oh well.

But even if the top guys and gals do understand it, their role is not simply one of allowing idea generation to happen by looking the other way – there are many other areas in which senior managers have an influence.

Take promotion, for example. Senior managers will often sit on assessment centers or selection panels, and they will groom their successors. The criteria for promotion may or may not be published, but the results certainly are: whenever an individual is promoted, their unpromoted former peers, and hoping-to-be-promoted subordinates, will spend hours working out just what it is that Lucy has that caused her to get promoted. Senior managers have promotion in their gift, and the criteria used in practice are highly visible. Is the key to promotion success in the day job, delivering a steady operating result, and beating the budget by just enough to be seen as a good manager, but without being given a hugely stretch target in the next year? Or is it to be seen to have taken a "risk" by working on an innovative project, outside the day job's normal line structure? Senior managers who say the right words about the importance of innovation, but who are seen to groom and promote those who play safe, are creating around themselves an environment in which two important levers – what senior management says and what senior management does – are pointing in different directions. With the inevitable result that people will take their cue from the actions, not the words, and play safe. Innovation surely won't flourish here.

Similarly, senior managers have a strong influence on budgets and the allocation of funds. If it's a struggle to get the budgets for training, or for bringing people together (remember the *BBC*? – see pages 155 and 156) for idea generation, then once again innovation will wither. That's not to imply that innovation requires profligacy and a general lack of financial control. On the contrary, financial control is a "best practice" discipline for innovative organizations too. The issue is the allocation of funds in the first place, and their protection thereafter – activities associated with innovation do require money, and that money should be made available without the necessity of wringing blood out of stones.

That leads to yet another role of senior management in innovation – protection. Innovation, as we have seen on many occasions now, is a fragile flower, and one of the most beneficial acts of senior managers is to protect innovative activities – especially idea generation – until they have borne fruit; they should not press for evaluation too soon, and they should protect the idea from being evaluated by others prematurely; they should also ensure that the time meant to be spent on innovation is actually spent – for example, by creating a context in which middle managers fully understand the importance of idea-generation sessions, and do not stop their staff attending because of some panic with the day job. These are all everyday signals that innovation is important and, as usual, the opposite behaviors – such as condoning absence at training courses, or allowing people to be pulled off innovation projects at short notice – send very strong signals about what is, and what is not, really important.

Senior managers also play a vital role in resolving cross-boundary conflicts, such as those associated with creating interdisciplinary teams, or providing access to information. The most exciting innovations are often at or over boundaries (see, for example, Chapter 5 of my book, *Unlock Your Mind*), and senior managers have it in their power to make that happen, or to block it.

And, finally in this section, there is the role of senior managers in mentoring and storytelling. Who are the heroes in your organization? And what is the nature of their heroism, the basis of their esteem? Senior managers, by virtue of the stories they tell, the role models they advocate, the praise they bestow, send any number of signals about what the organization really values. If innovation is part of the story, this becomes very visible, and everyone seeks to emulate those behaviors. But if it isn't – despite the mission statement and the corporate ads – they won't.

So, the role of senior managers is pervasive and subtle. If they are sincere advocates of innovation, and active participants in the process, great. But if they aren't, merely sitting back and letting it be isn't quite enough: they must ensure that they don't – probably inadvertently – send out all the wrong signals in lots of other ways.

Budgets

Innovation costs money, and this must be budgeted. Nothing is more frustrating than the statement "We can't take that initiative, we didn't budget for it." With innovation, of course, you can't predict – and therefore you can't budget for – specific, pre-identified, ideas. But you can predict, plan for, and allocate budgets to specific activities. In general, an innovative organization will spend money on:

- *Training*, including:
    innovation in general, and idea generation and evaluation in particular;
    other related topics such as systems thinking, project management, risk analysis and risk management;
    how innovation works in your organization; and
    communication, teamwork and culture.

- *Communication*:
    within the organization, to share ideas; and
    externally, to gather information from the outside world.

- *Knowledge transfer*:
    to help the "brain bank connectivity."

- *Idea generation*:
    primarily an allowance for workshops.

- *Idea evaluation*:
    to allow for all stages of evaluation from local, team-based evaluation, through feasibility studies, to fully-fledged business cases.

- *Development and implementation*:
    for projects which pass through the evaluation process.

- *Rewards*:

  for example, to reward new ideas.

- *Pipeline administration*:

  managing the pipeline of new ideas is possibly a new business process, and needs funds for creation, and then on-going operation.

How much should be allocated to each? Clearly, there are no generic answers – it all depends on context. But what does not depend on context are the headings. So, take a look through your budget, and see if sums of money and time allowances have been earmarked for each of these activities. Smart managers know that if it hasn't been budgeted for, it won't happen.

Performance measures

Smart managers also know that even if it has been budgeted for, it doesn't necessarily happen – that's what monitoring and control are all about. And the heart of monitoring and control is the system of performance measures, and the (hopefully corresponding) system of reward and remuneration. I'll talk about reward structures in the next section: let me deal with performance measures here.

To me, performance measures are the fundamental drivers of behavior: if I have a choice between two actions, I will take that action which is most likely to contribute beneficially to my performance measures. So, if a key performance measure is this period's profit, I will avoid taking actions which might jeopardize that objective, even if the action I fail to take might have improved next period's (or, more likely, some more future period's) profit. Or if a more subtle performance measure is the extent to which I can keep my immediate line boss happy, I will seek to do that, and decline activities such as working on a "special project" for someone else.

This is of course all familiar stuff, and smart managers know all the rules of this particular game. But when an organization is seeking to become more innovative, this will not happen in practice until some practical and realistic performance measures are in place, and layering in yet another set of objectives and measures makes life even more complicated.

These complications arise in three ways: time, method and consistency.

The issue of time is simple: innovation is not a quick fix, and the benefits of becoming more innovative evolve relatively slowly. Any organization seeking to become more innovative will therefore incur the costs and the pain long before they see benefits, and this cuts across all the everyday, period-by-period measures. Introducing performance measures that encourage and nurture innovation inevitably gives rise to conflict with those designed to encourage short-term performance, and squaring this particular circle requires thought, consultation and leadership, assisted by tools such as the Balanced Scorecard (see page 49).

The issue of method is less simple, and relates to what, precisely, you want to encourage, and therefore measure. The endgame, obviously, is business success, and this comes from the implementation of good ideas. This leads to the identification of output measures such as revenue attributable to new products, cost savings attributable to new processes, or whatever – measures that focus on the end result of the active and successful management of the whole Innovation Target.

But, as we all know, it takes time for this to happen, and so there is another set of performance measures which applies to the management of the Innovation Target itself – measures such as the number of new ideas generated; the number of ideas submitted for evaluation; the speed of the evaluation process itself; the number of ideas accepted; the number of ideas in development; and so on.

And in advance of the measures of the process are a series of input measures such as the amount of time spent on idea generation; the number of people trained and skilled in creativity and innovation; and the amount of time spent on evaluation.

And in addition to all of these, there are any number of behavioral characteristics that an innovative organization might wish to encourage – such as sharing knowledge, participating in teams, coaching innovation in others, being willing to accept the ideas of others – some of which can be measured relatively easily, others less so.

So many things we could measure – it's all overwhelming.

The immediate tendency, particularly of task-oriented folk, is to focus on output measures such as the profit attributable to new products. This is indeed a valid measure, but my experience is that this works well only in relatively sophisticated environments, which are culturally very attuned to innovation, and already have a well-stocked pipeline of ideas – the archetypal example is 3M who, as described in Ernest Gundling's recent book *The 3M Way to Innovation*, have a performance measure that 30 percent of the sales revenue in any one year is attributable to products that were not in the catalog four years before.

For organizations which do not yet have that degree of maturity with respect to innovation, my suggestion is that you introduce an increasingly rich portfolio of measures steadily over time, starting with input measures (most importantly, number of people trained in creativity and innovation, and the amount of time devoted to idea generation and evaluation), then moving on through the process measures (monitoring the flow through the idea pipeline), and only then introduce output measures. By adopting a staged approach, you reduce complexity, you minimize the burden of new systems, and you are most likely to stimulate the activities and behaviors you really wish to encourage.

The issue of consistency is more complex still – this being a question of how the objective of encouraging innovation can have an effect on performance measures throughout the organization. Suppose, for example, that you wish to stimulate innovation, perhaps as a pilot project, within a particular business unit – say, in a particular territory. You do all the right things, getting the business unit's leadership on side, agreeing the budgets, training the people, and encouraging idea generation. Suppose further that the boss of that business unit wants to back a particular idea, and seeks funds and approval from his own boss, who perhaps is managerially responsible for three territories.

But let's further suppose that the performance measures of the "big" boss have remained unchanged. What might happen? In a word, conflict – perhaps inadvertent, but conflict nonetheless. When the business unit boss seeks approval for something risky, which delivers benefits across organizational boundaries, but not for some years yet, as we have already seen, the "big" boss might take the view that this particular project does not meet his own objectives, and so turns it down.

This is just one example of the more general issue that the performance measures in one part of the business might not be fully aligned with those in another part of the business. As businesses grow and change, this can happen very easily, by accident. But one of the "little things" that an innovative organization gets right is to ensure that performance measures across the entire organization are mutually consistent.

Reward and recognition

The subject of performance measures leads naturally to that of reward and recognition: if we wish to encourage innovation, then surely those who contribute to it should be rewarded accordingly. Yes, they should, but – as often happens in this complex area – there is quite a lot to think about, the top six topics being:

- Should there be a special reward for innovation ("Innovator of the Year"), or should the reward be incorporated into the remuneration package?

- Who gets rewarded – individuals, or teams, or both?

- What form does the reward take?

- Who judges?

- According to what criteria?

- And what about sanctions and failure?

Special rewards

The first topic – special awards or rewards as part of the normal remuneration package – is a false dilemma: it is not a question of either/or but of both ... and. Special awards are, by definition, public and can become part of the folklore of the business, for the recipients of the award become heroes. This fits in with some organizational cultures, but not all, and the key issue to bear in mind is visible fairness – the recipients of such awards are necessarily relatively few, and all must be seen by their peers as deserving of such an award. Rewards as part of the remuneration package are public in that the existence of the reward as part of a bonus package will be well known, but – in most organizations – the amount awarded to any one individual will be private, and ought to be consistent with actual performance in the context of the agreed performance measures. There is also no exclusivity here: literally everyone in the organization can receive an element of bonus, if they deserve it, and if the profits are there to be shared around.

Individual or team?

Innovation at any of the four stages of idea generation, evaluation, development and implementation – let alone as regards the whole sequence – is almost never a solitary activity, and so to identify a lone individual as the recipient of a special award will inevitably disadvantage some people who will have contributed. The issue here is to strike a balance between, on the one hand, being seen to encourage innovation, and also to offer a reward to a deserving individual, and on the other, being seen to be fair. My experience is that public awards to individuals should be modest in value, but high on prestige (more value can always be assigned to the annual bonus), so as to avoid unhelpful jealousies and accusations of unfairness; public awards to small teams are in my view better, but even with a team award, there will always be someone on the outside. Most importantly, you must avoid the situation in which only the "boss" is eligible for the reward: bosses do not always deserve the credit for what was done by their teams.

THE NOBEL PRIZE FOR PHYSICS, 1974

Smart
things to
think about

On 10 December 1974, the Nobel Prize for Physics – the world's highest accolade for that science – was awarded in Stockholm to two professors from the University of Cambridge, Sir Martin Ryle and Anthony Hewish, "for their pioneering research in radio astrophysics: Ryle for his observations and inventions, in particular of the aperture synthesis technique, and Hewish for his decisive role in the discovery of pulsars."

No one would deny that Ryle and Hewish fully deserved their awards. But many would grieve for someone who was not invited to make a trip to Stockholm that December: Jocelyn Bell Burnett.

During October and November 1967, as a twenty-four-year-old research student at Cambridge, Jocelyn Bell (as she was known prior to her marriage) was studying some data from a newly-finished radio telescope she had helped construct for her PhD thesis adviser, Anthony Hewish. The data was comprised of wavy tracks made on strip paper, rather like the tracks made on certain types of medical equipment. On one particular track on *four hundred feet* of chart paper, she noticed *one half-inch* of a pattern she did not quite understand. Rather than ignoring it as "rubbish," she searched for other, similar hints of a pattern, and she discovered that these pulses, one and one third of a second apart, repeated every 23 hours and 56 minutes. This is in fact the interval over which the earth rotates with respect to the stars, and proved that the signal came from something fixed in the heavens, like a star, but hitherto undetected. Jocelyn had discovered a new category of celestial object – a pulsar – now known to be formed from incredibly dense matter. But a pulsar is not still – it is spinning very fast, and as it does so, it emits radio waves. This is the explanation of the pulsating radio signal that Jocelyn had discovered – the situation is just like someone on a ship, looking at a lighthouse, who sees pulses of light attributable to the rotation of either the lamp itself, or an associated mirror.

It was Jocelyn who had made the original discovery – but it was Jocelyn's boss who won the Nobel Prize.

What form of reward is best?

The form of any recognition for innovation also merits attention, for money, shares in the spin-off company created as a result of commercializing the idea, promotion, or benefits in kind (the all-expenses-paid two weeks in the Caribbean) have value to some, but not to all. Some people value time more than money, or a degree of independence, or the opportunity for some form of sabbatical break, perhaps for education, perhaps to spend time in another organization, perhaps to play golf. Christiansen, in *Competitive Innovation Management* (pages 158–159), starkly contrasts 3M, which allows individuals to spend up to 15 percent of their working time on projects of their own choosing, to "Northern Pharmaceuticals" (a pseudonym), whose employees, " … are expressly forbidden to work on their own projects, their time being 100 percent allocated to corporate projects." Which organization is the more innovative? You guessed. 3M.

Who judges?

Special, public awards need to be seen to be fair, so the judgements need to be made by, ideally, a panel of trusted people; rewards as part of the remuneration package are subject to the same rules as other elements of an annual bonus – usually, this is determined by the line boss, ideally after consultation with those in a position to give an informed view. This is where the performance measures come into the equation – I too have played the game: "I did this, this and this in accordance with my performance measures, so my bonus should be x." If an individual feels there are any disconnects between what he or she believes was done, how it was measured, and how this mapped on to the bonus actually awarded, then my experience is that their behaviors are driven by what was actually received. So beware the situation in which staff are exhorted to be innovative, but those who judge fail to recognize it.

What are the criteria?

The issues discussed so far are complex enough, but the most vexed concern the criteria for any award, from the public prize to the personal bonus. Is it a question of ideas generated – in which case, what about ideas that turn out to be very half-baked indeed? Is it a question of ideas that achieve commercial success – in which case, how long do you have to wait until this is determined, and what are the criteria of success? And what about ideas that aren't about specific new products, or those that reduce the costs of processes, or ideas that don't influence either revenues or costs directly – ideas about relationships, organization or strategy? And what about those people who haven't necessarily come up with ideas themselves, but who have created a context or an environment in which others have flourished? And what is the balance between rewarding outcomes and effort? Maybe it is appropriate to be seen to be rewarding well-intentioned endeavor, even if the outcome is as yet unknown, or even a "failure." This is deep water indeed, and I know of no magic universal answers. But smart managers aren't daunted by these types of real-world issues: the important matter is to be well aware of the issues involved, to assess them in the context of your specific circumstances, and to be as wise as you can.

What about sanctions and failure?

Before leaving this section, let me dwell for a moment on two related topics – sanctions and failure. Sanctions are less talked about than rewards, but they too play a role in making explicit what types of behavior an organization wishes to encourage, and discourage. I'm not talking here of building a culture of fear, or of penalizing people by withholding pay or benefits, but of the way in which individuals are alerted to problem areas, and the importance of ensuring that bonuses are true recognitions of achievement, rather than automatic outcomes of having survived another year.

Failure, too, is another tricky subject, especially in the context of innovation. Innovation is inevitably risky, and to me that means that things can genuinely turn out differently from what we might have hoped. Is this "failure"? Perhaps; but perhaps not. To me, the key issue is the distinction between negligence and genuinely unforeseen circumstances. No one can foresee the future with certainty, and so, in deciding to proceed with a new product, for example, no one can guarantee that the product will be as unique as we had all hoped, and reach the sales targets to which we all aspire. But you can, and should, take into account all available data, and you can and should identify all possible risks, and devise strategies and tactics to mitigate them. If, with hindsight, you can determine that certain information was available at the time a key decision was taken, and that this information was ignored, then this is negligence – once again, the stunning example of this is London's Millennium Dome: the 1997 business plan used a target of 12 million paying visitors, when all the benchmarks indicated that 4 million would be good going (see page 37). On the other hand, if you can genuinely look back and say, "Even with hindsight, looking at the information we had available at the time, we would still have taken the same decision," then this to me is not negligence at all, even if the idea turned out in practice not to be a success.

Not everything we try is going to be successful – innovation is all about risk. But if people associated with a project that did not work out as well as we had hoped – even though they did the best they could possibly do – are seen to suffer as a consequence (by being sidelined, being passed over for promotion, having their salary held or even cut, or being fired), then the signal this sends to everyone else in the organization is very powerful indeed. Don't take risks. Do the day job. Keep your head down. So, the issue of rewards is not just about rewarding those who get it right – it's also about being wise to those who appear to be getting it "wrong" too.

Project funding

This sounds simple: once you commit to innovation, you have to make funds available for projects, particularly feasibility studies and development projects. In practice, though, it can be clumsy, especially if an organization perpetuates its capital allocation procedures from its pre-innovation days.

Some thoughts to bear in mind, which correspond very closely to many of the themes discussed in Chapter 5 (see, for example, page 208), are:

- *Not everything has to go to the main board for approval.* Funding can be made available throughout the organization, at different levels, for appropriate amounts, for projects of differing scales and risk profiles.

- *Make decisions quickly.* Innovation does not ripen with age, so make funding decisions as quickly as possible once there is a robust enough proposal.

- *Make decisions close to the idea's origin.* This is desirable not only as regards speed, but also to avoid distortion of the message. If the funding source for an idea is a long way from its origin, the likelihood is that the approval process passes through many hands – and minds – on its journey from originator to funding authority. At each intermediate point, the idea can suffer from dilution, distortion, and a progressive loss of enthusiasm and passion.

- *Don't forget to make provision for funding organizational "orphans."*

  The previous three points collectively suggest a funding framework whereby sums of money to support innovation can be made available throughout the organization – this makes the processes local (and regional), fast, and close to the points of origin. In all likelihood, this will reflect the organization structure. That's fine, and this devolved process should work well for those ideas which naturally fit within the objectives and performance measures of that structure. But some ideas won't naturally "fit" – they might relate to cross-organizational new products or processes, or ideas that are simply too big for any one organizational unit to handle. There is therefore a danger that these ideas become "orphans" – potentially good ideas, but ideas that don't readily have organizational champions in a devolved structure. As we have already discussed (see pages 248–250), a smart organization anticipates this, and makes funds available specifically for such ideas: in addition to the funding process aligned to the formal organization structure, different levels of the organization (say, Divisional and Group) have pots of money available to be allocated to ideas which would otherwise risk being lost as orphans.

Training

Innovation and creativity are skills that can be learnt, but since the conventional educational systems do not teach them, it is up to organizations to remedy this in their internal training activities. Innovation and creativity are therefore important components of a smart organization's training and development programs. Once innovation is well-established as a natural part of the "way we do things around here," this program is likely to comprise a series of "master classes" to keep people refreshed, as well as some induction training for new joiners, but for organizations seeking to move from "here" to "there," there will be a backlog of skill enhancement that needs to be addressed by means of a special training initiative.

Who should be included in this program? And how might it take place?

My answer to the "who" question is "everybody" – everybody can contribute to innovation, and I see no reason why anyone, from the receptionist and the catering staff to the managing director and chairman, should be denied the opportunity. But I also recognize that different people have different levels of interest, so a series of different programs makes sense, with each module within the overall program specifically targeted at, and designed for, a particular community.

One community is that of the top management. I've already discussed their role in innovation, and the importance of ensuring that all senior managers are in the upper half of the diagram shown on page 52. In my experience, it takes about three hours to brief senior managers to the required level of insight, and this ideally takes place in a half-day session, either convened specially for this purpose, or embedded within a broader event.

There are many ways of delivering an organization-wide training program, but one that you might like to think about is to identify three further communities beyond top management:

- *specialists* – those people likely to have a particular interest in creativity and innovation, and who will act as local champions;

- *facilitators* – those people who have not only a particular interest, but can also act as facilitators and trainers of local groups; and

- *participants*– everybody else.

Specialists need to be fully confident in the tools and techniques of innovation, and require a training program of at least two days, so that they can deal with matters in the appropriate depth. As a result, they should be well equipped to lead, and contribute to, idea-generation workshops, and the evaluation process.

Facilitators need this level of training, and even more so. Many aspects of innovation, especially idea generation, are best carried out in small groups, and these usually benefit from active facilitation. Those who play the role of facilitator need to have not only skills and confidence in facilitation in general, but also a deep knowledge of creativity and innovation. The facilitator training courses I run usually take about five days, which allows time for simulations, video training, and plenty of discussion on how best to conduct *InnovAction!* workshops.

Those who are neither specialists nor facilitators are participants – encouraged to come up with ideas and to participate in idea generation and evaluation, but with no especial responsibilities. To play this role, people certainly need a modest level of training in the tools and techniques, so that they are equipped to participate, rather than to lead. In addition – and perhaps more importantly – people must be given a very clear and sincere message of encouragement, and that they are genuinely invited to participate in creativity and innovation. Part of this message is a clear explanation of how the innovation process works in your organization, so that people know what to do when they have an idea; how to suggest, be invited to, and participate in *InnovAction!* workshops; how the evaluation process works, and their potential role in it; and how participation in the innovation process is related to their appraisal and development, and to the remuneration and reward system.

This requires, of course, that all these organizational processes have been designed and implemented: this seems obvious, but it is not always the case – some organizations, with the aspiration of raising the levels of both skill and enthusiasm for creativity and innovation, launch significant training programs focusing on creativity tools and techniques, but without having first ensured consistency across the accompanying business processes. This training, of course, is fun and exciting, but it does not have the intended effect. If the organization has not built the processes for managing the pipeline, for wise and balanced evaluation, for funding and staffing projects, and for reward and remuneration, then what happens after people have been enthused? They start generating ideas, only to discover that there is no process for dealing with them; those ideas that do get evaluated may not be evaluated quickly and fairly; and people soon find that the systems for performance measures, reward and remuneration remain unchanged, and make no recognition of the new emphasis on innovation. The result of all this is disillusionment and distrust as another management fad bites the dust. This is doubly bad news – the failure of the training initiative to deliver the required results is bad enough, but even worse is the deep discrediting of innovation as a fundamental organizational goal, so making it even harder to implement innovation the second time around.

So, be smart, and don't confuse energy with effectiveness. Resist the pressure to roll out an organization-wide training program until all the other aspects of the innovation process are fully in place.

Managing projects

Here is a conversation you do not overhear in an innovative organization:

"Did you hear about Andy?"

"No. What happened?"

"He's been assigned to a special project."

"He's on his way out, then!"

Innovative organizations understand the importance of running both their line structure, and also a project structure, in parallel and in harmony. The line structure is there for continuity, and for delivering day-to-day operations; projects are there for special, one-off activities. Most innovation activities, before they become fully developed, fall into the project category, and for innovation to be successful, the organization must be able to create and manage project teams, lasting from a matter of just a few days, to many months or perhaps even a year or two.

The main difference between the line and a project concerns time: the line is in essence timeless, running in perpetuity, whereas projects have a finite time span, and have a definite start and end. This implies that, for a project to be successful, the project team must be convened, then managed, and ultimately disbanded. It is here, of course, that the main difficulties arise: the line and project teams both demand the very best resources, and if, as in almost every organization, "best" resources are in short supply, the demands of the line and the demands of projects are in direct conflict. The conflict can arise in many ways, for example:

- Departmental line managers can be reluctant to allow members of their team to be seconded to projects – why should a line boss release their best people?

- Individuals being asked to join project teams might be reluctant to do so, for all sorts of reasons – perhaps they feel that their lines of patronage for their next promotion will be broken; perhaps they fear that their line boss will feel they are being disloyal by their "resignation"; perhaps they are worried that their line job will no longer be available when the project is finished; perhaps they just don't want to take a risk in case the project is not seen to be a gleaming success (and we all know what happened to the last guy who volunteered for a failed project, don't we?).

Under conditions like these, the departmental manager, and the person invited to join the project team, can cement an alliance whereby: "I'm very sorry, but I just can't leave the line job." The result of all this is that the project gets staffed by rejects – all those people whose departmental managers are pleased to see the back of – and the likelihood that the project will be a success is severely jeopardized. And if the project does indeed turn out to be a failure, those who managed to avoid having been associated with it congratulate themselves on their lucky escape, and vow never to work on a project in their careers. No wonder the organization can't innovate.

Staffing innovation projects with the best people is probably the single most powerful, yet most difficult, action to achieve, since it goes to the heart of the organization. What, then, do smart organizations do? Lots of things, things like …

- ensuring that career progression is seen to include time in the line as well as time on innovation projects;

- building career development programs which incorporate line time and project time – although you can't predict what the nature of an innovation project might be in three years' time, an innovative organization will have full confidence in saying that "in about three years' time, you should plan for about six months on an innovation project";

- incorporating sensible succession planning so that there is never a problem whenever a particular person is seconded out of the line;

- ensuring that the reward structure for project participants recognizes their contribution to innovation projects, and is not unfairly harsh as regards "failure";

- ensuring that the reward structure for departmental managers recognizes their role in nurturing innovation and creativity in others, and in allowing their staff to move out of line roles;

- ensuring that people are not "out of sight, out of mind" whilst on projects; and

- ensuring that, towards the end of a project, people are successfully reintegrated into the line.

As so often in this chapter, none of this is rocket science – it's all no more and no less than managerial common sense. But it all needs attention, and if an organization is not used to staffing projects, these topics all work consistently together to help make innovation happen.

What about the project itself?

Smart quotes

"All projects suffer from one, and only one, problem. It's known as 'the big problem at the end'."

Martin Barnes, former chairman of the council of the International Project Management Association

The box says it all: this is so true. All projects start with a wave of energy and euphoria, and, especially these days with the ubiquity of tools such as PC-based project planning software, complete with umpteen pages of bar charts, dependency diagrams and task lists. And, sometime just before the end, so many projects are in a state of rancor, with prospective users feeling let down, financial managers wondering where the money went, and project managers feeling like they might have had a quieter life had they chosen to become professional heavyweight boxers.

This isn't a text on project management, but a few guidelines might be helpful.

Projects are intrinsically uncertain, and cannot be predicted with precision, in terms of both cost and elapsed time. Never produce (if you're a project manager) or believe (if you're on a steering committee) any plans which state: "the project will be delivered by this date for this cost." Rather, identify and scrutinize the range of times for delivery and the range of likely costs. One of the key roles of the project manager is, of course, to identify all the tasks that need to be carried out, their mutual dependencies, and their resource requirements. This is the basis of the project plan, and the resource estimate. But an even more important role is for the project manager to identify all the uncertainties and risks that will cause the project to take longer than the "earliest" time estimate and the "lowest" cost, and to devise strategies for their identification and management. As a result, the project manager can then estimate the "latest" time and the "highest" cost. The project steering committee needs to review the analysis of the project uncertainty for wisdom, and help the project manager's risk assessment. If the project is in familiar territory, and there is much relevant collective experience, then the range of uncertainty should be small; if, on the other hand, the project is truly new, the range might be very broad – that's the way these things really are. The project might, in fact, cost the projected maximum, and if this is far too much for the organization to bear, then maybe it shouldn't embark on the project in the first place. For if the project is started, and begins to move along the expensive trajectory, you should not be too surprised as the optimistic estimates are dashed. And if the organization decides it can't afford it, then the project should be cancelled – without destroying the career of the project manager, and all the members of the project team.

Hard-nosed managers – those who manage everything on time and within budget – are probably having apoplexy by now: how on earth can you condone, let alone advise, managing projects on the basis of ranges rather than deadlines? As soon as a range is mentioned, surely the project will immediately slip as the team slacks off?

I understand that, and that's why managing projects is a little more subtle. To keep the team focused and motivated, the project itself needs to be managed, on a day-to-day basis, to the "earliest" deadline, and the "lowest" cost: that way, everyone on the team is clear on what they have to do. The project steering committee, however, needs to be briefed on the possibility that the plans might need to be stretched, and one of their key roles is to release predetermined contingencies when necessary. The project manager needs to look in two directions at once, motivating the team to follow the "earliest" schedule, but keeping an eagle eye open for the signs of the necessity to go to the steering committee to recommend an extension. Pity the poor project manager, doomed to live in a permanent state of schizophrenia – striving to demonstrate leadership to the team to maximize the likelihood that the project can be delivered without the need for releasing contingencies; needing to be ever vigilant on assessing the risks; seeking not to appear to be "weak"; endeavoring to maintain the trust and respect of the steering committee, so that if in fact a recommendation to release contingency funds has to be made, the committee will do so, professionally and without blame. Not an easy role to play. No wonder some of the best people choose to stay within the safety and certainty of the line.

And the pressure increases as the project approaches completion. One of the most difficult decisions to take at the end of a project is to identify that it is indeed the end. In developing a system, there is always "one more bug"; in launching a new product, there is always a feature to tweak. When, precisely, is the system well-enough developed to be relied upon? When, precisely, is the product good enough to launch? To those who love tinkering, nothing is ever good enough; to those who are desperate for action, why oh why are we wasting all this time? The decision to cut-over from "development" to "live" is critical – if this happens prematurely, the damage to the business might be irrecoverable; if too late, time and money might be being consumed needlessly. Smart organizations understand this, and develop, well in advance of the time for the "go-live" decision, a set of specific acceptance criteria.

ACCEPTANCE CRITERIA

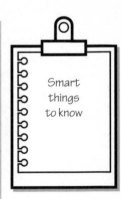

Smart
things
to know

Judging the end of a project is never a clean decision – nothing is ever perfect. The essence of the decision is to balance the business benefit of the launch (as represented by, for example, the sales of the new product, or the cost-savings of a new system) against the possibility of major failure. As ever, it is a question of risk.

A powerful way of managing the risk is by compiling, well in advance of the time the decision has to be made, a comprehensive list of "acceptance criteria." This is a comprehensive list not only of all the features of the new system (or whatever), but also of the associated performance characteristics. Suppose, for example, that the project is the building of a new call center. The list of features will be very long (certainly hundreds, and maybe thousands, of items), including all the features of the building, the systems infrastructure, training, and a myriad of other things too. Within that list will be a feature such as: "Response time on incoming calls," and the performance characteristic might be "96 percent of all calls received on any day to be answered within three rings, a further 3 percent within four rings, and no calls at all after five rings." The feature "Recruitment plans in place" might have the performance characteristic "The recruitment plan required to support months 3–6 of live operation has been defined, and signed off by the main board."

As the project nears completion, some form of test can take place at which all of these features can be measured, from which it is possible to determine which features have met the required performance levels, and which have not. This provides the steering committee with good, comprehensive information, on the basis of which they can assess the risk "throwing the switch" even if some features are not quite right. If the risk is assessed as unacceptable, further development work can be authorized; if the risk is acceptable, then implementation can proceed, even in the light of known teething problems.

This method really works, and I have used it on many occasions: notably for the opening of a new office for Goldman Sachs in Paris (a project carried out to very tight deadlines), and also in relation to the "go live" decision for the TALISMAN project at the London Stock Exchange, which, at the time, was one of the largest projects in the UK, representing more than 1000 man-years of effort.

One last word on projects: they do come to an end. Some organizations seem to forget this, and once a project team has been created, it continues, seemingly for ever (like some committees you might have come across!). Smart organizations don't fall into this trap. They know that projects are finite; they anticipate their natural end; they ensure that all the team members are fully and successfully reintegrated into the line subsequently, and – most importantly – they capture the learning from the project, so that they do not make all the same mistakes again.

Managing the pipeline of ideas

As you will by now appreciate, there is a lot to be done in organizing all the activities required for building and maintaining an unlearning organization. Some of these things are in the natural domain of the line – changes to the budgeting process, for example, are legitimately best carried out by the finance department, and changes to the reward and remuneration system by HR.

It may be, however, that your organization does not have a process for managing innovation itself – especially managing the pipeline of ideas, from idea generation right across the Innovation Target to implementation. In that case, one needs to be built. This, as usual, will require a champion, probably someone at board level, and naturally (but not necessarily) the individual with prime responsibility for the processes for business and strategic planning. It will also require a manager (probably full time), and a modest infrastructure.

The primary role of this new function is to manage the pipeline of ideas. This entails:

- ensuring the individuals throughout the organization are equipped to participate in idea generation and evaluation;

- acting as a central focal point where all ideas are logged;

- administering the information system that captures all the ideas, and monitors their progress from one stage to the next across the Innovation Target;

- reviewing, from time to time, the ideas "on the shelf" to determine if any should be revisited, given current or expected future circumstances; and

- acting as a central hub for information on creativity and innovation, providing support across the organization.

The role, as I have described it, is one of facilitation and networking: the role does not take responsibility for training, for example, but it is involved in making sure that training happens. The role therefore acts as a central co-ordinating hub, supporting the activities of the business units, and adding value by providing functions that the business units themselves cannot perform, such as acting as a central repository of all ideas, administering the system that tracks ideas as they move through the various stages of the Innovation Target, and – most importantly – providing a mechanism whereby ideas which have been shelved or rejected during the evaluation process (see pages 211–213) are not totally lost, but can be reviewed from time to time in case something has changed. Over time, the organizational repository of ideas can be immensely valuable.

What this role is *not* is the "central innovation department" – this being the part of the organization whose job it is "to have ideas." In my view, such a department is the antithesis of the unlearning organization, for it institutionalizes the excuse "having ideas is nothing to do with my job – that's what that central department is for." In an unlearning organization, creativity and innovation are everyone's opportunity, and the role of the central department is to support this, to champion it, and to provide the infrastructure to help make it all work.

Embedding innovation into the day job

The ultimate objective of creating a truly unlearning organization is to make creativity and innovation a natural feature of everyday existence, a totally normal aspect of "the way we do things around here." Innovation isn't something "special," something we go away to do at off-site meetings, or is the unique preserve of that department – where is it now? – oh yes, somewhere in marketing I think. Or did I hear that they closed it down last year? I'm not sure ...

Smart organizations and smart managers embed innovation in the day job, and they incorporate the tools and techniques, and the process, in the things that happen every day. They rejoice in it, they give it visibility, they publicise it. Take a look at your organization's internal newspaper, and see how many articles there are celebrating the success of innovation. Not too many? And how often does your organization get calls from the press or Business Schools asking for case studies?

The easiest way of embedding innovation into the day job is to start using the language of hats, at meetings and in conversation. "That's rather a black hat remark," "Let's all wear our yellow hats to think about the advantages of that suggestion" and "If I wear my red hat, I don't think I like that too much" are all perfectly natural statements, once the organization has sanctioned the use of the metaphor, and people have some insight as to what the colour-coding means. The *InnovAction!* process too can be used whenever there is a problem to solve, no matter how humble. All that needs to happen is for people to recognize that compiling a detailed description of what happens now is a very powerful way of helping people to ask, and answer, that magic question "How might this be different?"

Every organization, for example, is involved in some way or other with IT in general, and system and process design in particular. I discussed the role of innovation as regards business process re-engineering in Chapter 2 (see pages 62–66), and although process re-engineering may be rather less fashionable now, the processes of redesigning old systems and designing new ones will continue into the indefinite future. Take a look at the work-plans your organization has used for some recent design projects, and ask these killer questions:

What did we actually do with the maps we drew of the current process? Did we use them to ask, systematically, "How might this be different?"? Why not?

After we had done all the fact finding of user requirements and mapped all the relevant processes, and before we started the detailed design, did we allocate sufficient time to "searching for rearrangements of the puzzle" (see pages 106–112) to ensure we found the best possible design solution? Why not?

Have all our systems designers had formal training in innovation and creativity so that they can apply the tools and techniques with confidence on all our system and process design activities? Why not?

KILLER
QUESTIONS

In my view, innovation and creativity should be an intrinsic part of the thinking of all IT professionals, and tools such as *InnovAction!* should be standard components of the IT function's methodology. Given the ever-increasing role of technology as a source of competitive advantage, and the dependence of the rest of the organization on the quality of the IT team, this might be your view too.

Another opportunity relates to quality, where concepts such as total quality management, continuous improvement and lean manufacture, supported by processes such as quality circles, are well-established in many organizations, especially in manufacturing. The essence of all these initiatives is to strive for better processes, and encouraging those intimately associated with the processes to discover these improvements for themselves. As described in the next box, *InnovAction!* is totally consistent with this approach, and can inject additional energy and enthusiasm into what by now might perhaps be a somewhat tired process.

Smart things to think about

INNOVACTION! AND QUALITY CIRCLES

Many manufacturing organizations have gained great benefit from the various quality initiatives that have been developed over the last twenty years or so. One of the most powerful is the "Quality Circle," in which small groups, usually of shop-floor operatives, are encouraged to improve their own processes and methods by working collectively to solve local problems. There are any number of tools and techniques to support this, such as Ishikawa's fishbone diagram (to help break a more complex problem down into its constituents), and the "Five Whys" (if you ask the question "why?" repeatedly – rather like a challenging television interviewer tackling a particularly evasive politician – you will probably discover the underlying truths, as well as the assumptions that you rarely challenge).

The *InnovAction!* process is totally consistent with these, since its starting point is a complete description of what happens now – a description which will be in harmony with, and probably more complete than, the descriptions elicited by fishbones (which tend to describe what's wrong, rather than what is) or the five why's (which tends to seek explanations rather than descriptions). Where *InnovAction!* adds new value is by encouraging the team to ask: "How might this be different?" systematically for all the features – even those where there is no explicit problem to solve – remember the banana (see pages 120 and 121)!

Quality Circles have been used with success at shop-floor level in manufacturing industry, but it is very rare to find similar processes operating in other sectors, or in functions such as marketing or accounting, and even rarer at middle and senior management levels. Do these parts of the business have no opportunity for improving their efficiency and effectiveness? I wonder.

Kaoru Ishikawa, for many years an engineering professor at the University of Tokyo, was one of the leaders of the Japanese quality movement, especially as regards the use of Quality Circles and statistical techniques. He is perhaps best known for his *Guide to Quality Control*, and his advocacy of a "fishbone" diagram, a powerful tool for understanding the causes of problems, and in helping identify solutions: the "backbone" of the "fish" represents the problem to be solved, and the "radiating bones" represent the main and subsidiary causes underlying the problem.

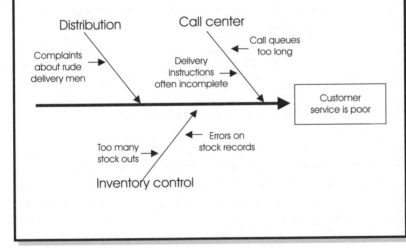

One activity, for example, that is very much within the domain of top management is strategic and business planning. There are many methods to support this fundamentally important process, and one of the most powerful of these – to my mind – is known as scenario planning. As I describe in the next section, the *InnovAction!* process can play a very natural role in this vital activity.

Innovation and scenario planning

In Chapter 2, we saw (see pages 74–76) that strategy formulation is itself one of the domains in which innovation can be enormously valuable. We also saw that there were three different ways in which innovation might apply to strategy:

- as a *result* of strategy formulation, in the sense of defining a strategic vision, and the corresponding actions, which are innovative as compared to your actual and potential competitors;

- as a *goal* of the strategy, in the sense of making innovation, and the creation of a truly unlearning organization, a strategic objective; and

- as applied to the *process* of strategy formulation itself, so that this is done in an innovative way.

Hopefully, this book as a whole will equip you to achieve the first of these, and this chapter in particular is all about the second. This section will focus on the third point – that of embedding creativity and innovation into the process of strategy formulation itself.

As I just mentioned, there are many ways of formulating strategy, and the business bookshops have many shelves full of learned tomes which will give you advice on how to do it. The process I wish to discuss here is called scenario planning, a brief overview of which is given in the next box.

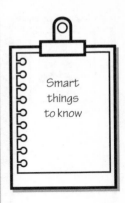

SCENARIO PLANNING

Scenario planning evolved during the 1960s as a result of the activities of Herman Kahn, at the American think-tank, the RAND Corporation; Peter Schwartz, at Stanford Research Institute, at that time a department of Stanford University in California; and Pierre Wack, at the industrial giant, Shell. All were grappling with the fundamental problem underpinning all planning: how can we best take decisions which are inevitably long lasting, when the future is in fact uncertain?

One approach is to attempt to remove the uncertainty by better prediction and forecasting: if only we can be "cleverer," then we can eliminate the uncertainty, and our decisions and plans will work. A second, diametrically opposed approach is to assume that prediction is impossible, and that the best tactic is to take short-term decisions, and to revisit them continually, adjusting them as circumstances change.

Scenario planning takes a middle course. It rejects the "we can predict" school as intellectually unsound, and the "we are powerless" view on the grounds that it can degenerate into the abdication of all managerial responsibility. The central tenet of scenario planning is that, although no one can predict the future with certainty, it is very possible to imagine a variety of possible futures which might come to pass. Each of these can be used to test various strategic policies and actions, and from this the management team can agree upon which policies and actions they wish to take, but with a very profound insight into the corresponding risks and uncertainties.

Smart things to know

Scenario planning, by the way, does not work in all organizations, especially those run by a boss who knows all the answers. But it does work well in organizations that share the values of the unlearning organization, and indeed, one of the leaders in the field, Arie de Gues, who for a time led the scenario planning team at Shell, is the author of an excellent book entitled *The Living Company*, which is totally in harmony with this philosophy.

Arie de Geus worked for 38 years with Royal Dutch/Shell, including a period acting as co-ordinator of Group Planning. His experience at one of the world's largest companies has given him great insight into the nature of decision-making and the management of change, and he is a great believer that planning is a process of learning, rather than one of prediction. He is the originator of the concept of "the learning organization," and is the author of a landmark article in the March 1988 issue of Harvard Business Review entitled *Planning as Learning*. His book, *The Living Company: Growth, learning and longevity in business*, explores the metaphor of a company as a living being with its own identity, existing within an ecology, and with a capacity for learning and evolution. His concept of "flocking" – bringing people together to allow them to communicate, listen and learn – is a powerful mechanism for encouraging the BBC (see pages 155 and 156).

Scenario planning itself has several associated methodologies (as described, for example in *Scenario Planning: Managing for the Future*, by Gill Ringland, and *Scenarios: The Art of Strategic Conversation* by Kees van der Heijden); central to the one I use this table:

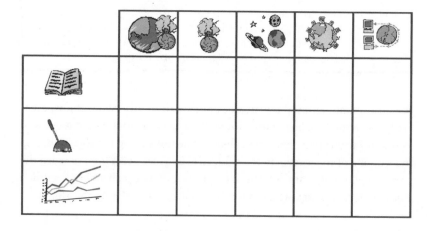

The columns represent "worlds," with the first column being "today's world," and the remaining ones possible alternative "future worlds." The three rows represent, respectively, "descriptions," "levers" and "outcomes."

Let me explain this by reference to the first column, "today's world." In the "description" row, the top left cell represents a complete description of the external context in which a business or organization operates – a description encompassing the current commercial and industrial structure, the nature of competition, the legislative and regulatory framework, the technological environment, and so on.

The "levers" row contains information relating to the "levers" that managers can pull, which reflect their decisions. These levers have two attributes: "names" and "settings." For example, one lever might have the name "staff establishment," and a setting of "3250," indicating that, as at today, the organization employs 3250 people. This number is a matter of managerial choice – depending on the strategy and policies of the organization, there could be more or fewer people. Other levers will represent, for example, products, services, channels to market, pricing policy and the like – collectively, the total set of levers reflects all the various decisions that managers can take.

The "outcomes" row contains information relating to the outcomes of the business, once again expressed in terms of "names" and "settings": as an example, one outcome might have the name "total sales revenue," and the setting "£5 billion." Other outcomes represent profit, market share, share price, credit rating, reputation, staff morale and so on, so that the total set of outcomes reflects all the results of running the business.

Overall, when completed, the first column, represents "today's world," showing a comprehensive description of what that world looks like, a list of the levers and their settings, and a list of the outcomes and their settings. This captures the essence of what is happening in the business today: in the existing world, by setting our levers at particular chosen positions, we achieve the resulting outcomes.

So much for "today's world" – what about the "future worlds"?

Let's assume for the moment that we have compiled descriptions of some possible, but very different, "future worlds," and that we have populated the entire top row of the table – how we can do this I shall describe shortly. The reason I skip over this for the moment is to demonstrate how this table, when completed, can help determine strategy.

Suppose for the moment that the levers stay at their current "today's world" settings in all the identified "future worlds." Having compiled a description of each world, you can ask the question "If my levers are at their given settings in a particular 'future world', will the outcomes be favorable or unfavorable?" If you have a good insight as to what a particular "future world" might look like, as achieved by having compiled its description, this is in fact an easier process that it might seem: it can be done by group discussion, or by analysis, for example by using models. If the answer is "favorable," then fine. But if the answer is "unfavorable," then this prompts the question "What do the lever settings have to be to create a favorable outcome in a particular world?" This too can be assessed by discussion or by analysis, and results in a process in which the lever settings are "reverse engineered," perhaps by trial and error but more likely by applying careful thought, to give a favorable set of outcomes in the chosen "future world."

If this process is repeated for each "future world," the table can be completed: each column contains a description of each world, associated with the settings of the levers which the management team believe will give favorable outcomes. In general, the lever settings will be different in each "future world," and that's why formulating strategy is not easy – if it didn't matter what decisions you take (as determined by the settings of the levers), then we'd all have a very easy job indeed.

How, then, do you determine the strategy? By discussing with your colleagues which lever settings you collectively believe in. And the completion of the scenario planning table makes this discussion very well informed: it acts as a "laboratory" against which you can test ideas, policies, potential actions. And as a result, you can agree which actions to take; for, at the end of the day, the strategy can only manifest itself as a series of actions in which you choose to move selected levers from "here" to "there" – there is nothing else that a manager can do.

Smart things to think about

CONNECTING LEVERS TO OUTCOMES

Levers represent management actions, for the *only* action a manager can take is to reset a lever from one position to another: you can hire more staff, you can retrain others, you can advertise more, you can open up new markets. These are all examples of resetting levers – the staff number lever, the skill lever, the advertising lever, the market lever.

Outcomes represent the results of these actions – the sales revenue outcome, the profit outcome, the share price outcome.

Unfortunately, there are no levers with outcome names such as "sales revenue," "profit," "share price" and the rest, for there are no actions managers can *directly* take to influence, for example, sales. The connections between the levers and the outcomes are indirect: you hope that by advertising more, market share will increase; you hope that having better-trained staff will increase customer satisfaction and hence sales. And to make matters even more complex, there are also all sorts of time lags between taking an action (in the current jargon, resetting a lever), and the hoped-for result (a beneficial outcome).

It is therefore a profound truth that *no lever is directly connected to any outcome*, and it is this absence of direct connections between the levers (what managers can actually do) and the outcomes (what managers want) that makes managing the challenge it indeed is. Yes, levers and outcomes are linked, but the linkages are indirect, complex, subtle, sometimes in mutual conflict, and often time-lagged. How, then, should all the levers be set to give optimal outcomes?

Smart managers have an intuitive understanding of how the levers and outcomes are linked, both logically and over time. Even smarter managers supplement their intuition with "systems thinking" – a powerful tool (see pages 16, 17, 28, 29 and 149) specifically designed to tame the complexity of understanding how the settings of all the levers determine the values of the various outcomes. Systems thinking is also the basis of "system dynamics modeling," a computer-based simulation modeling technique that can be used to explore how complex systems evolve over time.

Systems thinking and system dynamics modeling can play a very valuable role in scenario planning, for they can help specify how your levers are linked to your outcomes, under a variety of contexts, as defined by "today's world" and the various alternative "future worlds."

The process I have outlined does not require any prediction, for it does not require that the management team divine which one of the alternative "future worlds" will in fact come to pass. Nor is it a process in which managers place a bet, totally blind. Rather, it's a process in which the management team can thoughtfully and rigorously imagine what alternative "future worlds" might come to pass, and, as a result, determine policies and strategies in the full light of the inevitable uncertainty. And it does something else too – by creating a context in which managers can explore the future, by building what the scenario planners vividly call a "memory of the future," the management team is alerted to the way in which the future might evolve, so that as time actually evolves, you can be very alert to changes in the external context, you can spot the early signs of change long before your competitors, and you can react accordingly.

The heart of the process, clearly, is to imagine the "future worlds." How in practice is this done? Let me now answer this question, which I skipped over a few pages ago. But in fact, I don't have to. For you already know. By using *InnovAction!* of course!

The first row in the scenario planning table represents a detailed description of "today's world," and the various alternative "future worlds" – descriptions of the context in which your business operates now or might operate in the future, expressed in terms of the commercial and industrial structure, the nature of competition, the legislative and regulatory framework, the technological environment and so on. These descriptions can be formulated as a (very long!) series of bullet points, structured under various appropriate sub-headings.

The description of any "future world" must, of course, be different in some way from that of "today's world" – if it wasn't, the two worlds would be indistinguishable. And the easiest way of assembling sets of different descriptions is – you've got it – by asking "How might this be different?" of each of the bullet points in the description of "today's world." *InnovAction!* in action! That's why the first step in the process is to compile a good description of "today's world" – it's always best to start with what you know.

For sure, with a large number of bullet points in the description of "today's world," the process of asking "How might this be different?" can generate a huge number of alternatives. Also, during this process, it is very valuable to involve a broad range of people, including external technical experts, who can provide both specialist knowledge as well as contributing to the collective imagination (we're back to the *BBC* – see pages 155 and 156). Yes, after a short while it does get a mess, and, somewhat later, there are so many different possibilities on cards plastered all over the walls, it appears to be totally chaotic. But with reflection, the ideas cluster, and some self-consistent descriptions of possible "future worlds" emerge – the human brain is extremely good at organizing this sort of material.

InnovAction!, then, can lie at the heart of an innovative strategic planning process, and that's another way of helping embed creativity and innovation into the day job – in this case, the day job of the most senior managers.

Smart
things to
think about

> EMBEDDING INNOVATION INTO THE DAY JOB
>
> Imagine going into an organization, and seeing on the walls of the marketing department, a factory, the IT department, or wherever, long lists of "features of the way we do things," these being bullet point descriptions of how we manufacture our products, deliver our service, do our pricing, negotiate with suppliers, treat our staff, or whatever. And imagine further a banner right across these saying, "How might we do this differently? Please discuss new ideas with your colleagues, and e-mail your 'hatted' ideas to . . . "
>
> What stops this from being your organization?

So, what can you actually do?

This chapter, and indeed much of this book, has been directly or indirectly about organizational culture – the way the organization actually behaves, the unwritten but oh-so-powerful rules of behavior, the reality of how people are encouraged and rewarded, and discouraged and penalized. Yes, cultures can be changed, but it can be a long, slow process, especially if you believe in the (somewhat gloomy, but nonetheless realistic) message of the next box.

So how do you change something as amorphous as the corporate culture? How do you relax a tendency to avoid risks without betting the company? How do you encourage people to move out of the safety of the line, and be willing to cope with uncertainties of an innovation project? How do you break down the silos and the power bases, and encourage a richer spirit of sharing and teamwork?

My personal experience is that to try to change "the culture" is too big an undertaking: success is far more likely if you set out to change a series of specific processes, a step at a time, within a consistent overall framework. This is totally consistent with the message given at the start of this chapter: to become an innovative organization, to become an unlearning organization, you need to have two big things, the will to do it, and some financial headroom, and then lots and lots of little things need to be consistent and harmonious.

If the two big things are there, then, rather than tackling "the culture" as a whole, do a series of consistent projects to change those specific little things that will help – maybe it's the budgeting system to allow for innovation projects, maybe training, maybe the criteria for promotion. As these progressively and consistently become aligned, the culture – which is manifest by how many of these things work in practice – will shift too.

But where do you start? The checklist of little things (as an *aide memoire*, see the mind maps on pages 251 and 252) is enormously long; the task, surely, is daunting. Well, it might be, but I'd be truly surprised. In my experience, is it remarkably rare for *everything* on the checklist to be totally counter productive or dysfunctional: usually, some things are in good shape; some things are neutral; some things are a problem, but not hugely so; and some things require fixing.

So the starting point is the checklist. Use the checklist to scout round your organization, and do a quick diagnostic. For each of the items on the checklist, ask:

- How does this work now?

- Does this encourage innovation actively, is it neutral, or is it a positive disincentive?

- If it is neutral or negative, how might it be different? (Aha! ***InnovAction!*** strikes again!)

This enables you to segregate the host of little things into three categories – those that are fine, those that aren't fine but aren't causing pain, and those that are causing pain, and need to be fixed. When this is done, you can then define a series of well-focused, manageable, finite projects, with targeted deliverables, and a much higher chance of success. Some of them may be big and difficult – like changing the reward structure – but even if it is big and difficult (as indeed it is), it is still, with energy, appropriate resourcing and the right political support (the first being what you provide, and the other two being consequences of the two "big things"), manageable and doable. And you can do it, and it will succeed. And once that has happened, you can move onto the next project, and then the next, so that, over a sensible period of time, a series of projects have been successfully delivered, all of which have nudged those little things into alignment, so changing the culture, and resulting in your contributing to building a truly innovative culture, a real unlearning organization.

And you'll have built something else too – something I highlighted right at the start of this book, in the Preface. For you will have built your organization's own silver bullet machine, so you can manufacture those oh-so-valuable magic silver bullets again and again and again and again. That, surely, must be the ultimate competitive advantage.

TWELVE KEY FEATURES OF THE UNLEARNING ORGANIZATION

1   **The day job doesn't get in the way.** Unlearning organizations make time for thinking, exploration, innovation. They don't let the pressures of the day job stop this.

2   **"If it ain't broke, don't fix it" is not "the way we do things around here."** Unlearning organizations don't wait for things to break before they fix them. They are always searching for better ways of doing things, even if there is no explicit "problem" to solve.

3   **The only rule is "rules are for breaking."** Unlearning organizations recognize that rules, policies, procedures, processes, are artifacts of the time they were originated. All are constantly under review, and those that remain fit-for-purpose are retained, those that have passed their sell-by date are ditched.

4   **Negligence is distinguished from learning.** Unlearning organizations know that "failure" is a very broad term, and embraces many things. In particular, they distinguish between "negligence" (the deliberate departure from an agreed policy) and "learning" (what happens when an outcome differs from expectations). They do not condone the former; nor do they penalize the latter.

5   **They listen.** To each other, to the outside world. Actively. Bosses do not finish the sentences of their subordinates; peers use their ears more than their mouths.

6   **They share.** Resources, information, people, risk. They operate in highly connected networks rather than hierarchical silos; nothing is "mine," for everything is "ours"; everyone is comfortable playing whatever roles are fit-for-purpose at the time.

7   **They say "yes" more than they say "no."** Go to a meeting. Take a blank sheet of paper, draw a vertical line down the middle. Label the left-hand column "yes"; the right-hand column "no." Each time you hear the word "yes," or an equivalent positive remark, place a tick in the left-hand column; likewise for "no" and it's surrogates. In an unlearning organization, you will have far more ticks on the left than the right.

8   ***They don't rush to judge.*** Unlearning organizations know when to evaluate ideas, and do this only when there is a full and well-balanced view. They do not shoot from the hip, or jerk from the knee: they think from the head.

9   ***They have a wise approach to managing risk.*** Unlearning organizations fully recognize that innovation is all about managing risk. They also know full well that, in today's business climate – and especially tomorrow's – to maintain the *status quo*, though comfortable and familiar, is likely to be more risky than stepping wisely into the unknown. They do not expect every innovation to succeed, nor do they place any foolhardy bets.

10 ***Their performance measures support innovation, rather than discourage it.*** Unlearning organizations have enhanced their portfolio of performance measures to ensure that they support, rather than inhibit, innovation. Even to the (unusual) extent of measuring inputs (such as hours spent on idea generation) rather than outputs (number of ideas put into the suggestion box).

11 ***They are very good at managing both the line and projects.***
    "Did you hear about Pat?"
    "No, I don't think so. What's going on?"
    "He's been assigned to a 'special' project."
    "Well, he's on his way out then."
    That is a conversation you will not hear in an unlearning organization. Managing the line and managing projects exist easily side by side; being assigned to an innovation project is a symbol of regard; and risk-taking is rewarded.

12 ***They regard innovation as a core business process in its own right.*** Unlearning organizations manage innovation, in all its aspects, as a core business process, indeed as *the* core business process, forming the very heart of the organization's silver bullet machine. For they know that innovation – the ability to solve problems wherever they might arise, to be able to grasp opportunities however fleeting, to be confident in generating stunning new ideas again and again and again and again, and to deliver them too – is truly *the* ultimate competitive advantage.

Smart Stuff to be Seen in Your Bookcase*

There is a lot of good material on innovation, and here is my personal choice: the page numbers refer to those that are mentioned in text.

On innovation in general

?What If! How to Start a Creative Revolution at Work, by Dave Allan, Matt Kingdon, Kris Murrin, and Daz Rudkin, published by Capstone, 1999.
A lively discussion of ?What If!'s view on innovation: I particularly enjoyed the chapter on making ideas real.

Serious Creativity, by Edward de Bono, published by HarperCollins, 1993 (see pages 107, 177 and 180).
A compendium of de Bono's work over the last twenty-five years. De Bono is a prolific writer. Some of his works that are of particular interest are:

* and even smarter if you've read them!

Children Solve Problems, by Edward de Bono, published by Penguin Books, 1972 (page 107).
A wonderfully illustrated collection of how children aged between 5 and 14 solve problems such as "How to stop a dog and a cat from fighting," "How to weigh an elephant" and "How to design a bicycle for postmen." A powerful exposition of "the learning trap"!

Po – Beyond Yes and No, by Edward de Bono, published by Simon and Schuster, 1972 (page 178).
A series of thought-provoking essays.

Six Thinking Hats, by Edward de Bono, published by Viking, 1986 (page 213).
An exposition of de Bono's process for evaluating ideas safely, using the metaphor of wearing colored hats to legitimize the key roles.

I Am Right – You Are Wrong, by Edward de Bono, published by Viking, 1990 (page 155).
An impassioned plea for constructive and co-operative exploration and debate, rather than destructive and adversarial advocacy.

Letters to Thinkers, by Edward de Bono, published by George Harrap, 1987.
A series of thought-provoking essays.

Competitive Innovation Management: Techniques to Improve Innovation Performance, by James A. Christensen, published by Macmillan Business, 2000 (pages 243, 244 and 264)
Building the Innovative Organization: Management Systems that Encourage Innovation, by James A. Christensen, published by Macmillan Business, Basingstoke, 2000 (pages 243 and 244).

These two books are a matching pair, being based on Christensen's PhD thesis at INSEAD which studied twenty organizations, eight in depth (including 3M and Eastman Chemical), to discover what made some organizations highly innovative, and others less so. Very thorough, and highly informative.

The 3M Way to Innovation: Balancing People and Profit, by Ernest Gundling, published by Kodansha International, 2000 (page 259).
3M is widely regarded as *the* role model of the innovative organization, and although 3M is widely reported in case studies, this is the first full-length book on 3M to be published since 1955.

The Act of Creation, Arthur Koestler, published by Hutchinson & Co., London, 1964 (pages 95, 96, 177 and 191).
A book of genius in which polymath Koestler delves into the nature of creativity by exploring the bases of humor, art and science. Very many of the seminal ideas – for example those concerning patterns and the need to unlearn – are discussed most lucidly. There is a health warning, though: this is a book on philosophy rather than management, and more suited to reading on a flight to Australia, rather than a commuter train journey.

Radical Innovation: How Mature Companies Can Outsmart Upstarts, by Richard Leifer and Christopher M. McDermott, published by Harvard Business School Press, 2001.
This book covers similar territory to Christensen, being based on field-work at companies such as General Motors, General Electric, du Pont and IBM.

A Whack on the Side of the Head, by Roger von Oech, published by Creative Think, 1992.
A lively canter through a range of tools and techniques, accompanied by the wisdom of the Creative Whack Pack.

Creative Whack Pack, by Roger von Oech, published by Creative Think, 1992.
A pack of 64 "playing cards," each bearing an insightful message concerning creativity and innovation. Also available in disc format for use on personal computers.

Serious Play: How the World's Best Companies Simulate to Innovate, by Michael Schrage, published by Harvard Business School Press, 2000.
This book stresses the importance of making new ideas as real as possible.

Unlock Your Mind: A Guide To Deliberate And Systematic Innovation, by Dennis Sherwood, published by Gower Publishing, 1998, (pages 17 and 255).
My previous book on innovation, with quite a lot on systems thinking too.

On creativity tools and techniques

101 Ways to Generate Great Ideas, by Timothy RV Foster, published by Kogan Page, 1991 (page 181).
An easy-to-read compendium of tools and techniques, structured around 101 brief sections.

The Ultimate Book of Business Creativity, by Ros Jay, published by Capstone, 2000 (page 181).
A thorough description of 36 different creativity techniques, presented as algorithms, rather than with a framework.

Applied Imagination: Principles and Procedures of Creative Problem-Solving, by Alex F. Osborn, published by the Creative Education Foundation, 3rd revised edition, 1993 (page 154).
One of the creativity classics, by the originator of brainstorming. Contains much good stuff.

Techniques of Structured Problem Solving, by Arthur VanGundy, published by Van Nostrand Reinhold Company, 2nd edition, 1988 (page 181).
A veritable treasure trove of over 250 tools and techniques!

On strategy

Competing for the Future, by Gary Hamel and C.K. Prahalad, published by Harvard Business School Press, 1994 (page 75).
A management classic, and the origin of concepts such as core competencies.

Leading the Revolution, by Gary Hamel, published by Harvard Business School Press, 2000 (pages 75 and 163).
An upbeat, provocative, challenging and often witty view on strategy, with innovation as the key theme throughout.

Smart Things to Know about Strategy, Richard Koch, published by Capstone, 1999 (page 74).
An extremely lucid, pragmatic and insightful view of a complex subject.

On scenario planning

The Living Company: Growth, Learning and Longevity in Business, by Arie de Geus, published by Nicholas Brealey Publishing, 1997 (pages 285 and 286).
A powerful rallying call to those who believe in the importance of the human spirit in organizations – even large ones. The central metaphor is the organization as a living being.

Scenarios: The Art of Strategic Conversation, by Kees van der Heijden, published by John Wiley & Sons, 1997 (page 286).
A well-written discussion of scenario planning by a leading member of the Shell scenario planning community.

Synchronicity: The Inner Path of Leadership, by Joseph Jaworski, published by Berrett-Koehler Publishers, 1996.
Joseph Jaworski is an American lawyer who was invited to run the Group Planning function in Shell for a few years. This largely biographical book is a fascinating story in its own right, and also gives great insight into organizations and management.

Scenario Planning: Managing for the Future, by Gill Ringland, published by John Wiley & Sons, 1998 (page 286).
A comprehensive description of most of the different methods of scenario planning.

The Art of the Long View: Planning for the Future in an Uncertain World, by Peter Schwartz, published by John Wiley & Sons, 1996.
Peter Schwartz was one of the originators of scenario planning, working firstly at Stanford Research Institute, then at Shell, and most recently with GBN – the Global Planning Network. Part biography, part history of scenario planning, this is indeed a good read.

On other relevant managerial tools and techniques

The Mind Map Book: Radiant Thinking, by Tony Buzan, published by BBC Books, 1995 (page 21).
A lavishly illustrated exposition of Mind Maps.

Use Your Head, by Tony Buzan, published by BBC Books, 1998 (page 21).
More on mind maps, and some related intellectual skills too.

Tony Buzan's Book of Genius: and How to Unleash Your Own, by Tony Buzan and Raymond Keene, published by BBC Books, 1995 (page 15).
A coffee-table style book, to my mind most interesting for its potted biographies of 100 luminaries.

Guide to Quality Control, Kaoru Ishikawa, published by the Asian Quality Organisation, 2nd revised edition (1986) (page 283).
The source book for the fishbone diagram, and many other techniques for statistical quality control too.

The Change Masters: Corporate Entrepreneurs at Work, by Rosabeth Moss Kanter, published by George Allen & Unwin, 1984 (page 120).
When Giants Learn to Dance: Corporate Entrepreneurs at Work, by Rosabeth Moss Kanter, published by Touchstone Books, 1990 (page 120).
Two management classics, still highly relevant today.

The Balanced Scorecard, by Robert S Kaplan and David P Norton, published by Harvard Business School Press, 1996 (page 49).
The authoritative source for this important concept.

The Fifth Discipline, by Peter Senge, published by Currency Doubleday, 1990 (pages 148 and 149).
A persuasive and articulate exposition of the role of systems thinking in management, alongside the four other key disciplines of "personal mastery," "mental models," "shared vision" and "team learning."

The Fifth Discipline Fieldbook, by Peter Senge, Charlotte Roberts, Richard Ross, Bryan Smith and Art Kleiner, published by Nicholas Brealey Publishing, 1994 (page 149).
A companion to *The Fifth Discipline* packed full of examples, explanations, discussions and anecdotes.

The Dance of Change: The Challenges of Sustaining Momentum in Learning Organisations, by Peter Senge, Art Kleiner, Charlotte Roberts, Richard Ross, George Roth and Bryan Smith, published by Nicholas Brealey Publishing, 1999 (page 149).
An extension of the *Fieldbook*, with yet more examples, explanations, discussions and anecdotes! These two books are, to my mind, amongst the most interesting and informative management texts on the market today.

On e-commerce

Smart Things to Know about E-commerce, by Mike Cunningham, published by Capstone, 1999.
There are a huge number of e-books on the market now: this sister volume is one of the most readable, intelligible and practical.

On learning and the mechanism of the brain

The Organisation of Behaviour: A Neuropsychological Theory, by Donald O. Hebb, published by John Wiley, 1949 (page 103).
In which Hebb explores his hypothesis that the process of learning is one in which neural connections are formed and progressively strengthened.

Consciousness: How Matter Becomes Imagination, by Gerald M. Edelman and Giulio Tonini, published by Allen Lane, The Penguin Press, 2000.
An up-to-date exposition of Edelman's latest research into the mechanisms of the brain – but quite a tough read!

The Human Brain: A Guided Tour, by Susan Greenfield, published by Weidenfeld & Nicholson, 1997.
An easy-to-read and erudite exposition, written by the *doyenne* of British science.

Oulipo

A Void, by Georges Perec, translated by Gilbert Adair, published by The Harvill Press, 1995 (page 77).
The 276-page novel which contains no "e."

The Exeter Text, by Georges Perec, translated by Ian Monk, to be found in *Three*, published by The Harvill Press, 1996 (page 78).
The short story (only 54 pages this time!) in which the only vowel is "e."

And just in case we start taking ourselves too seriously

Dilbert: The Joy of Work, by Scott Adams, Boxtree, 2000.
Try in general Chapter 8 ("Bringing humor and creativity to your job"), and in particular pages 76–77!

Index

References in **bold** refer to boxes; in *italic*, to drawings or figures; and those that are <u>underlined</u> refer to entries in *Smart Stuff to be Seen in Your Bookcase*.

Innovation Target 9–83, *10*,
    22, *56*, **105**, 124
  and e-business 77–83
  as a description of
    innovation as a four stage
    process *10, 22, 56*
  management of 41–54,
    278–80
  process measures of 258–9
innovative organizations
    238–52
  and the importance of rules
    242–3
  characteristics of **238, 239**
  demands of managing 242,
    243
Innovator of the Year award
    261
input measures
  of innovation 259
Inspector Morse **111**, 112
intellectual creativity 95, **191**
intelligence quotient (IQ) 15,
    19
internal relationship
    innovation **68**, 71, **71–2**,
    72–3
Internet 80–82, 98, 111
  as a new "piece" from the
    outside **98**, 111
  as used by Amazon.com 81,
    98
interpersonal behavior
  and innovation 31, **51**, 140,
    241
introversion (Myers-Briggs
    characteristic) **45**
intuition (Myers-Briggs
    characteristic) **45**
IQ 15, 19
IRR's 228
issues to be managed
  and evaluation **214**, 218–20,
    221, 223
  example of 231
ISTJ, Myers-Briggs type 44, **45**
IT
  case study of cost
    effectiveness at Yorkshire
    Electricity **194–5**
  embedding innovation in
    281, 281

jigsaw puzzle **97**
jokes
  humour and creativity **191**,
    191
journeying
  idea generation technique
    190
judgement
  importance of in evaluation
    25, 42, 62, **227, 228**
  in an unlearning
    organization 297
judging (Myers-Briggs
    characteristic) **45**
"just one sheet of paper"
    fallacy 4–5

knowledge 99, **102**, 105, 112,
    114, 123, 129, 130, 141,
    152, 182, 259
knowledge management and
    sharing 71, 183
knowledge transfer 256
knowledge-based industry
    and brain bank connectivity
    (*BBC*) 156
Koch, Richard 74, 74, <u>303</u>
Koestler, Arthur 95, *95*, 96,
    177, <u>301</u>
Koestler's Law 6, 95–8, 112,
    171, 182
  and drama, humor and
    intellectual creativity 95
  and *InnovAction!* 126, 127,
    130, 137
  and learning 98, 112
  business implications of
    96–7

landscape metaphor for
    learning **101–2**, 128–9,
    135, 147, 154, 178, **188–9**
language 93
  and embedding innovation
    into the organization 280
  and evaluation **219–20**
  use of during *InnovAction!*
    147, **148**
lateral thinking **107**
  and *InnovAction!* 176–81
  convergence with
    InnovAction! 177, 179

leadership
  importance of to make
    innovation happen 258
Leading the Revolution 74, 75,
    162–3, <u>303</u>
lean manufacturing 282
learning 98–104, **99–100**,
    100–101, **101–2**, 114,
    130, 141, **152**, 182
  and *InnovAction!* 126
  and unlearning **104**, 105–12
  as a process of hard-wiring
    neurons **100–101**
  distinguished from
    negligence 296
  from implementation 34,
    39–41
  landscape metaphor **101–2**,
    128–9
  rejoicing in 117, 127
  what you can't see when
    trapped 104
learning organization 238, **286**
learning trap **104, 121**
  how to escape from 105
learning, team **149**
Let it be, step 5 of
    InnovAction! **118**, 125,
    134, 153, **153–7**
levers
  and systems thinking **290**
  how they are connected to
    outcomes **289–90**
  in scenario planning 286–92,
    286
life 92, 94–5, 113, 114
line management
  as contrasted to project
    management 272
linkages between brains
  and creativity **155–6**, 156–7
listening
  importance of in an
    unlearning organization
    296
  importance of in
    InnovAction! 148
literature 92–3, 95, 113
"little things" to make
    innovation happen **244**,
    247–50, *251*, 252, 294
  how to tackle 294–5

organizational innovation 55, 56, 66–9, **105**, **143**, 250
  and e-business 82
  budgeting example 173–6
  importance of people's feelings 220–22, **222**
originality
  of new ideas 58–62, 66–7, **210–11**
"out of sight, out of mind"
  and staffing innovation projects 274
outcomes
  and systems thinking **290**
  how they are connected to levers in scenario planning **289–90**
  in scenario planning 286–92, 286
output measures
  of innovation 258
outside world
  as a repository of component parts 111, 182
outsiders
  value of using in *InnovAction!* 162, 182

Pages, Yellow 80
panel, assessment 144. 145
panel, selection 253
participants
  in innovation 269, 270
patterns 85–115, **191**
  and *InnovAction!* 126, 129
  and Koestler's Law 8, **96–7**, 98, 112, 127
  component parts bundled together 99, 127, 129, 161–2
  unbundling of in *InnovAction!* 154, 161–2
Pearson Television, game show *InnovAction!* case study **201–3**
perceiving (Myers-Briggs characteristic) 45
performance measures 49
  and making innovation happen 248, *251*, 257–60
  and organizational innovation 67, 257–60

as applied to innovation 11, 35, 38–9, 232
conflict between 249, 260
consistency of 260
in an unlearning organization 297
output measures of innovation 232
periodic table of the elements **115**
personal mastery **149**
piano 13, 90, 91, 92, 99, **102**, 113, 114
pipeline of ideas 257, 270, 278–80
  and making innovation happen 248, *252*
planes
  example of "po" 177–8, 179–80
planning, business 284–92
planning, scenario 284–92, 285, 286
planning, strategic 284–92
plant (Belbin type) 46
PLUTO – pipeline under the ocean **226**
"po" 177–80
policies and procedures
  to make innovation happen 247–50, *251*, *252*
  consistency of 248–50, 294–5
pragmatism
  of the evaluation process 210, 211, 213
premature evaluation 30, 44, 254–5
  during *InnovAction!* 123–4, 152, 153
Price is Right, The 201
prince
  new piece in chess 139
princess
  new piece in chess 139
printing press 77
prisoner of success **104**
Prize, Nobel 5–6, **103**, 263
problem-solving 42, 181, **191**
process design
  embedding innovation in **281**, 281

process innovation 31, 55, 62–6, **105**, **143**, 250, **281**, 281
  budgeting example 173–6
  importance of people's feelings 220–22, **222**
process re-engineering 62, **63**, 64–6
  embedding innovation in **281**, 281
processes **281**
product development 55, 58–62, **105**, **143**
product innovation 55, 58–62, **105**, **143**
product positioning **56–8**
professional firm
  organization structure **68**
  relationship innovation in 68–9, 71, **71–2**
project approval 27, 29
  see also project funding
project funding 267–8
  and making innovation happen 248, *251*, 249–50
project management 41, 256, 271–8
  and making innovation happen 248, *252*
  in contrast to line management 272
project manager
  role of 274, 275–6
project teams 31–2
project, TALISMAN **277**
projects 274–8, **274**
  and risk assessment 275
  cut over from development to live 276
  end of 276, 278
  management of 271–8
  management of contingencies 275–6
  role of steering committee 275, 276
  uncertainty of **274**, 275
promotion
  policies on 253–4
proof, burden of
  during evaluation 216
provocative operation – "po" 177–80